P9-CMX-114

BIG
TENT

Also by Mallory Factor and Elizabeth Factor

*Shadowbosses: Government Unions Control America
and Rob Taxpayers Blind*

BIG TENT

THE STORY OF THE CONSERVATIVE REVOLUTION—AS TOLD BY THE THINKERS AND DOERS WHO MADE IT HAPPEN

Edited by

MALLORY FACTOR

and Elizabeth Factor

BROADSIDE BOOKS
An Imprint of HarperCollinsPublishers
www.broadsidebooks.net

BIG TENT. Copyright © 2014 by Mallory Factor. All rights reserved. Printed in the United States of America. No part of this book may be used or reproduced in any manner whatsoever without written permission except in the case of brief quotations embodied in critical articles and reviews. For information, address HarperCollins Publishers, 10 East 53rd Street, New York, NY 10022.

HarperCollins books may be purchased for educational, business, or sales promotional use. For information, please e-mail the Special Markets Department at SPsales@harpercollins.com.

FIRST EDITION

Designed by William Ruoto

Library of Congress Cataloging-in-Publication Data has been applied for.

ISBN: 978-0-06-229069-4

14 15 16 17 18   OV/RRD   10 9 8 7 6 5 4 3 2 1

To our loving and wise children:
you inspire us to work for a better America.

PROPERTY OF
LIBRARY OF THE CHATHAMS
CHATHAM NJ

CONTENTS

◆ ◆ ◆

Contents

Contents

Contents

x

WE THE PEOPLE

Edwin J. Feulner

◆ ◆ ◆

Conservatives believe that America is an exceptional nation because, unlike any other nation, it is founded on an idea—the idea that "all Men are created equal" and are endowed by their creator with "certain unalienable Rights," among them life, liberty, and the pursuit of happiness. To secure these rights, a government is given "just Powers from the Consent of the Governed."

In these few words in our Declaration of Independence, we find the first principles that have guided America for nearly two and a half centuries—liberty and equality, individual rights and limited government. The idea that political power ultimately rests with the people and not with any monarch or parliament was truly revolutionary.

The Constitution builds on the idea that the people are sovereign by beginning with the words "We the People"—and in bold letters. The people, the preamble states, have established a constitution to do six things: form a more perfect Union, establish justice, insure domestic tranquility, provide for the common defense, promote the general welfare, and secure the blessings of liberty "to ourselves and our posterity." These are monumental goals never attained before or even conceived in recorded history.

And yet the authors of the Constitution, meeting in hot humid Philadelphia in the summer of 1787, believed they could be achieved. They had faith in the ideas that had inspired a tiny country of four million scattered along the coastline of a new world to challenge and defeat the most powerful nation in the world. And they had faith in the people who now sought a new and exceptional kind of political governance.

Who were the "people" in whom the Founders had such confidence? John Adams said, "Our Constitution was made only for a moral and religious people. It is wholly inadequate to the government of any other." Our form of republican government, he was saying, requires not merely the consent of the governed but their ability to govern themselves.

So the first responsibility—the first duty—of the "people" is to ensure that they remain a moral people.

The Founders placed great hopes in the Constitution, but they knew that no piece of paper could ensure liberty. Only a people, steeped in the principles that animated the Declaration, could do that. Further, liberty depended not upon individuals living in isolation but on what the Anglo-Irish parliamentarian Edmund Burke called the "little platoons" of society.

Social virtues are nurtured in families, sustained in religious congregations, and fostered in the everyday flow of work, hobbies, and life. Long before the Declaration, foreign observers noted the number and the vigor of America's social institutions—what Alexis de Tocqueville called "voluntary associations"—and the everyday democracy of marriage, vocation, and community.

The Founders believed that if the institutions of civic virtue remained free and strong, the American people would remain self-governing and free. But freedom was not guaranteed. As Ronald Reagan said in his historic speech about the "evil empire" of the Soviet Union, "Freedom is never more than one generation away from extinction." So the second duty of the people is to pass the torch of freedom to the next generation.

Many on the Left claim they favor civil society. But Progressives see the maintenance of civil society as the primary responsibility of government—giving it the right to speak for the people and to assert a moral authority greater than that of the people. Progressives argue that only the state can produce good works, an assertion roundly rejected by conservatives, who point, for example, to the trillion-dollar failure of the "Great Society" to end poverty.

Big Government invariably weakens and even impoverishes the people in body and spirit. In sharp contrast, the little platoons of society—our families, our churches, our communities—strengthen and enrich all our lives. The lesson is clear: government must encourage not discourage these social institutions if it wishes to foster a civil society based on a free, independent, and patriotic people.

The third duty of the people, then, is to remain faithful to the first principles of liberty and equality, individual rights and limited government, to nourish the family and the other little platoons of society, and to encourage a love of country.

In his Farewell Address in January 1989, President Ronald Reagan called on the nation to foster what he called "informed patriotism." The president believed that with the end of the Cold War there was a renewed spirit of patriotism, but that was not enough. Patriotism, he said, had to be "well grounded" in popular culture and to recognize that "America is freedom . . . and freedom is special and rare." American freedom, he declared, began with the American memory, and if that was not preserved, Reagan warned, the result would be the erosion of the American spirit.

Where does the preservation begin? he asked. In the home and around the kitchen table. If parents have not been teaching their children what it means to be an American, Reagan said, they have failed in their obligation to be good parents.

It is critical that we know and study the Constitution so that we can defend what we have achieved under it—a government of, by, and for the people. We must pass along our history to the next generation so as to preserve the ordered liberty bequeathed to us by the Founders.

THE CONSERVATIVE CONTRIBUTION

And this is what conservatives have been doing for the past six decades, although it has been no easy task. Especially in the beginning, conservatism was ignored, dismissed, and derided.

In the introduction to *The Liberal Imagination*, published in

1950, the reigning liberal critic Lionel Trilling wrote that "liberalism is not only the dominant but even the sole intellectual tradition" in the United States. What he called the "conservative impulse" was not thoughtful at all but made up of at best "irritable mental gestures which seem to resemble ideas."

When Russell Kirk wrote the magisterial *The Conservative Mind* three years later—offering Edmund Burke, Alexis de Tocqueville, John Adams, Alexander Hamilton, and John Marshall as eminent conservative thinkers—the liberal historian Arthur Schlesinger Jr. said in his review that this "great scurrying about" for respectability produced only "an odd and often contradictory collection of figures" that did not rise "to the dignity of a conservative tradition." We should be grateful to Professor Schlesinger for providing so clear an example of ideological denial.

In *The Liberal Tradition in America*, the liberal historian Louis Hartz explained that by conservatism, what was really meant was European feudalism, which was not only absent from but altogether foreign to the American experience. Meaning, I suppose, that Hartz considered American revolutionaries such as John Adams and Thomas Paine to be European "feudalists."

In *Conservatism in America*, the historian Clinton Rossiter concluded that because America was "a progressive country with a liberal tradition," conservatism in the United States was simply "irrelevant." If so, we may ask, why did Kirk's *The Conservative Mind* and Whittaker Chambers's *Witness* stay on the *New York Times* best seller list for weeks?

As my Heritage colleague Matthew Spalding has written, the leading minds of the American academy have invariably misunderstood conservatism, the conservative movement's role in American politics, and the relationship of conservative thought to the American political tradition. For example, a team of professors from the University of California at Berkeley, Stanford University, and the University of Maryland argued in a leading psychology journal that conservatism is a pathology stemming from fear, aggression, uncertainty avoidance, irrational nostalgia, and the need for "cognitive closure."

Thankfully, the picture today is far different from when Lionel Trilling and other liberals dominated the intellectual scene. Those "irritable mental gestures" are widely recognized as a legitimate and influential set of conservative ideas, enunciated by popularizers like columnist George Will and editor William Kristol; defended by prominent scholars such as Princeton's Robert George, Stanford's John Taylor, and the Hudson Institute's Yuval Levin; and embodied in powerful think tanks like the Heritage Foundation and the American Enterprise Institute.

The stirrings of modern American conservatism began with a trio of books and the creation of a journal. First in 1944 came Friedrich Hayek's *The Road to Serfdom*, providing an ethical defense of free markets and a classical liberal critique of planned economies. A liberal Harvard historian called publication of that book "a major event in the intellectual history of the United States." Whittaker Chambers revealed his story and his soul in 1952 in *Witness*, presenting the contest between communism and democracy as a life-and-death struggle between good and evil.

Perhaps the most influential conservative book appeared the

following year—Russell Kirk's *The Conservative Mind*, which provided American conservatism with an impressive patrimony reaching back to Edmund Burke and John Adams. *Time* called it a "wonder of conservative intuition and prophecy." With one book, Kirk made conservatism intellectually acceptable. As publisher Henry Regnery and conservative strategist William Rusher both pointed out, he gave the conservative movement its name.

The new journal of opinion was *National Review*. Its editor in chief was William F. Buckley Jr., who for the next fifty years inspired conservatives, young and old, with his wit, his élan, and his willingness to take on any and all challengers in debate. The historian George Nash has written that in many ways the rise of the modern conservative movement is parallel to the prominence of *National Review*.

Through its philosophers and popularizers, conservatism influenced a generation of political leaders in both major parties. Daniel Patrick Moynihan, a liberal Democratic senator from New York, conceded reluctantly that "something momentous has happened in American life; the Republican Party has become the party of ideas."

No greater proof of this intellectual shift can be found than the 1964 elections. In July, Senator Barry Goldwater of Arizona won the Republican nomination for president and changed the landscape of American politics. In the fall campaign and against the longest of odds, he insisted on offering a conservative choice, not a liberal echo.

Like a stern prophet of the Old Testament, Goldwater warned the people to repent of their wasteful ways or reap a bitter harvest of debt and decline. Anti-communist to the core, he urged a strategy of victory over communism by a combination of means, including military superiority over the Soviets and the encouragement of the peoples behind the Iron Curtain to "overthrow their captors."

In the field of domestic policy, he talked about the partial privatization of Social Security, a flat tax, the phasing out of farm subsidies, and the need for morality in government. Denounced as extremist in 1964, such proposals have since entered the mainstream of America's national policy debate.

Goldwater laid the political and philosophical foundation for a political revolution that culminated in the 1980 election of Ronald Reagan as president and the 1994 Republican capture of the U.S. House of Representatives under Speaker Newt Gingrich. In his memoirs, Goldwater insists that he did not start a revolution, that all he did was to begin "to tap . . . a deep reservoir that already existed in the American people." That is like Thomas Paine saying he did not ignite the American Revolution with his fiery pamphlet *Common Sense*.

Barry Goldwater carried only six states in his run for the presidency and was consigned, along with his radical ideas, to the ash heap of history by most political observers. But just sixteen years later, presidential candidate Ronald Reagan carried forty-four states, campaigning on conservative ideas and conservative solutions for an America suffering economically at home and unable to block communist gains in country after country. Once described as the "forbidden faith," conservatism was now the chosen political label of 40 percent of Americans.

The Reagan administration brought a generation of ambitious young conservatives to Washington, D.C., to fill congressional staffs, serve in the executive branch, edit publications, and join think tanks—with, I am pleased to say, many passing through the doors of the Heritage Foundation. The new conservative administration exposed the ineptitude of an overblown government, cut high tax rates, and stopped the appointment of activist judges. It refused to accept the permanent division of the world into slave and free, calling for victory in the Cold War.

The congressional elections of 1994, producing a Republican House of Representatives for the first time in forty years, confirmed that conservatism was not an aberration based on the engaging personality and persuasive rhetoric of Ronald Reagan but the most serious, sustained political movement in America since the early twentieth century.

Conservatism's intellectual, political, and institutional success might tempt one to think that it was somehow ordained. Not so: the gains were won by the courage and perseverance of men and women who risked reputations, careers, and sometimes their very lives to break with convention.

The story of the modern conservative movement is the story of film actor Ronald Reagan, who carried a revolver after being threatened by pro-communist goons in Hollywood; humanitarian Barry Goldwater, who flew desperately needed food and supplies to starving snowbound Navajo in northern Arizona; backbencher Newt Gingrich, who waged an often lonely fourteen-year struggle to bring about a GOP House majority.

American conservatism, it needs to be emphasized, is far

different from the aristocratic conservatism of Europe or the authoritarian conservatism of Latin America. Here are some of its canons:

Conservatives are highly suspicious of promised utopia and earthly salvation. The purpose of politics is not to gain redemption but to carve out a system of justice under the rule of law, a moral order, and freedom, recognizing that human beings are neither perfect nor perfectible. When governments seek utopia, they end in oppression because man and society are infinitely complex and cannot be reshaped by any institution of experts. To think otherwise, as Hayek wrote, is a fatal conceit.

Conservatives—whether traditionalist, libertarian, neocon, or any other kind of conservative—understand that power is a zero-sum game. When power is assumed by government, it is lost by individuals. There must be a stopping point in every program and plan beyond which no government should be allowed to go, not merely because of budgetary concerns but because of the inevitable loss of freedom.

Conservatives believe there is an intimate connection between private property and freedom—economic freedom is an essential part of human freedom. As the Heritage Foundation's Index of Economic Freedom has documented for two decades, when given the chance, freedom works everywhere, producing more prosperity and more freedom for more people than any other economic system.

Conservatives believe in the necessity of change but not in radical change based on abstract theories and the passions of the moment. They prefer settled institutions, values, and traditions, reflecting what G. K. Chesterton called "the democracy of the dead." They decline to follow the lead of any arrogant oligarchy who happen to be walking about. Such prudence, the philosopher Michael Oakeshott wrote, produces "the politics of repair" rather than "the politics of destruction."

Many conservatives share a sense of reverence, a belief in two worlds—one physical and one spiritual—that stand in judgment of our own. When the author Ralph de Toledano was sent proof sheets of a novel he had written, he noticed that his New York publisher had removed the capital letters from Heaven and Hell. Toledano corrected each and sent back the proofs. His publisher called and said, "Ralph, we have a set of style rules over here we must observe. Why do you insist on capitalizing Heaven and Hell?" "Because," replied Toledano, "they're places. You know, like Scarsdale."

According to George Santayana, there is a sentiment of gratitude and duty in the human spirit that we may call piety. That piety is common among almost all conservatives and sustains our respect for the living, the dead, and the yet-unborn.

These are some of the themes of American conservatism. I find all of them compelling and none of them contradictory. The danger comes when one conservative value—whether freedom or moral order or piety—becomes an absolute, something to which everything else is sacrificed. Conservatives have usually avoided that danger because of a great conservative virtue—prudence—that balances valid and competing truths.

Near the end of his life, Whittaker Chambers wrote that escapism is laudable perhaps for "humane men," but only for them. Those who remain in the world, he said, must not surrender to the world but maneuver within its terms. Conservatives must decide, Chambers wrote, "how much to give in order to survive at all; how much to give in order not to give up basic principles."

All great conservatives have been practitioners of prudence who sought a golden mean, a balance between competing truths, in their politics and in their philosophy.

Friedrich Hayek was more than a Nobel Prize winner in economics—he was a philosopher and a prophet. He was intrigued by the mind of man, the markets he has made, and the way those markets have made man and society what they are. He used economic precepts to unveil the totalitarian nature of socialism and explain how it leads to serfdom. Using meticulous scholarship and powerful logic, he stopped the advocates of economic planning in their tracks, leaving them without a theoretical leg to stand on.

Russell Kirk was never a liberal and always a conservative from the hour he began to reason. He committed his life to conserving "the three great bodies of principle . . . that tie together modern civilization"—Christian faith, humane letters, and the social and political institutions that define our culture. In one of his many Heritage lectures, Kirk urged all of us to defend our culture and preserve what the poet T. S. Eliot called "the permanent things."

Despite the incivility, materialism, irreverence, and immorality all around us, Kirk was not discouraged about the future. He predicted that if conservatives "take up the weapons of reason and imagination," they have every reason to anticipate victory. He drew his optimism in part from Edmund Burke, who reminds us that the goodness of one person, the courage of one man, the strength of one individual, can turn the course of history and renew a civilization. Among the conservative individuals who changed history were George Washington, Abraham Lincoln, and Ronald Reagan.

The history of Great Britain in the last quarter of the twentieth century is the biography of one woman and a conservative—Margaret Thatcher. Committed to the ideas of limited government and the free market, Prime Minister Thatcher transformed Britain during her eleven and a half years at No. 10 Downing Street.

She tamed the trade unions despite a violent miners' strike in 1984, refusing to cave in to radical demands. Her government sold off British Telecom, British Gas, British Airways, and British Steel, producing vastly improved service and profits. She assumed control of the money supply, reduced the government's budget deficit, trimmed state spending, cut taxes, and reduced government regulations. Freed of the nanny state, Britain embarked on its longest economic expansion in the postwar period. It produced more new jobs in the 1980s than the other members of the European Community combined. Her successful application of conservative principles is a lesson for everyone, including our own leaders.

Most elected officials come and go in Washington, making only the faintest of impressions. Only rarely does a politician advance an idea that changes the path of the nation—such a political leader was former congressman Jack Kemp of New York. Following discussions with economist Arthur Laffer and *Wall Street Journal* editor Robert Bartley, Jack became convinced that supply-side economics with its focus on tax cuts was the key to national prosperity—and political success for whichever party promoted it.

Presidential candidate Reagan agreed and made the Kemp-Roth tax cuts (the latter sponsor being Senator William Roth of Delaware) a central initiative of his campaign. The Economic Recovery Tax Act of 1981 sparked the longest period of peacetime economic growth in U.S. history, lasting more than two decades.

In an address to members of Heritage's President's Club in November 1994, Jack Kemp offered a vision of the American idea rooted in the thinking of the Founders:

We must return to people their resources so that they will accept their responsibility.

We must return to people power so that they will rebuild the institutions of a free society.

We must return to people authority so that they will create the moral capital to help renew our nation.

Last, I turn to President Reagan, who transformed conservatism from a middling intellectual movement into a powerful political movement. He exposed the bankruptcy of modern liberalism and proved that true liberty is the motivating force of a just and prosperous society. Through the power of his words and the impact of his deeds, he buried Leninism and ended the Cold War without firing a shot.

He was called the "great communicator," but substance not style was critically important to him. "I wasn't a great commu-

Foreword

nicator," he insisted, "but I communicated great things, and they didn't spring full blown from my brow. They came from the heart of a great nation—from our experience, our wisdom and our belief in the principles that [have] guided us for two centuries."

Reagan had the gift of reducing politics to a fundamental level and speaking a plain language that touched mind and heart. At the center of our conservative message, he said, echoing Edmund Burke, "should be five simple familiar words . . . family, work, neighborhood, freedom, peace."

Throughout his presidency, Reagan turned again and again to the wisdom and philosophy of the Founders. Indeed, more than once, he sounded like one of them, never more than in his Farewell Address to the American people. "Ours was the first revolution in the history of mankind," he said, "that truly reversed the course of government, and with three little words: 'We the people.' 'We the people' tell the government what to do," the president said, "it doesn't tell us."

The idea of "we the people" underlined everything that Ronald Reagan tried to do as president. That same idea underlines the modern conservative movement, inspired by the great documents of our republic—the Declaration of Independence and the U.S. Constitution.

PREFACE

John W. Rosa
Lieutenant General, USAF (Retired)
President and Class of 1973
The Citadel

◆ ◆ ◆

America is in the midst of a great debate over values and principles—as it always has been and, by our foundation, always will be. At my institution, The Citadel, this debate sets the stage for knowledgeable instruction, which in turn allows our Corps of Cadets to consider their positions and participate in the discussion.

One might assume that because we are the Military College of South Carolina, we are regimented in terms of thought, but nothing could be further from the truth. The Citadel is a bastion of free thinking and diversity of opinion with a mission to educate and develop principled leaders for all walks of life.

At The Citadel, we promote true academic freedom: the ability to think and speak freely on campus in order to help

our young people master the skills necessary to become leaders who embody our core values of honor, duty, and respect.
Since 1842, the members of our Long Gray Line have included
great leaders in the military, boardrooms, and public institutions. Therefore, we take our responsibility to develop men
and women of strong character very seriously. We have an obligation to share with them the teachings of great thinkers from
all points of view. This prepares them to act morally and ethically whether defending the nation's freedoms or protecting
the trust of shareholders and citizens.

In that spirit, I am pleased that Mallory Factor, the Governor John C. West Professor of International Politics and American Government at The Citadel, put together a course on the
conservative intellectual tradition in America. The guest lectures from that course evolved into the essays in this book,
and as you will see, they extend beyond partisan conservative
matters. Moreover, while the authors may consider themselves
conservatives, their philosophies vary widely.

The timeless debates of our society are discussed in these
essays: the questions of liberty vs. standards, equality vs. opportunity, fairness vs. freedom, and interventionism vs. isolationism. The authors seek not to resolve these debates, but to
illuminate them and draw attention to the fact that the great-
ness of America lies in its diversity of opinion and its attempt
to seek the purest form of liberty as envisioned by the Founders
and by the millions who have fought to preserve it.

THE MEANING OF CONSERVATISM

Mallory Factor

◆ ◆ ◆

In the spring of 2012, I had the privilege of exploring the American conservative intellectual tradition in depth in a seminar with top cadets at The Citadel, the Military College of South Carolina. I came to this examination as a person who wrestles with these issues every day and who discovered his conservative principles in his youth by reading Milton Friedman and then by studying the conservative canon.

The cadets came to this seminar for many reasons. Some of my cadets were "cradle conservatives"; others were trying to understand a different point of view. Many had already seen combat in the service of their country. Others would be deployed after graduating that spring. As brave young Americans, the cadets provide important contributions to our examination of the conservative tradition. Together, we spent the semester probing exactly what the conservative intellectual tradition is, how it arose, where it is going, and what it means for our nation's future.

Our seminar was made especially meaningful by the incredible conservative leaders who came to The Citadel to address our class. Each of these leaders took the time to visit the campus, eat with our students in the mess hall (a unique Citadel experience), and meet many cadets, in addition to addressing our seminar. Our cadets not only met with these leaders but also had the opportunity to ask them questions on camera during our Q and A sessions, which their parents and friends were then able to watch on C-SPAN and online.

I was deeply honored both to give this opportunity to these cadets to host these leaders and to listen and learn from the ensuing discussion. Our guest lecturers told us their personal stories about building and strengthening the conservative movement. I was amazed by how profound and interesting their insights were. Their lectures were so original and meaningful that we have assembled them for you in this book.

You will see almost immediately the wide breadth of experience and viewpoints of our contributors. Yet, as we will discover, the conservative movement's adherents share certain core beliefs. What the core beliefs of the conservative movement *are* will be at the center of our exploration in this book.

WHAT IS CONSERVATISM?

The political Left attempts to link conservatism with racial intolerance, classism, bigotry toward women, sexual prudery, anti-intellectualism, religious parochialism, and general cultural backwardness. But this is not what the movement is about. The conservative movement is not about people who have refused to embrace progress and have been left behind. The movement is *actually* about people who hold tight to core principles and hold essential truths that are needed to save our nation from tyranny.

Conservatism as a political and social philosophy is ancient. The personal human impulse to defend and fight for one's most cherished convictions is natural and timeless. Conservatism as a guiding philosophy for social life, education, cultural institutions, and government is equally natural and ancient.

The label *conservative* comes from the Latin prefix *con*, meaning "with," which, when combined with *servare*, "to guard, keep, or save," conveys the idea of attentively guarding something for purposes of safekeeping. Perhaps because of this association with guarding, many people confuse conservatism with blindly upholding tradition.

But *traditionalism* fails to capture our movement adequately. Conservatives recognize that tradition may be wrong or without meaning. Conservatives have often opposed the status quo and advocated a return to first principles. When the tradition is lacking truth or morality, conservatives are often moved to become revolutionaries, as we will see in these essays. Tradition may be missing essential truths and the moral substance toward which conservatives strive, and may need correction. Conservatives have reverence and respect for tradition but are not inseparable from it.

Conservatives have numerous reasons that they fight, and within this book you will find many of these reasons. Conservatives want a government that is ordered and functions according to the rights given to us by our Constitution. Conservatives want our government to defend the nation and provide "essential" services, but not to encroach on functions that should be reserved for families, religious institutions, and private enterprise. Conservatives want government to protect freedoms, property, and livelihood, but not to choose winners and losers, redistribute property, or impede commerce. And conservatives want government to leave them alone to use the fruits of their liberty and to worship as they see fit.

Conservative principles of personal freedom and limited government stand in stark contrast to the Democrat Party's slogan at its 2012 convention: "Government is the only thing we all belong to." If the American people start believing government is the only answer, it will be a wretched ending indeed for the American experiment.

CONSERVATISM: THE AMERICAN PHILOSOPHY

Conservatism isn't merely another American philosophy. It is *the* American philosophy. Our Founders came out of the British tradition, and conservative principles were in their tradition, their experience, and their DNA. The American Founders were trained in the tradition of ordered liberty, many from reading Cicero and Cato in Latin in their youth and from studying the English common law. Even today, many of us respond to conservative principles because we live in a society that has been ordered by these principles for centuries. Up until recent times, immigrants to America and their children internalized these principles as well by living in our nation, where the rule of law is respected and individual freedoms are cherished and defended.

Conservative principles are the heritage and tradition of the West, but they are not common to all nations. Other peoples who do not share our experience of ordered liberty may have a harder time understanding and applying its principles. As a result, successfully adopting a republic or parliamentary system as their form of government may not be intuitive and natural for other peoples, who have not inherited the West's governmental and philosophical history.

The ideas that hold conservatism together are rooted in man's most important values and the values upon which our nation was founded: truth, liberty, and freedom. These are American principles. While the French Revolution rejected monarchy in favor of democracy, it also rejected individual liberty in favor of collective rights. Much like modern leftism, the French Revolution had at its root the belief that the great ills of life were due to inequality of station and wealth. Our Founders instead suggested the great ills of life were caused by arbitrary justice and the lack of consistent application of the rule of law. And our American Revolution was a revolution about the preservation of individual freedoms through limitations on government.

To find conservative principles in our nation's founding, all we need to do is look to the Declaration of Independence. That brief, 1,337-word document explains what it means to be American—and why America is a nation bound together not by geographic boundaries, which have changed over time, or by common ethnic heritage, but by common ideals. The Declaration of Independence tells us that people are entitled to a "separate and equal Station" by "the Laws of Nature and of Nature's God." This comports with the conservative principle that our rights as men spring from our creator.

Our nation's foundational document created our government as the guarantor of our rights, not as the grantor of rights. The Declaration reads: "That to secure these Rights, Governments are instituted among Men, deriving their just Powers from the Consent of the Governed." When government fails to protect man's inalienable rights, believed the Founders, government must be abolished.

Even as the Founders declared their independence from Great Britain, they recognized that overthrowing great and historic institutions must be undertaken only with extreme care and justification. "Prudence, indeed, will dictate that Governments long established should not be changed for light and transient Causes; and accordingly all Experience hath shewn, that Mankind are more disposed to suffer, while Evils are sufferable, than to right themselves by abolishing the Forms to which they are accustomed," the Founders wrote. Only great violation of rights granted by God and nature could justify such change.

In the Constitution, the Founders sought to enshrine conservative principles in a governmental system that delegated as much power as possible to the individual and local forms of government. Only the issues of great national import—war and peace, debt and trade—were delegated to the federal government. These remain conservative principles today, just as the Constitution still provides the framework for our system of government. But to bring us back to the principles of limited, principled government set forth in our Constitution, our political leaders and the electorate will have to fundamentally change their expectations of the role of government in our lives, which expanded dramatically over the last century.

THERE IS NO MIDDLE ROAD FOR TRUTH

Society and government must have a moral foundation. Thus, the failure to recognize or value a moral foundation is a threat to the virtue, good, and beauty in our nation. These ideas have been explained by many thinkers over time. They have been captured by William F. Buckley's landmark *God and Man at Yale*, Whittaker Chambers's seminal *Witness*, and Russell Kirk's magisterial *The Conservative Mind*. And they are identified, as well, by many of the contributors to this book.

Conservatives understand that the truth cannot be denied. Henry Regnery, in his introduction to Russell Kirk's *The Conservative Mind*, wrote that a colleague once explained to him that "a conservative knows that two plus two always, invariably, equals four, a fact of life that a liberal, on the other hand, is not quite willing to accept." And in his greatly influential work *Witness*, Whittaker Chambers explained that when you find truth, you must stand up to defend it: "A witness, in the sense that I am using the word, is a man whose life and faith are so completely one that when the challenge comes to step out and testify for his faith, he does so, disregarding all risks, accepting all consequences."

That there are objective truths that must be defended, sides that must be taken, and enemies that must be defeated is a fundamental conservative principle.

The man who refuses to judge, who neither agrees nor disagrees, who declares that there are no absolutes and believes that he escapes responsibility, is the man responsible for all the blood that is now spilled in the world. . . . There are two sides to every issue: one side is right and the other is wrong, but the middle is always evil. The man who is wrong still retains some respect for truth, if only by accepting the responsibility of choice. But the man in the middle is the knave who blanks out the truth in order to pretend that no choice or values exist, who is willing to sit out the course of any battle, willing to cash in on the blood of the innocent or to crawl on his belly to the guilty, who dispenses justice by condemning both the robber and the robbed to jail, who solves conflicts by ordering the thinker and the fool to meet each other halfway. . . . In any compromise between good and evil, it is only evil that can profit.

These words could have been expressed by English parliamentarian Edmund Burke. They were in fact written by Ayn Rand, whom many in the conservative movement consider a fringe thinker outside our tradition, but whom others consider to have given voice to certain of our core principles most clearly and articulately.

Media pundits and even Republican consultants may advocate compromise on principles from time to time—to achieve a meeting in the middle, to work across the aisle, or to achieve greater victories down the road. But many conservatives realize that there is a greater peril in taking a middle-of-the-road approach than in standing fast for truth. Margaret Thatcher expressed her reluctance to take a middle road from a practical perspective: "Standing in the middle of the road is very dangerous; you get knocked down by the traffic from both sides." Conservatives understand that the truth cannot coexist peacefully with evil, engender no conflict, and improve our election prospects while still remaining true.

WHAT ARE THESE ABSOLUTE TRUTHS?

Conservatives have always attempted to warn the world that truth is by its nature absolute. As just one example, consider the conservative message on excessive U.S. government debt. Conservatives and the Left battle constantly these days over the need to address our national debt and stop deficit spending. The press, academia, Hollywood, and other leftist circles regularly vilify conservatives as reactionary and intransigent in their focus on reducing our national debt. But the truth is this: spending that greatly exceeds income and resources, if continued, will eventually result in the default and bankruptcy of any entity. This is true for an individual, a family, a company, a nonprofit, or a government. This fact is an iron truth and would be an iron truth even if there were no conservatives and leftists to argue about it. This view is not a *conservative* position. It is a *true* position. Insistence that our nation can continue to spend beyond our means without incurring harm, by contrast, is not a *leftist* position. It is a *false* position that, if continued, will eventually destroy the full faith and credit of the U.S. government. How can such manifest falsehood about our budget persist at all, much less be adopted as a widespread view by the Left? If you look closely, there are many falsehoods thrust upon the American people by the Left, press, and Hollywood working together to advance a common agenda.

But if essential truths exist, are they somehow too oppressive for modern life? Conservatives argue that the truth is not only real but liberating. A society built on true principles allows liberty, individuality, and freedom to flourish. After all, the fundamental equality of all men and women before God and nature, even amid their differences in wealth, talent, social status, language, professional success, intelligence, education, skin color, ethnic heritage, or political power, is an essentially conservative notion. The Left's unrelenting focus on equality of *outcome* is merely the Left's twist and corruption of the true principle of equality of opportunity that is held by conservatives. So it is with many policies of the Left that lead us, by turns, down the road to a collectivist and godless society.

WHAT CONSERVATISM ISN'T: THE LEFT'S FALSE PICTURE

Critics on the left often attack conservatism as overly concerned with keeping taxes low on the rich and preserving wealth. Defending economic freedoms is depicted by the Left as cheating the poor or supporting crony capitalism—using government to enrich yourself with government favors and backroom deals. By appealing to envy instead of aspiration, the Left suggests that conservatives are trying to hold on to their wealth and aren't paying their fair share to support government and the less fortunate.

But conservatives are really protecting economic freedom, one of conservatism's core tenets. Conservatives understand that people should be allowed to keep the fruits of their own labor and use them as they wish to the greatest extent possible; that is the only way for prosperity to grow. And conservatives don't defend crony capitalism, which goes against conservative ideals and is itself a form of government intervention in the marketplace. Crony capitalism is really just another form of corruption, enabled by an overly large and lavishly funded government.

Critics often confuse the conservative movement with the Republican Party, but party politics is separate from the pillars and principles of the conservative tradition. Admittedly, Republican politicians can be found who have voted against foundational conservative principles. These politicians and their votes do not demonstrate the impracticality of conservative principles, as the Left argues; rather, they illustrate that politicians are fallible, maybe even more so than the rest of us. Some conservatives are willing to keep politicians in office who vote with Republicans on most important legislation, even if they cast occasional votes that go against conservative principles. Others would rather see politicians like these replaced with people who are true to the conservative tradition.

The Republican Party contains many conservatives, but the party doesn't represent faithfully all tenets of the conservative philosophy. As Governor Haley Barbour explains in his conclusion to this work, though, the conservative movement needs the Republican Party to elect conservatives who put these principles into practice. This is certainly true for the time being at least. The first and foremost goal of each party is to win elections for its team, and the Republican Party does win elections for conservatives (and for some non-conservatives as well). We will explore this tension between the politics of the grassroots base and the politics of the party establishment throughout this book.

HERETICS AND INFIDELS

Conservatism is a vibrant ideology, but a word of caution is required about the movement in practice. Many conservatives would rather burn heretics from the different wings of the movement than unite and fight the enemies who are actively attempting to tear down the country.

In our movement, conservatives of one stripe put in place litmus tests on certain issues important to them to keep out other conservatives who don't agree with them. The result is that the conservative movement often seems fractured and divided in the popular media and imagination. There are paleocons and neocons, evangelicals and atheists, traditionalists and libertarians, foreign policy "hawks" and isolationists, academics and activists, supply-siders and gold standardists, the Tea Party and the Republican Party, media pundits and Fox News watchers. And it is certainly true that some of these groups really dislike one another.

Must conservatism put aside its internal conflict to win the future? Many today claim that our movement should be a big tent and the tent's flaps must be thrown wide open. They hark back to Republican strategist Lee Atwater's 1989 line regarding conflict within the Republican Party: "Our party is a big tent. We can house many views on many issues."

While Atwater was speaking of party, the conservative movement also can be seen as a big tent. Conservatism is advocated by people with a wide range of views on defense spending, national security, foreign policy, legalization of drugs, abortion, marriage, immigration, and many other issues. We debate all these issues among ourselves, clashing fiercely with those who disagree with us, and sometimes failing to come back together to advance our movement's core principles.

This vibrant and lively internal debate stands in stark contrast to the orthodoxy of the Left, which seems to adopt the position of "no enemies to the left." On the left, special interest groups join a grand coalition. Each group gets legislation that benefits it in return for its support of other coalition members' interests. This approach assures that all groups on the left get their piece of the government pie, whatever the cost to the nation as a whole. The conservative movement has never worked this way.

Having strong core principles is important for our movement, but the ultimate goal has to be winning the power to govern. Conservatives must govern to bring the liberty and freedoms that we speak about to the American people, and to do this, we must stand united.

THE PILLARS

The conservative movement's focus on a moral foundation and absolute truths may sound outdated, extreme, and downright bigoted to contemporary non-conservatives. Who are these people that still claim to know absolute truths and stand resolutely as witnesses to them? In the following chapters, you will find out. Here are assembled contributions from some of the most prominent conservative voices of our generation, urging a nation to return to its original moral and spiritual heritage. In their own individual ways, the contributors here bear witness to their vision: each has invested a large portion of his or her life and resources articulating and promoting that vision, and each in one way or another has sacrificed in its service.

As the contributors to this work explain, there have to be some pillars we all agree on or the whole tent falls down. We want our government to be based on a foundation of essential truths. We want to preserve liberty and freedom in our nation. We want our federal government limited in its powers to those granted under the Constitution and for government to get smaller and less intrusive in our lives. And when leaders in our movement fall away from these core principles, we step back, reexamine our course, and select new leaders. Our tent, too, has its bounds.

For someone new to conservatism, we hope this book will help you understand this important movement. The contributors' lives serve as worthy models for those wishing to learn about the tradition that created the United States as the world's last, best political hope.

To non-conservatives, the contributors may appear as a uniform and monolithic group. But consider for a moment just what a big tent our movement is and what a wide range of viewpoints our contributors represent. To be sure, righteously celebrating diversity is fashionable today, but we are talking here about real diversity of opinion, not of group identity. Indeed, it is hard to imagine all contributors to this book standing in the same room with one another, nodding in agreement on many issues. Yet they share common truths. All believe in preserving and upholding American freedoms and ideals for future generations.

Some in the conservative movement may bristle at one or more of the people whom we have assembled to address the conservative intellectual tradition. These conservatives would argue that we have been too inclusive. A number of conservatives, friends among them, have even told us that they can't be involved in this project, because of the presence of one or more of the other participants. People hold differing views, though, on exactly which participants and subgroups must be cast out to accurately reflect the conservative movement today.

To all who think we have been too inclusive and drew the line to include too many, we ask that you read the essays of those whom you consider beyond the pale and look for fundamental principles on which you agree. The "vast right wing conspiracy" has its breaches, but we have learned an immense amount about our tradition from this group of thinkers.

Other conservatives will claim that we have excluded some essential strand of the movement or overlooked the contributions of key figures. And to those who think we have been too selective, we say you are right. Many more voices should be heard and listened to about conservative principles. And we hope that you will continue the exploration of our common tradition.

Our journey in this book traces the conservative intellectual tradition from its ancient roots through the American experience and on into the future. If you have begun to perceive the wasteland produced by the vague, lawless leftism now pervading American and global culture; if you are growing weary of knaves in the middle who blank out the truth and pretend no choice or values exist; if the fading portraits of our Founders intrigue you but often seem like little more than relics of an earlier time; if you sometimes worry that, without a course correction, America, too, may be left on the ash heap of history, read on. We will show you something different from the shadows and illusions of leftism. We will show you a mighty, eternal river of truth.

BIG
TENT

CHAPTER 1

• • •

Conservative principles are rooted in Western civilization. These pillars of belief in liberty, tradition, rule of law, and God are interrelated and evolved gradually over our long history. These principles descend to us from our ancient past, our Judeo-Christian heritage, our English common law experience, and the American founding.

Publisher Alfred S. Regnery explains the traditional pillars of conservatism, their historic origins, and how the core beliefs of contemporary conservatives stem from these earlier pillars. He shows how conservative convictions flow naturally from an appreciation of God's supremacy and of a natural law that exists above man's law.

Regnery also highlights efforts to unite the conservative movement behind common principles, such as the Mount Vernon Statement, which was signed by representatives of all major branches of the conservative movement, including Regnery himself, in February 2010. This statement echoes an earlier commitment to common principles known as the Sharon Statement, signed by young conservative leaders in the fall of 1960 at the Sharon, Connecticut, home of *National Review* founder William F. Buckley. According to the Mount Vernon Statement, the principles of the American founding "define us as a country and inspire us as a people. . . . They are our highest achievements, serving not only as powerful beacons to all who strive for freedom and seek self-government, but as warnings to tyrants and despots everywhere."

Alfred S. Regnery is one of the most iconic members of the conservative movement and comes out of a rich publishing tradition. Regnery's father was Henry Regnery, who helped create the conservative newspaper *Human Events* in 1944 before founding his own publishing company. Henry Regnery's firm published William F. Buckley Jr.'s *God and Man at Yale* in 1951 and Russell Kirk's *The Conservative Mind* in 1953.

Alfred Regnery is the former president and publisher of Regnery Publishing, Inc., as the firm founded by his father is now called. During his tenure, the firm produced twenty-two *New York Times* best sellers. He is also a former publisher of *The American Spectator*, the monthly conservative journal. Regnery served in the Justice Department during the Reagan administration, worked as counsel to the Senate Judiciary Committee, and has been in private law practice. He is the chairman of the Intercollegiate Studies Institute.

THE PILLARS OF CONSERVATISM

Alfred S. Regnery[1]

◆ ◆ ◆

Conservatism has, over the past fifty years or so, become the dominant political philosophy in the United States. Any newspaper or magazine article, any television news or background report, or anything else having to do with politics more often than not will mention the word *conservative*. Politically, almost every Republican candidate running for office—whether for the county clerk or president of the United States—will establish his position in the political spectrum relative to how conservative he is. Even Democrats, particularly in the South and West, distinguish between members of their party as more or less conservative, albeit less commonly than twenty years ago. Similarly, in economic policy, tax policy, foreign affairs, social issues, and the culture more generally, the "conservative" position provides a common measuring stick.

This conservative primacy in American politics and culture didn't just happen. It is the result of decades of hard work by those who are often referred to as "the conservative movement"—the great body of organizations, committees, political activists, politicians, think tanks, periodicals, talk-show hosts, bloggers, and the rest who are actively involved in conservative politics.

Although conservatism as we know it today is relatively new, emerging on the scene only after World War II and becoming a political force only in the 1960s, it is based on ideas that are as old as Western civilization. Its basic tenets—the intellectual foundations on which this movement has been built—stretch back to antiquity, were further developed during the Middle Ages and in eighteenth- and nineteenth-century England, and were ultimately formulated into a coherent political philosophy at the time of the founding of the United States. In fact, in a real sense, conservatism *is* Western civilization.

There are four fundamental concepts that serve as the four pillars of modern conservatism.

THE FIRST PILLAR: LIBERTY

Conservatives believe that individuals possess the right to life, liberty, property, and freedom from the restrictions of arbitrary force. They exercise these rights through the use of their natural free will. That means the ability to follow your own dreams, to do what you want to do—so long as you don't harm others—and to reap the rewards. Above all, it means freedom from oppression by government and the protection by government against oppression. It means political liberty, the freedom to speak your mind and advocate any political position that suits your fancy. It means religious liberty to worship as you please. It also means the liberty not to have to do any of those things.[2]

Liberty also means *economic* liberty, the freedom to allocate resources by the free play of supply and demand and the free market system that follows from it; it means the freedom to own property and to use it accordingly.[3]

Conservatism embraces the notion that the pursuit of virtue is central to human existence, and that liberty is an essential component of the pursuit of virtue. Virtue is a necessary element in the pursuit of freedom—it ensures that freedom will be pursued for the common good—and when freedom is abused and must be controlled, virtue provides a standard for restraint.

Over the course of history, people came to realize that the greatest threats to liberty are the impositions of government, whether monarchial, democratic, or otherwise. On the other hand, people also realized that there are some things the government must control. Finding the right balance in this tension between order and liberty is often at the root of questions of the desirability of more or less government. At the end of the day, in choosing whether to have more security or more liberty, the conservative usually inclines toward liberty.[4]

THE SECOND PILLAR: TRADITION AND ORDER

Conservatism is devoted to *conserving* the values that have been established over centuries, resulting in an orderly society. It believes that human nature has the capacity to build a social order that respects human rights and is able to repel evil. Order consists of a systematic and harmonious arrangement, both within one's own character and in the state. It entails the performance of certain duties and the enjoyment of certain rights in a community, as implied by the phrase "the civil social order." It is absolutely necessary for life and the pursuit of our dreams. Order is an achievement but is easily taken for granted; it is perhaps more easily understood by looking at its opposite. Disordered existence is confused and miserable. If a society falls into general disorder, many of its members will cease to exist at all. Disorder helps to explain why order depends upon virtue—if the members of a society are disordered in spirit, the outward order of society cannot endure. Disorder describes well what conservatism is not.[5]

THE THIRD PILLAR: RULE OF LAW

Conservatism insists that a predictable and consistent legal system is necessary for ordered liberty. A lawful society consists of a government of laws, not men, as John Adams described it. It is one in which people know what the rules are, and in which rules are enforced uniformly for all citizens. Rule of law means that government itself, along with the governed, is subject to the law, and it means all people are to be equally protected by the law.[6] Rule of law promotes prosperity, and it protects liberty. Simply said, rule of law provides the conditions for uniform justice.[7]

THE FOURTH PILLAR: BELIEF IN GOD

Belief in God means adherence to the broad concepts of religious faith, things like justice, virtue, fairness, charity, community, and duty—concepts absolutely foundational to conservative thought.[8] Conservatism is tethered to the idea that allegiance to God transcends politics and sets the standards for politics. For conservatives, the reality of a supreme transcendent authority, higher than any earthly authority, naturally limits the legitimate authority of the state. No government can demand absolute obedience or legitimately attempt to control every aspect of our lives. This belief in God does not conflate faith and politics, and it does not mean that religious disputes are necessarily political disputes, or vice versa. Nor does it mean that all conservatives believe in God, or that they have a monopoly on faith. It *does* mean that conservatives believe that there is a moral order that lies behind political order, and that order establishes the natural limits of all human authority.

Man is fallible. If you believe that man is on top of things, that man is at the top of the heap—then you must believe that man can't make mistakes, that man has all the answers. The foundational tenet of liberalism is that man can do anything. Individually, of course, that's impossible. But the Left believes that man *collectively* can do anything, and that acting collectively through government, man can create heaven on earth. He can answer all of the problems that people have, and he can do it in such a way that there really aren't any mistakes or errors. There is a reason that communism requires atheism; if rights descended from God, and heaven were not possible on earth, communism would fall flat philosophically.[9]

Each of the four pillars is related to the others—indeed, they are interdependent. Conservatism provides a conceptual framework that incorporates them into a whole. Liberty, for example, is a gift of God that is safeguarded by, and dependent on, the rule of law. The rule of law itself reflects and is dependent on natural law, the law written on every man's heart from a transcendent source beyond human perception, which is reflected in every orderly and civilized society.[10] This higher law distinguishes between good and evil and finds particular expression in tradition, custom, and human laws. Tradition and order are best expressed by the common law, the law that was developed over centuries by reasonable people in their everyday lives and experiences, and which establishes rules for order consistent with the past. And tradition and order are central components of belief in God. What could demonstrate tradition and order more fully, for example, than the Old Testament and the history of the Jews, or the teachings of Christianity, and particularly the Catholic Church?[11]

THE FOUR CITIES THAT FOUNDED CONSERVATISM

It can be helpful to look at these conceptual pillars of conservatism from a historical perspective. Russell Kirk, probably the preeminent conservative thinker of the twentieth century, spoke of four great cities where the foundations of conservatism were laid: Jerusalem, Athens, Rome, and London. According to Kirk, what originated in those four cities culminated in a fifth great city, Philadelphia, in the late eighteenth century. Those four cities provide an excellent illustrative account of the philosophical underpinnings of modern American conservatism, how they were knit together, and how they evolved into contemporary conservatism.[12]

The first city is Jerusalem, from which the concept of a transcendent order originated, along with the notion that true law is divine and that God is the source of order and justice. Jerusalem's contribution to conservatism is essential, reminding us that man is subservient to God, that man does not have all the answers, and that there is a greater power to which we owe our lives and all that we have. The Hebrews in the Old Testament taught that God made a covenant or compact with his people; he provided laws by which they should live, and from that revelation man developed modern ethics and modern law. The Hebrew notion of compact is present in the very basis of Western political order.[13]

The second city is Athens, where the ancient Greek philosophers, particularly Plato and Aristotle, developed the Western understanding of the basis of the social order, what is required for people to live together in society and thrive. In the Greek mind, ethics and politics are fundamental to human existence: ethics establishes one's character, and politics is the means by which man attains his desires. Aristotle, whose work is profoundly influential in conservative thought, understood the needs of the individual person and his relationship to community. His account of man as a social animal recognized that man discovers his talents and their potential only as part of a broader community. Despite their philosophical contributions to conservatism, the Greeks add little to the appreciation of liberty; in their attention to natural human gregariousness, some Greeks were quick to conflate society and the state, even to the point of total subjugation of the person to the state.[14]

The third city in this historical progression is Rome, which esteemed the republic as the highest form of government. The Roman Republic introduced the separation of powers in the wielding of political authority and a system of checks and balances for the control of political power. Rome also embodied the idea of the rule of law as necessary for the preservation of both order and liberty, and as both reliable and consistent. Until the Roman Republic collapsed in 43 B.C., Roman philosophers such as Cato, Marcus Aurelius, and Cicero developed the appreciation for virtue as a necessary component in the rule of law. For the Romans, the virtues were necessary to maintain internal order by restraining human passions, making it possible to sustain external order and therefore conditions for preserving liberty. In this way, Roman civilization defined ordered liberty in a world where anarchy and disorder reigned. Following the republic, the Roman Empire contributed little to an appreciation for liberty but retained a great deal about the use of power in upholding order.[15]

Finally, London helped to establish the foundations of conservatism from the Middle Ages to the end of the eighteenth century and beyond. Starting with the Magna Carta in 1215, the English developed the concept of the common law and an appreciation for the universality of law applied equally to all, whether the king or the lowliest citizen. Magna Carta and the common law tradition also expressed the notion of the permanence and supremacy of law, meaning that existing law endures and must be obeyed by all.

In 1765, William Blackstone, Oxford professor and a judge, published his *Commentaries on the Laws of England*. In that massive work, he proposed that all law was rooted in the natural law and was properly shaped by Christian ethics, and he declared that man had innate rights to personal security, personal liberty, and private property. He allowed, however, that those rights were not absolute; according to Blackstone, life in society requires sacrificing certain rights as the price for the mutual commerce that society makes possible. This form of social contract is fundamental to American politics and is central to conservatism.[16]

The influence of British political thinkers on conservatism is great. Central to the conservative intellectual tradition are John Locke, John Stuart Mill, David Hume, Jeremy Bentham, and, most important, Edmund Burke. An Irishman and member of the House of Commons, Burke is probably the closest to being the intellectual father of American conservatism. His writings concerning the wisdom of tradition and order are his most important contributions to conservative thought. Specifically, he recognized that the collective wisdom accumulated over the centuries dwarfed that of any one person, and he understood that such collective wisdom was crucial to maintaining an orderly and productive society. To Burke, habit, instinct, custom, faith, reverence, and what he called "prejudice"—the accumulated practical knowledge acquired through experience—were more important than abstract reasoning. Together, they formed tradition and, for better or worse, constituted man's very nature. In other words, the good of a society is dependent upon tradition—especially a tradition of obedience to laws. For Burke, reasonable laws provided the benefit of security, which compensates for the diminishing of perfect freedom. Arbitrary and unreasonable laws, which restrict liberty without the assurance of security, on the other hand, are to be feared the most.[17]

Among the most important lessons we learn from Burke was the value of the classical virtue of prudence—the art of practical wisdom, calculating the eventual results of policies and actions, of avoiding extremes, of shunning haste. Prudence is the statesman's virtue; it equips and enables him to make sound judgments about the right means to achieve the right ends. Without it, politics may not be aimless, but it lacks a sure path to achieve its purposes.

THE FIFTH CITY

The lessons of Jerusalem, Athens, Rome, and London together found expression in a fifth city, Philadelphia, where the Declaration of Independence and the American Constitution were drafted, debated, and adopted. It is, of course, where the United States was founded. The Founders, who are also rightly described as the fathers of the American conservative tradition, were highly educated and well-read men. They had studied the Bible; they had read the classics and the British political philosophers. They knew the history of Western civilization and melded the orders of the soul, what they had learned from the Bible; the mind, the teachings of Greece and Rome; and the polity, what had filtered down through Western civilization, largely by way of Britain. They used this combination to form the great experiment of a state predicated upon reverence for liberty, morality, and justice. This American creed is the foundation of American conservatism.[18]

The Declaration of Independence dissolved the political relationship between the American people and Britain, establishing a new, independent nation. It articulated the moral vision of the emerging nation, and suggested the form of government that would later be established. It also established a theory of what a legitimate government should be, and then spoke, both in general terms and in terms of specific complaints, about how British rule had violated those principles.

The Declaration articulated a list of twenty-eight abuses—issues such as taxation without consent; denial of trial by jury, of religious liberty, of freedom of speech, and so on—that settlers had come to America to escape. The social contract, in other words, had been broken and the colonists declared that they owed no further allegiance to the king of England.

The second paragraph in the Declaration is arguably its most important, setting forth the most basic belief of the Founders:

We hold these Truths to be self-evident, that all Men are created equal, that they are endowed by their Creator with certain unalienable Rights, that among these are Life, Liberty, and the Pursuit of Happiness.

Here, the Founders are making a claim about natural law, a higher law than human law and a standard for all legitimate human law. The Declaration proposes that to secure these God-given rights, governments are instituted by men—in other words, natural law is prior to and the foundation on which man-made law is built. Only governments that secure the consent of the governed are legitimate, and the governed have the God-given right to change or abolish governments that forfeit their legitimacy.

The Declaration therefore disallows any divine right of kings, any absolute power of the state. Instead, all legitimate authority derives from the people. It makes it clear that man is born with these rights, that every person has equal rights, and that each is entitled to exercise those rights as he sees fit. Government's only legitimate function is to secure those rights, and it must do so with the consent of the people. The Declaration therefore limits the power of government not once but twice: by its ends, or purpose, and by its means, i.e., our consent.

Eleven years later, after the war was won and independence secured, the Constitution was designed to reflect the principles set forth in the Declaration of Independence, establish the structure of the new national government, and spell out how it would function. The challenge was creating a government powerful enough to protect the rights established by the Declaration from both internal and external threats, while providing sufficient restraints on the new government to secure those rights against it.

Toward that end, the Constitution establishes a system of

vertical and horizontal checks and balances. It identifies three branches of the federal government with duties particular to each, which limit each other, and sets forth the role of the states, reserving for them general police powers to accomplish what the federal government is not specifically tasked with doing. It provides citizens with a set of protections against government power and a way of protecting themselves against the abuses of that power. It enumerates the powers of the federal government, and gives it none that are not enumerated.[19]

THE TWO MOST PERFECT CONSERVATIVE DOCUMENTS

The Declaration of Independence and the Constitution, taken together, were the work not of a moment, an hour, or even a generation. They reflect the wisdom of two thousand years of Western thought, political struggle, and hard-won knowledge about man and the state. The Declaration of Independence and the Constitution may be the most perfect and most successful conservative documents in the history of the world. They are also an expression of the four pillars of conservatism. These two compact documents provide a practical codification of the doctrines of modern American conservatism.

First, they express devotion to the concept of *liberty* and the necessity of protecting liberty from the abuses of state power. The Founders recognized that government was necessary, but they also recognized that without strict limits its powers could threaten the very freedoms it was designed to protect. The Bill of Rights, of course, secured the most essential liberties from being infringed on by the government.

Second, they preserve the *rule of law*. Protecting the freedoms granted under the Constitution requires a fixed and certain rule of law. As the Founders saw it, a system in which the ruling power could alter the Constitution and the law as it pleased, and thus expand the scope of its authority, was incapable of sustaining freedom. The legislative mechanism ensured that there could be no arbitrary decrees and that justice would be settled by fixed rules and duly authorized judges. The Constitution could be amended, but only by means of an arduous and cumbersome process.

Third, they honor *order and tradition*. As mentioned, the Constitution was the culmination of more than two thousand years of Western civilization and Western thought. Further, the Founders recognized that a government was needed to provide defense, administer justice, and otherwise maintain an ordered state of affairs in which people could go about their business safely. It established continuity and the stability of leadership, providing for an orderly process of choosing leaders, making laws, and administering the new republic.

Finally, they reflect *belief in God*. Both documents reflect the great reverence of the Founders and their understanding of the Bible. The Declaration of Independence opens with reference to the Divine by saying men are "endowed by their Creator" and closes with reference to "the Laws of Nature and Nature's God" and an appeal to "the Supreme Judge of the World." The Constitution, although less explicit than the Declaration, enshrines the liberties discussed in the Declaration and protects them. It explicitly safeguards religious liberty as an integral part of a free society, and it reflects the Founders' confidence that the free exercise of religion would have a positive impact on society and government.

It is fitting that many conservatives call themselves "Constitutional Conservatives," that the Tea Party has adopted the Constitution as its iconic text, and that the conservative legal community showcases the Constitution as its fundamental document. The Constitution sets forth the basic tenets of conservatism in clear and unambiguous language; it is brief but complete, and still stands as the very bedrock of American conservatism. There is no better expression of what conservatism in America stands for than what the Declaration of Independence and the Constitution embody.

AMERICAN MODERN CONSERVATISM: A HISTORY

A brief history of the modern American conservative movement helps to connect these historical reflections to the form that contemporary American conservatism takes in the twenty-first century.[20]

As World War II drew to a close, America was culturally conservative, but not so politically. The growth of government and political domination of economic activity were accelerating. All three branches of the federal government were controlled by left-leaning Democrats. Communist Russia and

"Uncle Joe" Stalin were still considered benevolent, and Great Britain was largely a socialist state. Opinion makers and the universities were largely in agreement concerning politics and economics. In short, liberalism was in control of all the organs of influence.

In the midst of this, conservative intellectuals began to critique what they viewed as a dangerous drift of the United States toward socialism. Among them was a group of libertarian economists, led by Friedrich Hayek and Ludwig von Mises, both Austrians, who wrote about the virtues of capitalism and free markets. Socialism, Hayek wrote, was the "road to serfdom" and free market economics provided the only way for Europe to rebuild and for the United States to combat the growing communist and socialist threat from Russia and Europe. These libertarians advocated limited government instead of socialism, self-reliance instead of the welfare state, private property and entrepreneurship instead of government involvement in the means of production and central planning. The alternative, they wrote, was chaos and global poverty.

Another group of emerging conservatives perceived the primary threat to the West and to Western civilization in the spread of communism, which exerted its influence around the world in an attempt to subvert American culture and the American way of life. For anti-communists, communism represented everything abhorrent to Western values—it was tyrannical, repressive, socialistic, and atheistic. It employed terror, deceit, and subversion to achieve its ends and was determined to force its ideology on the rest of the world. Communism's goals entailed the destruction of tradition and order in the rest of the world, and it defied the rule of law.

The anti-communists also believed that modern liberalism was a progenitor of communism and, by sharing the same substantive goals, was more often than not complicit in its spread. These men were appalled at the peace that followed World War II, particularly the fact that Roosevelt and Churchill had surrendered most of Eastern Europe to the Soviet Union.

The growing strength of Soviet Russia, the fall of China to communism, and the lack of will on the part of American and European liberals to stand up to the communists alarmed the anti-communists. They also perceived threats to American internal security and considered the fact that the federal government was being infiltrated by communists and other leftists to be to the detriment of our national interest. The anti-communist movement became the most public and popularly persuasive feature of the emerging modern conservative movement.

Yet another group of conservatives was concerned about the loss of American values and the importance of tradition and faith for purposes of preserving Western civilization and culture. These traditionalists saw in unprecedented social permissiveness and vulgarity a threat to American identity. They believed in ethics and honor, the power of the church, and the need for traditional education and higher learning. In a word, they were concerned about the decline of Western civilization itself, and were devoted to the recovery of tradition and order. These traditionalists included people like Russell Kirk, William F. Buckley Jr., and Richard Weaver, among others.

These men were concerned with ideas not only as an intellectual exercise but for their practical implications. They challenged the intellectual status quo and sought to use their ideas to change the world. Although they did not think much of his theory of economics, they agreed with John Maynard Keynes's claim that "ideas are more powerful than is commonly understood. Indeed, the world is ruled by little else. . . . Sooner or later, it is ideas, not vested interests . . . which are dangerous for good or evil."[21] Lamenting what had happened to the United States and indeed to the rest of the world during the first half of the twentieth century, they believed that cultural and political liberalism was at odds with American ideals at home and abroad. Liberal ideas, they thought, were responsible for the assaults on individual liberty, limited government, free markets, and Western culture itself.

Into the early 1960s, many of the conservatives who would occupy the stage for the balance of the twentieth century developed a coherent and highly respected portfolio of academic books, articles, and lectures and, in the process, set the stage for the upsurge in conservative politics that would follow.

It is clear that in addition to reverence for liberty, suspicion of growth of the state, hostility toward communism, and a commitment to the power of traditional ideas, another force motivated much of what conservatives were doing at the time: *reaction* to and against change in the world, largely being advanced in one way or another by the Left. That reaction is what prompted many conservatives to feel that they needed to fight. Things were going wrong, in their eyes, and needed to be fixed.

By the early 1960s, conservative momentum grew, and conservative organizations were formed; conservative magazines and book publishing companies were organized; a lecture circuit was established. In short, the beginnings of a "movement" developed. Explicitly "conservative" politicians came into prominence, and in 1964 Senator Barry Goldwater, the country's most visible conservative politician, was nominated as the Republican candidate for president. Although he lost, his campaign solidified the movement politically, attracted thousands of bright young conservatives to national politics, and transformed the Republican Party from a politically moderate party dominated by easterners into a more conservative party largely animated by people from the South and West.

During the 1960s and '70s, the movement continued to grow. And in the 1980s, Republicans nominated, and subsequently elected and reelected, Ronald Reagan, the most conservative politician ever to have reached a national standing in politics. When Reagan finished his second term, having included in his administration thousands of conservative appointees, the conservative movement had, over forty years, transformed itself from an intellectual movement in the 1950s and '60s to a political movement in the 1960s and '70s, and finally into a governing movement in the 1980s. In the process, it solidified a coherent philosophy still in evidence today. It is no exaggeration to say that most of today's influential conservatives—politicians, academics, activists, donors, writers, and the rest—got their start working for Ronald Reagan in some way.

THE TENETS OF MODERN
CONSERVATISM

Given how far modern American conservatism has come from its beginnings, it is worth considering the extent to which it has been transformed by its successes and by the inevitable changes of more than sixty years of history. Yet the pressing issues of our day are not particularly different. Fittingly, the core beliefs held by contemporary conservatives stem from those timeless four pillars already described.

Many conservatives make it a point to identify themselves as "Constitutional Conservatives." This is a good starting point for examining the tenets of contemporary conservatism. First, conservatives today universally advocate a return to limited government based on the rule of law. We are currently experiencing a rapid growth in government—the creation, if you will, of a government intended to satisfy every need and desire of the populace. It is at the forefront of conservative philosophy to object to such growth. Limited government is the focal point for the ongoing struggle between governmental power and personal liberty. Ronald Reagan was right to say that the government that can give you everything you want can also take away everything you have.

The second tenet of modern conservatism is a close corollary to the first: economic freedom. Economic freedom posits a combination of free market capitalism, lower regulation of business and economic activity, and fiscal responsibility. Conservatives are generally tax cutters because they believe high taxes do not simply fund government with the resources to do things it should not be doing, but also stifle economic growth and progress. That's why conservatives tend to favor entrepreneurship over big business, which often embraces government regulation because it stifles competition.

Big business's willingness to help big government and vice versa has been termed "crony capitalism" by some. A few years ago, *The American Spectator* published an interesting piece called "America's Ruling Class—and the Perils of Revolution."[22] It divided the country into two segments in a different way from what has been commonly described. The author described the ruling class as being about 30 percent of the population, largely comprising people who are graduates of elite universities, and who occupy the legal community, big business, Wall Street, academia, or the media. Most of these elites have a vested interest in sustaining big government precisely because it's good for them.

The author put the rest of the country into what he called the "country class." These are the people earning a living, going about their own business, and on the whole not having much to do with the government. He suggested that the country is polarized between these two classes.

Conservatives do not approve of this elite ruling class. That is in part why libertarianism is an extension of conservatism into economics. Libertarians resist the idea of government picking winners and losers in the marketplace and believe in freedom remaining as unfettered as possible. They strive to maximize individual freedom by removing government restrictions on business, personal behavior, and all other individual activity.

A third tenet of modern conservatism is limited and judicious use of the courts. Activist courts have arrogated unto themselves responsibilities far beyond what was constitutionally given to them—so much so that they in effect now make policy. The Founders would not recognize the courts today. Activist judges who intrude into matters and decide issues that are outside their proper jurisdiction are now common. Far too many political issues are decided in the courts rather than being settled by the political branches of government. Consequently, the judicial philosophy of federal judicial nominees occasions some of the most hotly contested battles in Congress. In reverence for "rule of law," conservatives insist upon judges who decide cases according to the Constitution and the law, not in light of ideological aspirations.

The fourth tenet of modern conservatism is concern about the restoration and maintenance of American virtues and traditions. Contemporary conservatives who are motivated to political activity out of concern for social issues generally adhere to these tenets but are especially devoted to family values. Abortion, gay marriage, moral permissiveness, and related issues are prominent concerns among social conservatives, as are education policy, adoption and foster care, and government intrusion into personal and family matters. Many are evangelical Christians, and much of their concern is animated by their faith.

The fifth tenet of modern conservatism is strength on foreign policy. Conservatives are often divided on just what this means. Historically, conservatives believed that war should be avoided if at all possible, but were dedicated to a strong national defense. "Peace through strength" is a conservative mantra. But a new strand of conservatives, the so-called neoconservatives, joined the movement in the 1970s and '80s. Many neoconservatives were former Democrats, often liberals on domestic policy but anti-communists and hawks who identified with other conservatives on foreign policy during the Cold War. Neoconservatives tend to be more inclined to use military power for purposes other than simply defending American interests, and are known to embrace such impulses as nation building.

No clear lines of demarcation distinguish the different branches of conservatism, and most conservatives don't fit neatly into one or another camp. A general consensus remains because, for the most part, they can usually find enough to agree on for the purpose of upholding the four central pillars of conservatism.

In an effort to sustain an appreciation for and commitment to these principles, conservative leaders gathered not long ago to draft a statement of conservative belief and purpose, a statement that was subsequently signed by hundreds of thousands of citizens across the country. The Mount Vernon Statement articulates, in broad terms, principles that most conservatives embrace. The statement begins by reaffirming the principles of the Declaration of Independence and the Constitution, and emphasizing the fact that the Constitution unites conservatives through the natural fusion provided by distinctly American principles. It reminds economic conservatives that morality is essential to limited government, reminds social conservatives that unlimited government is a threat to moral self-government, and reminds national security conservatives that fiscally responsible government is key to America's safety and leadership role in the world.

The Mount Vernon Statement offered a set of policy prescriptions that remind us that conservatives will continue to have to apply these timeless principles to the age in which they live. The increasingly unprecedented growth of government and the decline of Western civilization are driving young people to conservatism—so much so that the contemporary conservative movement has as much if not more energy than it has ever had in the past.

In order to build on those past successes, and sustain them into the future, contemporary conservatives would do well to remember these foundational pillars and apply them with prudence, patience, and perseverance.[23]

CHAPTER 2

◆ ◆ ◆

According to political historian David Norcross, American history does not begin in 1776 or even 1750. It doesn't even begin in 1620 when the Pilgrims arrived on the *Mayflower* or in 1492 when Columbus discovered North America. It begins in 1066 when William of Normandy invaded England and became King William I. The point is that our history is inextricably tied to English history and law.

Norcross traces the origins of the English Revolution to 1215 when English nobles forced King John to sign the Magna Carta. He speaks eloquently of the strands of history and Anglo-American political thought that connect these events to our revolution and provide context for the life and thought of British parliamentarian and philosopher Edmund Burke.

Burke was an Irishman, educated at Trinity College, Dublin, who became an English MP and a self-proclaimed Englishman. He is widely regarded as the father of English conservatism, but Norcross makes the strong case that he should also be considered the father of American conservatism.

David A. Norcross has served in many roles in the Republican National Committee in his over thirty years of association with the RNC, including service on the Executive Committee, as general counsel, as chairman of the RNC Rules Committee, and as chairman of the Committee on Arrangements for the 2004 Republican National Convention. Norcross was formerly a lawyer in private practice with Blank Rome LLP. He was chairman of the Republican National Lawyers Association, general counsel to the International Republican Institute, and general counsel for the Center for Democracy. He served in the Judge Advocate General Corps in Ethiopia, and attended the University of Pennsylvania Law School.

EDMUND BURKE AND THE ORIGINS OF MODERN CONSERVATISM

David A. Norcross

◆ ◆ ◆

Who is a conservative, and who is more conservative? Much time and intellectual energy are spent on these questions, usually with little satisfaction. Instead, let us consider the philosophy of a classic conservative as a means of comparison. You could do no better than Edmund Burke as a template for what conservatism really is. Now, clearly not every conservative knows a whole lot about Edmund Burke. Many have probably not read Edmund Burke, but Burke and his principles describe the classic conservative. Political philosophy—right, left, center, how far right, how far left—is a pretty personal thing; it's pretty complex. The use of labels is probably, while not the best of ideas, just too tempting. Do not expect the practice to go away.

In New York, as chairman of the 2004 Republican Nominating Convention, I was required to deal with Republicans of all stripes: left, right, and center. One of the ways I did that was by not trying to put any of them into a particular box. But Burke will give us a yardstick, a box you can use to see whether principles or people fit. This will give you a way to judge how they think.

HISTORY BEFORE BURKE

You cannot understand Burke without an understanding of English history. And you cannot understand the politics of America, and therefore American history, unless you understand Burke.

American history really didn't start in 1776 or even 1750. Arguably, it started with the Norman conquest of England in 1066; all of the ensuing developments of representative government in England led to the government we have in the United States today. Consider that in 1688, just forty years before Burke was born, there was an English "revolution," the so-called Glorious Revolution. It was, for the most part, bloodless but represented real change in leadership; Michael Barone calls it "our first revolution."

In 1688, the English, in essence, chose their king. It is interesting to read Burke's explanation for how they selected a king but didn't elect the king. What they did was follow the bloodline (which was a very strong, and perhaps imperative, tradition and guide for the English), to select a person who satisfied the requirements of the bloodline and yet would be a king to do what the leaders determined needed to be done. They sought to be rid of James II and his Catholicism and to replace him with a Protestant who was interested, they thought, in the development of English culture and commerce. The con-

tinuation of English culture and the desire for commercial opportunity are constant threads throughout English history and
indispensable elements of Burke's philosophy.

So, in 1688, they selected a king. But in 1649, only forty
years before, King Charles I had been executed and a different
leader chosen very definitely by the sword. Oliver Cromwell led
a bloody and bitter civil war to create "the Commonwealth,"
and he sought radical change in the culture and traditions of
England. That war saw bloody battles and massacre and ultimately led to the emigration of thousands of Royalists. It was as
bitter and hotly contested a change in England as had occurred
before or has since. In 1660, the English leaders rejected the
brutality of the Commonwealth and restored the traditional
monarchy by offering the crown to the son of the executed
Charles I. When the leaders restored Charles II to the throne,
there was no sitting Parliament. But a group of leaders came
together and devised the Restoration, restoring the crown to
Charles II. They then, in a measure most respectful of tradition, passed an act legitimizing their actions. In essence, they
said, "We weren't really Parliament when we chose the king,
but now that he's chosen and he's here and we're in place, we're
going to say we were Parliament." We have had transitions
in this country from president to president not as smooth as
that was.

In the course of forty years, England had had three chief
executives selected by the "people" and still managed, at the
end of much tumult, to protect (or restore) traditional English
values, including representative government and commercial
opportunity.

You would think that between the time Charles I was executed and the time it put William and Mary on the throne (1689), considering the turmoil of the civil war, the country would have lost its bearings and its respect for very basic traditions. But it did not—so strong were the foundations of its society. The country continued to be a commercial and military success. It continued to grow and prosper without any serious disruption at home in terms of commerce or the day-to-day life of the citizenry.

In 1714, not long before Burke was born, England picked a whole new royal line. William and Mary died childless; Queen Anne had no children; so the English came to another roadblock. They picked the House of Hanover; they found a German elector; and they chose him to be their king: King George I. Burke is careful to say they didn't elect him, but they selected him. So now there were four leaders changed in the course of fewer than one hundred years, and England soldiered on. The merchants in England continued to be successful, England continued to grow, English commerce grew. The country thrived during that period, notwithstanding the possibility for extreme turmoil. There was in fact little disruption.

This is the world into which Burke was born, the world in which he became a politician. He spent many, many years in Parliament, was in leadership only a very short period of time, and was in opposition much of that time. Burke's philosophy was shaped by those extremely important, potentially disruptive, events through which England survived—not only survived, but thrived. Through that whole period, Parliament gained strength, in part, because it had been the vehicle for selecting the new leaders.

Thus, we see that one of the Burke basic tenets is that government is necessary. There is a divergence on this point between Burke and Paine. Burke, much like Blackstone, said any government is better than no government. Clearly, in the hundred years before Burke was born, and when he was becoming active in politics, a smoothly functioning government was essential, and was essential to the continuation of people's comfort and people's commercial development. You can't understand U.S. history without understanding that period of time and the growth of the power of people to select their leaders by means that were not revolutionary, even if the Glorious Revolution was called a revolution.

At all times and through all of those potential upheavals, the preservation of existing freedoms was foremost in the English psyche. And that's how it became part of our psyche. Burke understood as no one else in his time—that might be unfair to Blackstone—that the preservation of existing freedoms was essential to progress and the goodness of human life.

Understand that throughout all of this turmoil, every time there was a bump in the road, Parliament developed a little more power. If you think about it, from the regicide of Charles I to the Britain of today, and to where we are today, in terms of the power of the people, and of legislative bodies, you will understand that it is that development that shaped Burke's philosophy and that has shaped Britain, and the United States, and for that matter Australia, New Zealand, and Canada as well.

BURKE'S PHILOSOPHY

Burke gained prominence during the period of the Enlightenment, the so-called Age of Reason. At that time, society was
just beginning to embrace Romanticism. Burke was not really
a man of either of those philosophies, which makes him all the
more interesting. He was pretty much a man of his own philosophy, his own thought, and his own "undisciplined reading,"
as he called it.

He had debates with Rousseau, who was much more a believer in the innate goodness of man. Burke was not, inciden-
tally. Burke realized that man (and woman, lest I be accused
of leaving half of mankind out), left to their own devices, and
with no government, wouldn't lead very happy lives, wouldn't
understand progress, and wouldn't progress. So for Burke the
Romantic notion that you can create government out of reason
alone—which I believe is essentially where the French were after
the French Revolution, and before they destroyed the model—
was never an alternative. Burke never separated human reason
from historical experience. Those two things, history and experience, along with a third, tradition, are the keys to Burke.

History is a means to preserve the progress that had already
been achieved. What is it that we are trying to preserve? What
is it about our way of life that is most important to us? To Rousseau, it was probably man's ability to figure out how to make
everything better. To Burke, it was the actual progress that had
already been achieved, and also the capacity of mankind to keep
good changes coming, to build productively on the past.

Tradition is typically thought of as something dry and dull.

But it isn't dry at all—it's the everyday life of today looked at forty years hence. One great concern today is that we may be abandoning traditions and years of experience that have kept us progressing. Ironically, "Progressives" don't really understand progress.

Burke and his knowledge of tradition, history, experience, and survival in times of potential upheaval describe why Great Britain today and the United States as well as Canada, Australia, and New Zealand are so very different from virtually any other model of government in the world. Yes, those nations have a monarch, and we have a president that we elect every four years, but have you ever asked yourself, "Why are there such difficulties in other parts of the world with what we assume as second nature?" It's because it *is* second nature. And it is second nature because we have respected history and tradition and experience.

There is a continuum of development in the United States, a continuum that Burke not only would have understood but, I suspect, would have expected. One of the notions of conservatism is that it is a rejection of change; this is the simplistic explanation of conservatism you hear from liberals. But that isn't truly what conservatism is. Conservatism is a resistance to the rejection of history, tradition, and experience. Regardless of how you feel about the health care plan (Affordable Care Act), I think you must concede that it is a significant change in a tradition that involves a very large part of American economic society. Conservatives consider whether that change is good or bad based on its rejection of prior norms. Liberals just see all change as progress.

Some change *is* progress, of course. When the American Revolution was over, the crown was offered to George Washington. If you think about Burke's philosophy, and you think about Americans who knew about Burke, you can certainly understand why somebody said Washington would make a good monarch. The secret to our success and to our foundation is that we got past that with a pretty radical change. What would have happened if George Washington had accepted monarchy? It might have worked. But I think at that point, we understood that we could make the change; we could keep the traditions; we could embrace the progress with a new kind of executive.

Burke was a kind of contrarian Whig. For Burke, opposition was fine, even if it was within your own party. Being able to think your own thoughts and present your own ideas was a good idea. He saw political parties as a way to limit the monarch. He, like the rest of the Whigs, was a constitutional monarchist. He got into a significant dustup with the king over this. The three Georges pushed back on the growth of the importance and power of Parliament. They were looking for a bit more control. Burke saw that as a very bad idea indeed and fought against it successfully. It's easy to see why he did: having the king become a tyrant clearly was not what Burke saw as progress respecting history, tradition, and experience.

BURKE AND HUMAN NATURE

One can't separate human nature from human experience. The French tried. The French Revolution threw it all out. The revolutionaries threw out the church; they threw out the king; they threw out the nobility, killed most of them; they did a do-over. And the do-over didn't work. And Burke saw that it wasn't going to work. Thomas Jefferson thought highly of the French Revolution, had some significant disagreements about it; Burke and Jefferson had serious combat over his position on the French Revolution.

But Burke wasn't hidebound. He was not a man who didn't understand or appreciate change. He supported the American Revolution; he was appalled by the French Revolution. And he was appalled when the French got done, because there was nothing left of history, of tradition, and there was no experience to guide them on the new course.

With reason and the human mind and knowing that man is good, the French tried to create something new. The something new is now known as the Reign of Terror, decried by Burke, who watched it. And then, when that was over, they fell into . . . Napoleon. Napoleon certainly would not have been a Burke favorite.

You look at the French Revolution and you look at the American Revolution and you see the difference: the French tore everything down and threw it out. In today's parlance, they threw the baby out with the bathwater.

Burke was troubled by the French Revolution because human nature is central to governance, and man is not inherently good. Burke, by the way, said that the king wasn't nearly as bad as we read in the history books. Burke did believe that liberty was God's gift. Burke's opposition to the French Revolution was a very contrarian notion. It was so contrarian,

Burke broke with the leader of his party over his opposition to the French Revolution. Ultimately, the party came back to him and the English king actually said, "Burke, I've read your book. I think you're right." Burke's *Reflections on the Revolution in France* is a seminal treatise on conservatism.

Burke's reaction to the French Revolution galvanized an already conservative inclination that had been developed because of the history that was so proximate to his life and that was so clear to him, followed by, during his lifetime, the American Revolution, in which he supported the colonists. He didn't support freedom for America; he supported the rights of Englishmen who lived in the colonies. That was different, but it was consistent with his philosophy.

OF REVOLUTIONS GOOD AND BAD

The English Revolution actually started in 1215 when the barons told King John, "You've got to stop taking stuff away from us. You're taking our power away; you've got to give us something." Now these were enormously wealthy, landed people. This was major change, but it was gradual, even surviving the reign of Henry VIII. Parliament survived, waxing and waning; more powerful, less powerful. The Glorious Revolution, with little bloodshed, shuffled one king off to France in a reasonably happy frame of mind, and then substituted a new one with the proper bloodlines.

Consider three more upheavals: the Russian Revolution, the American Civil War, and the Arab Spring. First, the Russian Revolution pretty well tracks the French, with even worse long-term results.

Second, I want you to put the Civil War into the mix. It was, in many ways, a failed revolution, and it has taken a long time for us to get over it—assuming the majority of us are over it. But it still was no great challenge to the fundamental institutions of government. Both South and North followed Burke's principles: history, tradition, experience. And when it was all over, unpleasant as that was, and difficult as it was, the South was able to come back to the tradition and experience and history they understood, though they clearly would have preferred a different result. But it wasn't the institutions that got challenged in that war—and Burke would say, "That's why we got through it."

Third and last, consider the Arab Spring. The Arab Spring, thus far, appears to be ignoring all of Burke. The Arabs don't have the tradition. My question is whether their religion will let them accept a form of government not dominated by religion. And I readily admit that in the Burkean sense, religion is a huge part of their tradition, and, in fact, a part of their tradition with which they now struggle.

I was called upon in Tunisia, Nigeria, and Russia to try to give advice on how to develop political parties. In both Nigeria and Tunisia, the question was that they wanted political parties, but they didn't want any opposition. Political parties are perforce made up of the government and opposition. So when you have a tradition that doesn't accept opposition, it's difficult to export our democracy. That doesn't mean we shouldn't try, but in my view they are going to have to endure a long period of trial and error before they get there. Burke nailed it: the tradition isn't there, the history isn't there, and the experience isn't there.

Stability. All of the last revolutions that we have talked about resulted in terrible bloodshed, upheaval, and an overthrow of existing ways of life. They were a result not of slow development, or gradual development, but of radical change.

If the Progressives were willing to move forward slowly, to progress with some attention to history, tradition, and experience, then I would have no quarrel with them, and neither would Burke, because Burke was certainly not antiprogress. Where the question becomes critical is an example like ObamaCare. Is that progressive? Is that within the bounds of our history, tradition, and experience, or is that too much? Obviously, we have two very vigorous sides to that question, but when is progress bad? "When it's too fast" is the glib answer to that.

BURKE ON ECONOMICS

Let's talk about something else in which Burke was a believer. Before Jack Kemp, Bill Roth, and Ronald Reagan, Burke was a supply-sider. "Who," he said, "is to judge what profit is appropriate; surely no one on earth."

I spent some time in the former Soviet Union as the Russians were overthrowing communism. I remember being asked, "I want to ask something I don't understand about the United States. Talk to me about potato chips."

I said, "Okay, let's talk about potato chips."

"How do you know where to send the potato chips? How do you know that? How do you know that Joe's Grocery Store gets eight cases and Mallory's Grocery Store gets sixteen? How do you know that? Who tells you that? Who's in charge of that?"

Obviously, the markets are in charge of that. Burke understood that. While he was in Parliament, some bright spark decided that they were going to put a tax on corn because there was too much of it, and they were looking to enhance revenues as governments then and now are wont to do. Burke was appalled. There was a shortage of grain, the grain price went up, and then Parliament's solution was: let's build a bunch of granaries around the kingdom, and then we can take the corn and put it in the granaries, and then let it out as people need it.

Burke's reaction: "Are you crazy? When the government buys the corn, the government goes into business against itself." So it pays too much for the corn; now it's got to give the corn away, and the people must pay for the extra corn anyway. It's a market lesson. By the way, the corn tax did not work, and they didn't build the granaries. Burke's opponents wanted "compulsory equalization." This has faint echoes today. Burke said, "Equalizers never raise what is low; they pull down what is high." That is precisely what happened. We would do well to consider that history.

All markets are related. Consider ethanol and corn. There is an ethanol subsidy; thus, farmers grow a lot of corn, and it's used to make ethanol. The price of food goes up; the price of feed goes up for the corn-eating critters we eat. You really can't mess around in a market, says Burke, unless you're willing to accept the consequences. And the consequences seldom, if ever, provide what it is that you thought you wanted when you started to tinker with it. Most consequences it sometimes appears are unintended. Legislators would do well to consider that carefully.

Lest you wonder about labor, labor is a commodity. If there isn't enough labor, and I need it, I'm willing to pay more. If there's too much labor, I'm going to be able to pay less. And you've heard this argument today on the minimum wage. If you impose a minimum wage, and I'm an employer, I can avoid the consequences of that by refusing to hire as many people. So Burke was right about that. Labor is indeed a commodity.

Think about labor unions. I've never been a very big supporter of labor unions, but it seems to me that the willingness to withhold labor if it's a commodity is a legitimate way to address the employer. That is unless the result of your withholding work gets you a wage that is too high for the product to be salable—then everybody will suffer.

Again, if you're going to intervene, try to understand the consequences of your intervention and whether they are good and whether your intervention is more than you need to do or just about right. If you guess wrong, you may be sure the market will sort it out in the end.

Burke also said two other things: "Once you look to the government for bread, you will always expect it." That's worth thinking about today. And this is worth thinking about even more: "Do not inflame the poor versus the rich. We are in it together." That's all got to do with markets; it's all got to do with our history, our tradition, our experience. If we ignore or abandon those principles of Burke, we do it at our risk, and we need to carefully consider whether we're willing to accept the consequences.

BURKE AND THE CHURCH

With regard to public education and civil policy, Burke thought that the church should not meddle. But he was clearly a very religious man in the sense of a belief in God, the importance of the history and tradition and experience of the church, and what these had meant in England.

We have growing secularism in the United States. Can you teach without reference to faith? Can you maintain society as we know it without religion? That's part of our history, tradition, and experience; that's a huge part of our history, tradition, and experience. It's why people keep talking about the Judeo-Christian ethic of the United States. If you take it away, with what do you replace it? I have no idea.

While Burke's religiosity has been questioned by some, he had a clear understanding that religion is an essential element in keeping order in society. He was less interested in denominational differences than in religion's social utility as a way to order man's relationships with his fellow man. The question comes down to what happens to a society if you remove religious tradition and observance. If you take religion out of the equation, what is the replacement? I worry about the rise of secularism in the United States. I began to worry about it in terms of the fundamental role that religion plays in our society. How important is it? The only thing I can think of is Rousseau and his perspective that man is basically good and inclined to do the right thing, with or without societal or religious control. But is that true? Burke rejected that notion. If Burke is right, and I think he was, where do we find the substitute for the institution of religion?

BURKE'S INFLUENCE ON AMERICA

Who made a more important contribution to our revolution and to the form of government that followed—Burke or Paine? Who contributed more to the philosophy that sparked and sustained our revolution? Paine's contribution and Burke's contribution are entirely different. I believe Burke's contribution to be far greater than Paine's. From my perspective as a politician, that's true. But that's not really a fair comparison. Paine's rhetoric was rather over the top, but it also encouraged the colonists to take the steps that they needed to take. You can legitimately wonder whether Burke's philosophy—reasoned, wordy, very prolix—would have gotten the colonists where they needed to be in terms of freedom from Britain, and recall that Burke was never in favor of American freedom from Britain.

Burke started with the notion that government is what keeps man in line so that man has the opportunity for improvement, while Paine takes a more grudging view of government's organizing and controlling. It figures, because Burke wanted to progress; Burke didn't want us to be free of England. Paine wanted to throw the bomb! He certainly was not opposed to any kind of government; he certainly wasn't much in favor of a centralized executive, but he would have centralized power in one great legislature, which looks a lot like France.

Burke provided the serious, philosophical underpinning of early American political society and for the conservative movement that is as appropriate and important today as it was in 1775 and 1776. While Burke may have made a greater contribution to the result, it was surely Paine who lit the fire.

Any form of government that is democratic includes the possibility that the majority will go too far. We are presently positioned to jettison Burke's principles and take that step too far. We have already proved the point that "when you look to the government for bread, when you get it, you will always look to it for bread." That's how we got where we are. Is our next step reconsideration of Burke's basic principles as they apply today? Will we abandon the lessons of history, experience, and tradition in search of a progressive utopia?

If we are true to Burke, we will not go too far. We will realize that we cannot abandon tradition, history, and experience.

CHAPTER 3

◆ ◆ ◆

Admiration for the American founding period is perhaps the most unifying sentiment for the conservative movement. The idea of a group of English citizens risking, as it is said in the Declaration of Independence, "our lives, our fortunes, and our sacred honor" still stirs the blood of conservatives of every stripe.

Conservatives may argue over the role of the state in upholding virtue, or the balance of power between the states and the federal government; conservatives diverge in their opinions over the role of American military power overseas; conservatives may disagree in strident terms over deficit reduction versus low taxation. But conservatives agree that the Founders—the men who broke from England, declared independence, and then formulated the Constitution of the United States—are worthy of admiration and emulation.

Former Speaker of the House Newt Gingrich explains the impact of English tradition on the American founding and on the legacy of the Founding Fathers. The American

Revolution represented a battle, Gingrich argues, to uphold the rights and responsibilities with which citizens felt they had been endowed, and which were being trampled on by a usurping government.

Newt Gingrich is well known as the architect of the Contract with America that led the Republican Party to victory in 1994. From May 2011 to May 2012, Newt Gingrich was a candidate for the Republican nomination for president. He is an analyst for CNN and cohost of *Crossfire*. As an author, Speaker Gingrich has published twenty-four books, including fourteen fiction and nonfiction *New York Times* best sellers. Newt and his wife, Callista, host and produce historical and public policy documentaries. Recent films include *Nine Days That Changed the World* and *Ronald Reagan: Rendezvous with Destiny*. He resides in McLean, Virginia, with Callista and has two daughters and two grandchildren.

THE AMERICAN REVOLUTION
AND WHAT IT MEANS

Speaker Newt Gingrich

◆ ◆ ◆

The Revolutionary period is in many ways the richest and most important period of American history. It's almost the DNA of modern America and the way in which we have evolved since then. With the possible exception of Lincoln's resurrection of the Declaration of Independence, there's no period after 1800 that is quite as dynamic intellectually in setting the stage for the America that evolved during that period.

Think of this as a story in which there were a group of people who discovered themselves being in a particular situation. They were living a life of freedom. They were living a life of community. They were living a life of self-government. They were living a life of enormous practicality. And all of a sudden, the British Empire began to disrupt their ability to continue living that life.

You have to see the American Revolution, in a remarkable way, as a conservative reaction to British imperial tyranny, actually protecting a past status quo. It was unlike the French Revolution, in that the American revolutionaries weren't trying to rebel to create a different future. They were trying to sustain what they saw as a powerful past.

There are a couple of reasons that this occurs. Part of it is captured by Paul Johnson in his wonderful *History of the American People*, where he says that by the 1770s, Americans were probably the lowest-taxed people in the history of the human race, and they resented every penny.

One useful organizing model for how real Americans have acculturated is DNA. America can absorb people from other countries, and literally in a matter of years, immigrants can learn to be American in a way you never learn to be French or to be German or to be Chinese. America has a unique intellectual and cultural DNA, and this is the core of the American experience.

THE BRITISH HISTORY OF AMERICA

What is that American experience? It began with a very long evolution of a British or English sense of personal freedom, going back in many ways to the Magna Carta, in some ways going all the way back to Angle and Saxon laws preceding the Norman invasion. There's a lengthy sense of individuality and a lengthy sense of individual rights that is expressed as "I have some rights that even the king can't take from me." In the Magna Carta in 1215, the barons had the king sign a document that says there are certain rights he can't take from them, and he can't get extra money without their approval.

Early on, this is actually a deal for the great lords that gradually, over hundreds of years, spreads also to be a deal for the commoners. By the seventeenth century, this is beginning to be a real power struggle. Michael Barone has written a terrific small book on the Glorious Revolution of 1688 in which he describes James II seeking to establish absolutist power. That was combined with a sense that he was Catholic; the country was largely Protestant. So the British act to stop him. They bring in a Dutch prince who is coming from a country that has such a thoroughly screwed-up governing system that almost nobody can make it work. And the Dutch pride themselves on being this little bastion of self-government in which the oligarchs protect themselves through all sorts of constant arguments and pettiness and cheapness.

When William arrives in the Glorious Revolution, he arrives with a sense of the limitations of kingship. He is himself comfortable manipulating the Parliament rather than trying to run over it. Thus, you begin to get into charters and agreements that create a very deep framework for what followed.

That back-and-forth created modern government People like John Locke began trying to figure out a solution to the last several hundred years of governance. They said to themselves, "We don't want to go back to the English Civil War because that was horrible; we don't want to go back to Cromwellian dictatorship because that was terrible; we don't want to see European absolutism—that violates who we are as English." Instead, they pushed for a nationalist sense of liberty that is deeply tied into the sense of being English.

THE NEW WORLD

Now, this wasn't all good. People were subordinated and, if necessary, killed because they didn't understand the British view. The period engenders sending people to the New World. Somebody once said the most important thing to understand about America is we're the people who left, and the Europeans are the people who didn't. There's almost this pattern; you're getting very aggressive, very risk-taking people, who come here in very small boats. If you ever go to Williamsburg and to Jamestown and you see the size of the boats that came across the Atlantic, you understand why, when the first permanent colony was established, they stopped at Cape Henry and they put up a cross to thank God for having gotten across the Atlantic. They were really shaken by how hard it was to get here.

When they got here, they were in the New World, and they felt it was a new world. There's a famous story of Captain John Smith opening a letter to discover he's been put in charge of the colony by the people who paid for the colony. This is a private enterprise operation. It is one of the things I hark back to in thinking about alternative ways of organizing similar great adventures like space, because these colonies are being founded by private entrepreneurs with grants from the king. The king doesn't have the power and the bureaucracy to do it, so he says, "Here, you go see if you can make it work."

So Smith was put in charge. The aristocrats who were there came to him and said to him, "We've already paid our way over here. You cannot make us work. We're aristocrats." (I always tell my liberal friends, it's ironic: the people who don't want to work are the aristocrats, not the poor.) And Smith looked at them and he said, "Look, we don't have a big enough surplus of production in the New World to take care of you, but I can't make you work. You're right; you signed this document. So here's the deal: if you don't work, you won't eat," which is actually a paraphrase of Paul. They thought about it for a couple of hours and came back and said, "Okay, tell us some more about this work stuff."

This is the beginning of the whole American DNA that is very work-oriented, very self-reliant, very inquisitive. We've always been a country that wanted to have private property rights. Jefferson wrote not "the right to pursue happiness" but the "right to private property" in the first draft of the Declaration of Independence. The reason is, if you have private property rights, no tyranny can take away from you what is yours. The rule of law begins to be protected from the smallest property up; it's not protected by the largest theory down. So this is the context in which you see the development of these ideas of freedom.

ORIGINS OF THE FOUNDING FATHERS

The Founding Fathers, by the time they began to argue seriously with Great Britain around 1770, were inheriting 160 years of practice in which they were routinely governing themselves. Washington started very early in life on the frontier. He went out at sixteen or seventeen as a surveyor in the Wild West— which back then was western Virginia. He then engaged in leading military expeditions, the first of which was a disaster, the second of which was Braddock's Expedition, where they got slaughtered by the French and Indians. He learned an immense amount about trading along the frontier. He led the Virginia militia in a successful anti-Indian and anti-French campaign.

Then Washington announced for the legislature and wanted to go to Williamsburg to serve in the provincial assembly. The tradition was that you bought drinks for all of your neighbors and they then elected you. Washington announced grandly that he was a military hero and above the indignity of buying drinks. He promptly came in last, because he didn't understand the rules of the game. The next time he ran, he bought more drinks than anybody in the history of Virginia.

Washington did not make the same mistake twice. When he was a young man on the frontier, he surrendered Fort Necessity. Nobody who knew anything about military strategy would have done it. Washington screwed up. He went back home; he actually wrote a pamphlet explaining why he surrendered. Then he was asked to be the senior colonial adviser to Braddock's Expedition, which left Carlisle, Pennsylvania. He told Braddock, "You know, I personally would not advise marching forward in a row in bright red uniforms down a road. The French and Indians are going to fire from behind trees, and you're just setting yourself up as a big target."

Braddock answered, "You're obviously a colonial; you don't understand British or European tactics. This is a great, professional army. We don't fight like bandits. We're not going to do the things you do."

Well, of course, exactly what Washington suggested is what

happened: they were ambushed from every side. Braddock was killed almost at the very opening of the battle. Washington was the senior officer remaining. He had roughly 1,500 troops. Washington rallied all the troops, and he got them off the field without having a total massacre. Washington had two horses shot out from under him; there were four bullet holes in his coat at the end of the day. Ten years later, he ran into an Indian chief at a powwow and the chief said to him, "God must want you for something. Every one of us was trying to shoot you. You're this huge guy. I personally shot at you six times. I do not understand why you're here."

Washington wasn't just lucky; he knew how to work a room. Governor Byrd used to make money because he would bet strangers a shilling that Washington could break a walnut between his thumb and his first finger. Try it sometime at Christmas when you have lots of walnuts; you'll see: it's virtually impossible. Washington was so physically strong he'd break them. And Washington was quite personable; he was a guy who sat around with the guys.

He was also an advocate of liberty. Everyone should read Addison's play *Cato*. *Cato* is a play about Cato the Younger, who refuses to give in to Caesar, ultimately flees Caesar during the civil war, and goes all the way over to North Africa. His son is killed by Caesar. And Caesar eventually finds him and tells him, "Look, if you'll just accept that I'm the leader, then you get to live the rest of your life happily. I'll give you honors. I'll give you money. It's important to validate my government that you concede." And Cato says, "No, I'd rather die a freeman than live having put my knee down to you."

Now what makes it interesting is that *Cato* was Washington's favorite play. He read it repeatedly. It was deep in Washington's being; there was a sense of nobility.

Then they began to notice this cloud on the horizon. The cloud came from two directions. It came first of all because the British monarchy was increasingly dictatorial and increasingly arrogant. And it came second because the British governing class was increasingly successful and increasingly arrogant. Now these are two different, parallel problems.

The rise of the British government in the eighteenth century followed the period when William takes over in 1688, at which point it was a very weak central monarchy. But with the rise of the Hanovers, the centralization of the monarchy began anew. They learned that they could manage the government by corruption. For them, corruption was public resources for something other than the public good. For them, it meant, "Would you support my government? By the way, I happen to have a job in the treasury" or "I need to get this done; your cousin, I understand, needs to be an ambassador somewhere."

All of these things begin to permeate the society. About 1740, there is an enormous intellectual explosion, which asserts itself in the Whig critique of the British government. One of the arguments that Gordon Wood in particular makes is that you cannot understand the American revolutionaries unless you understand that they are the Whig critique. They are taking up the same exact critique that the Whigs had.

The Whigs were deeply criticizing large government, and saying large government is inherently corrupt government. They said large government breeds favoritism and centralized power, and violates the rule of law. They said that it violates the notion that private property rights should be equally protected, because now people were being taxed in order to give power and money to people who weren't. It became a very bitter fight. Remember, this was still an era when you had to be very careful how you phrased things, because to overtly criticize what is "the king's government" was to criticize the king, and it wasn't far from there to treason, and it wasn't far from there to getting hanged.

So there was a fairly delicate game under way.

THE REVOLUTIONARY WAR

By 1776, Washington's army drove the British out of Boston. They got to Brooklyn, but were beaten by the British army. A divine intervention occurred. This is Washington's language; he said, "Providence intervened." The reason was the British navy, which was going to massacre them, was in the East River. But their back was to the river. A huge fog came in. The Marblehead fishermen who would later take Washington across the Delaware rowed the entire army at night across the river, escaping the British.

Now there were 30,000 effectives in Brooklyn. They lost in Brooklyn; they lost in Manhattan; they lost in White Plains; they lost in the Palisades; they were driven across New Jersey. By the week before Christmas, they were down to 2,500 effectives, a third of whom did not have shoes. They were wearing burlap bags, leaving a trail of blood when they marched.

The generals met with Washington and there was this great hashing back and forth between Washington and the council of war. The generals all said to him, "We're in deep, deep trouble. We don't know what to do. There aren't many of us left." Washington said, "I've got this idea. We're going to cross the river at night, during a snowstorm. We're going to march nine miles at night. We're going to surprise the Hessians. We're going to capture all of them. It's going to be a great victory; it'll revive the morale of the war. It just requires a three-pronged assault across an icy river at night."

And every single one of the generals said, "We can't do that." And finally Washington said, "Look. If we don't win something, this army will disappear in two or three weeks. When the army disappears, the revolution will be over. When the revolution is over, everyone in this room will be hanged. Therefore, we have nothing to risk, because we have certain death on one side and a chance to win on the other, crossing the river."

Washington was someone who's actually very subtle. He understood the Napoleonic principle "Morale is to material as three is to one." So anytime you have a choice between an army with high morale and low equipment, or an army with low morale and high equipment, always pick high morale.

They crossed the river that night. Their password was "victory or death"—and they meant it. They marched nine miles. They found that there were two ravines. They thought there was one; there were two. They had to manhandle the artillery. They had a driving snowstorm from their rear. If you were war-gaming this, if you were doing this in a classroom, you would have the Hessians mobilized and they would annihilate Washington about eight o'clock that morning. But because the snowstorm was so enormous, the Hessians didn't post guards. Here's part of the problem: Europeans had coerced soldiers; you couldn't put them out in a snowstorm because they'd go berserk. They were really trapped into fighting in open weather where sergeants could keep track of your men. Americans were fighting for freedom, plus Americans were all deer hunters. They just thought of this as a snowstorm. They had been out in snowstorms their whole lives.

The result was a crushing victory. They captured 800 Hessian professional soldiers at the cost of one American. Within two weeks, word of the victory had brought 15,000 volunteers. Washington drove the British across northern New Jersey, and the war was saved for the moment.

Washington was in the field for eight years. He spent one week at Mount Vernon. I wear Washington's commander-in-chief flag from Valley Forge to remind myself and other people. When the Founding Fathers met at the Constitutional Convention and they wrote "commander in chief," the guy presiding over the convention was Washington, the commander in chief.

THE FOUNDING PHILOSOPHY

Now why were they doing all this? They were doing all this because they were really angry. And the reason they were so angry is they had grown up accustomed to what they thought of as the natural rights of Englishmen. They all thought of themselves as English. They all thought that they were part of this extraordinary worldwide empire. They identified with the Parliament. They even identified with the king and the House of Lords.

Back in 1770, the British, out of arrogance and ignorance, began to behave in a way that said to the Americans, "No. You're not us." Benjamin Franklin went to London to petition for the provinces, left as an American Englishman, and returned an American, because he realized that even though he was a world-class scientist, independently wealthy, a very successful businessman, a writer of considerable note, and the founder of various institutions, he was a provincial. And he would never, ever be accepted in British high society. So he said, "Fine. You want to make me an American? I'm an American. Now that I'm an American, I want my independence because I don't trust you to govern me."

And so around 1770, starting with the Boston Massacre, you really began to see a ramping up of organization. You got committees of correspondence. This was not some highly centralized, organized product. This was a mass movement. For example, five months before the first shot was fired at Lexington and Concord, the New Hampshire folks went to the British fort in New Hampshire, surrounded it. There was a very small garrison and a very junior officer who looked out and said, "Okay, I quit." This small garrison leaves, leaving all the guns and all the ammunition to the New Hampshire militia. It doesn't become the first shot heard round the world because there were no shots fired. The guy just surrendered. And that didn't bubble up. It didn't become part of the folklore. But, in fact, New Hampshire also wrote its first state constitution before the Declaration of Independence. Out here in the wilderness, they were saying, "We're not paying to London."

Thus, the British now had this escalating crisis. The Americans were starting to know one another; they were driven together by one common theme, a Burkean one: "We have inherited rights that are coming to us from God and that constitute a fundamental contract. You, the king, and your government, are breaking our rights."

So from their standpoint, the revolutionary behavior was the king and his government, because they were simply living out what they already believed, in a sense.

Here's what the Americans would have told you in the mid-1770s: "The royal government is corrupt. The royal government is violating our rights." Interestingly, while the number one complaint was no taxation without representation, the number two complaint was judges who were dictators on behalf of the king. There were more complaints about judges than any other single problem except taxation. And why was taxation so big? It's ironic. The British, who didn't understand at all what was going on—this is how you get into establishment revolutionary environments—believed that they had footed the bill for the French and Indian War, and that the colonies should pay for that. The Americans believed that the British behaved like an empire, and should pay like an empire.

But instead of saying, "Gee, this is a political conversation. Maybe we'd better find a way to talk with each other," the British imperial government decided on coercion. Now why were they doing this? Because they'd done it everywhere. They coerced the Irish; the last great massacre was in 1693. They just finished coercing the Scots with the Battle of Culloden in 1744. They made it a hanging, drawing, and quartering offense to wear a kilt. They had crushed the Welsh earlier.

And this is why, by the way, the Second Amendment ended up being so important. In a terrific book called *Paul Revere's Ride*, it's pointed out that the British had routinely coerced peasants. They marched out of Boston in April of 1775 to coerce peasants. Except they didn't find peasants. They found citizens. And they didn't find people who were unarmed—they found an armed, trained militia that had spent over six months preparing for the battle. And they got beaten, badly, and they had lost men all the way back to Boston. And now they had a crisis, because how can you be the greatest empire in the world and have a rabble in America stand up to you?

That's how this process begins.

Now what did the Americans think they were doing? They were protecting themselves from an aggressive attack. They were not on offense. They were not asking anything new. They were defending the rights that they had been living for 160 years. And they were saying to the British government, "What are you doing to us? We're just being who we are. We've always had the right to vote. We've always had the right to decide our taxation. We've always had the right to solve our problems locally. You're sending us these foreigners to judge us; they're confiscating our houses; they're imposing troops to live in our homes; you're taking away our money." And here's the underlying core idea that is at the heart of this: it goes back to Addison's *Cato*: "If I concede that you have the arbitrary power to take a penny from me, then I have conceded that you have the arbitrary power to take everything from me."

In a sense, if you read Lincoln on slavery in the 1850s, Lincoln was capturing the rhythm of the Founding Fathers' argument with the English, which was to say, "I can't allow you to cross this line."

There were two different conversations under way. The British were saying to themselves, "Aha! Americans are cheap. So what we'll do is we'll give tea to the East India Company. The East Indian Company, in return for a monopoly, will reduce the price of tea. So although we'll still have a tax, it will now be cheaper than it was. Therefore, the Americans will have no complaint because, after all, tea will now be cheaper."

But the Americans were saying, "Wait a second. The argument isn't about money. The argument is about rights. We'd rather pay more for a tea without a tax than less for a tea with a tax." Which totally confused the British, and that's why you have the Boston Tea Party. They were making a moral point. They were not going to tolerate British taxes being seductively brought in with a monopoly that lowers prices. This was now a political fight over the very nature of our rights. And that's what then led to the Declaration of Independence.

THE NATURE OF THE REVOLUTION

There's a very important thing to recognize about the Founding Fathers, who were truly one of the most remarkable groups, if not the most remarkable secular group, in history. They began by saying, "We hold these truths to be self-evident." These were pretty pious people. A surprising number of them were actually preachers. They weren't trying to find a theory. They weren't trying to find a philosophy. They weren't trying to find an ideology. They were trying to understand the truth by which humans are able to govern themselves.

They said that all men are created equal. At a time when you have a king, think about how radical this was. This document arrived in London and the king and his ministers and the dukes and the earls and the barons and the lords were all sitting around reading this document that says, "All men are created equal." They just drove a knife into the heart of the British hierarchal structure and every European hierarchal structure.

It was completely different from the French Revolution, in which the revolutionaries changed the calendar. They were determined, in every way, to create a new world. The Founding Fathers, in the Burkean tradition, said, "This is crazy!" The greatest of all sins is hubris, the idea that you can replace God. The French were explicitly doing that, saying, "Let's drive out God. Let's eliminate the Christian calendar. Let's invent a brand-new world; we'll have a brand-new language. Brand-new titles." It is a disruption comparable to the first cycle of the Soviets and the Maoist Chinese, or the Nazis. You have this relentless effort to create the new person. The Founding Fathers would say— and did say, pretty routinely—"There are no new people. We are all children of God. We all represent an organic tradition."

Next, think about "they are endowed by their Creator." This was a direct assault on kingship. Under the historic medieval system, power comes from God to the king. The king lends power to those he favors, but the king is absolute. The Americans just said the exact opposite: power comes from God to the citizen. So in America, the citizen is sovereign. Now, they didn't think they were saying something radical. They were saying something "self-evident." This is how they'd been living for six generations.

And the rights were unalienable. That meant no judge, no king—in the modern world, no president, no bureaucrat—can get between us and God. These were people living in a culture of liberty, in a culture of practical common sense, in a culture of getting things done. They ultimately absorbed Adam Smith's *The Wealth of Nations*. And they sort of understood this model, this new model of a free society with a free market with an invisible hand, and they were amazingly practical people.

This is where our modern academic classes are such a mess. These were not folks sitting around thinking in the abstract. They were sitting around thinking, "What is going to work?" and they blended two things: "What are the historical truths and what are the practical requirements, and how do we blend them?"

THE CONSTITUTIONAL SYSTEM

The Declaration is a freestanding document. It's an idealistic document. It states the "why" of America. Then the Founders had their first cut at the "what" of America, the Articles of Confederation. They did not work very well. Valley Forge vividly illustrates what a mess it was, how impossible the Congress was, how incompetent the system was. But it held together enough to win the war.

Washington went home, ready to be a private citizen. King George III said, "If he gives up power, he'll be the greatest man of the century." Washington's officers came to him at Newburgh and said, "Let's mutiny. Let's take over the government. They're not paying us; they're impossible; the Congress is irrelevant." Washington came to their meeting in a schoolroom, pulled out his glasses slowly—to illustrate that he had grown old in the service of his country—and read a letter. And he says in the decisive turning point in American history, "I did not rebel against George III to become George I." Period. The officers all said, "Got it. We're for you."

He went home. The system still wasn't working. His friends said to him, "We've got to do something." He said something very profound. He said, "We're not ready. The American people have not grown tired enough." And so he waited several more years. They then met and decided that they should amend the Articles of Confederation. They gathered in Philadelphia. Washington presided. And in fifty-five days of closed meetings with no press, they virtually all decided to remake the document.

Now remember, Washington spent eight years trying to get the Articles to work. So you had a guy who had both the prestige of the revolutionary leader and the experience of having tried to do it. After a couple of days they decided, "This is stupid. We're not going to reform the Articles of Confederation. We're writing a new document."

This was, in fact, a coup d'état. They didn't have the authority to do this. But they said, "We are the leadership class of the country, and we're going to do what we think is right." And then they said something that is central: "Although we're the leadership group and we're going to go ahead and write this document, it will work only if the people ratify it. So we now have an obligation to go out and say to the people, 'This is what we believe we should do but we cannot do it without your approval.'"

And so they went into every single state and they waged a campaign. They wrote the most elegant campaign pamphlet in history. Someday just pick up the Federalist Papers and think to yourself, "In a country where only a third of the people were literate, this was a campaign pamphlet." Not a thirty-second TV commercial—an enormously complex, sophisticated book that came out as a series of newspaper articles for the purpose of winning an election. And they slowly, gradually won it.

By the way, the people who were opposing them were very honorable people. Patrick Henry, for example, was the leader of the anti-Federalists in Virginia. And the argument of the anti-Federalists was very simple: you do not want centralized power; it will inevitably over time grow too big, too corrupt, too tyrannical. And I would suggest to you that Patrick Henry would look at the current Obama administration; he'd look at the recent ruling against the Catholic church; he'd look at the two trillion dollars in deficits; he'd look at the corruption of Solyndra; and he'd say, "See, I told you. Took a couple of hundred years, but the mess has now occurred."

You can make an argument that the anti-Federalists stuck

closer to the Whig critique than did the Federalists, but the Federalists were trying to solve a really big problem. How do you have just enough government to be effective and not enough government to be a tyranny? And that is the permanent balance of tension in the American system.

WHO AMERICANS WERE AND WHO WE ARE

The American Constitution was designed for a volunteerist society of people who were profoundly religious, and who were bound by their culture to behave in certain ways. All the Founding Fathers believed this. And when you go back, if you look at de Tocqueville, when you contextualize the culture within which they were operating, they had certain invisible assumptions about life. They assumed that people would have some sense of virtue. They assumed that there would be some overriding religious belief system. Washington describes it; John Adams describes it; even Jefferson describes it. In the Northwest Ordinance of 1787, they wrote, "Religion, morality, and knowledge being important, it is essential that we have public schools."

Recently at the Capitol Visitor Center, some secular staff person cut out the first three words and put up, "Knowledge being essential . . ." But that's not what the Founding Fathers said. They said "Religion, morality, and knowledge being essential."

This was an unusual moment in history when the historic

background gave the Founders a sense of rights that were being
threatened, and they were actually conservatives fighting to re-
tain the rights that the emerging British tyranny was threatening. They were culturally committed to a limited government
with a big citizenship. In other words, they would have argued,
you want big citizens and small government; you don't want
big government and small citizens.

Our move away from this started with the Progressive
movement and the effort by the intellectual class to begin to
take power away from politicians and turn it over to bureau-
cracies. There was a growing belief among the intellectual class
that only they knew how to take care of the poor. Therefore,
with each passing year, they aggregated more and more power
to do for us what we weren't smart enough to do for ourselves. That grew, starting in the late 1890s and then accelerating through Woodrow Wilson. There was a brief hiatus in
the 1920s, then it reaccelerated with FDR, took a break again,
accelerated again with Lyndon Johnson, and then Obama is the
apotheosis of this whole movement. He seems to be prepared
to take over every aspect of your life and tell you what, in his
personal opinion, you would do if only you were as smart as
he was. I think that the country is finally beginning to act in
revulsion at that kind of centralized power.

Revolutionary philosophy actually had grown out of the
experience of the time. It was then driven into our DNA. Now
we're in danger of losing it with the rise of the modern welfare state and the scale of modern bureaucracy. And that's one
of the great issues of our generation: Are we, in fact, going
to continue to be Americans in the sense that Paul Johnson

described them? Or are we gradually going to become subjects in the European tradition, rather than citizens in the American tradition?

Americans believe that citizens control the government, and the government is their servant. Subjects are controlled by the government, and they are the servants of the government. It is a fundamental dividing line; it is a dividing line that all of the Founding Fathers believed was real. They all believed that historically, they had inherited citizenship and that it was the British government that was acting as a revolutionary force in trying to take it away from them. And that's why you end up with the model we have today.

I always say that the Declaration of Independence guarantees us the right to pursue happiness. Now, in the eighteenth-century Scottish Enlightenment where it comes from (and I've actually seen in the Library of Congress the book from Jefferson's library, which is underlined on this topic), the pursuit of happiness is wisdom and virtue, not hedonism and acquisition. The Founding Fathers believed that a wise people could remain free, but a foolish people would become part of a dictatorship. In that framework, I always tell audiences, they guarantee the right to pursue happiness; they don't guarantee you the attainment of happiness. This is a good example of the distinction with the French, the Nazi, the Soviet, and the Chinese revolutions. There's no provision for happiness stamps for the underly happy. There's no provision for the Federal Department of Happiness. I always tell audiences, if you had told the Founding Fathers that someday we'd have a politician walk into a room and say, "I'm going to take away from the overly happy and redistribute to the underly happy," they would have thought you were crazy. Their very society was based on inequality. It was based on a meritocratic opportunity to rise.

I would argue that organic conservatism, not some abstract intellectual theory, but organic conservatism, asserts that our rights come from God, that we are a community of equally sovereign people, that we have an obligation to solve things and we shape government to fit those things that we conclude government can solve better, but we do not owe government. Government is, in fact, a subordinate to us. This entire model is an organic, cultural, historical model that can be carried back into the British tradition but that really flourishes in the late seventeenth and early eighteenth centuries as the Whig tradition. And then it becomes captured in the DNA both of American government and of American citizenship and American culture.

De Tocqueville captured it remarkably well in the 1830s, and I think he was stunned by it. We were different. We were Americans; we weren't just the western wing of European civilization. We were something new, and that's why we could absorb people from anywhere, because you can learn the culture of being American. And *it's not the structure*. The structure is just this fabric within which the American culture operates, but it's the culture that really has made so much difference.

THE CONTINUING REVOLUTION

I'll just close with one last observation, which gives you a flavor of how deep this is. When the British were conquering the Scots, they drove many of them to flee, and they fled off into Philadelphia and then came down the Great Wagon Road and ended up in South Carolina and North Carolina, along the Appalachians. One of them was a young man in South Carolina named Andrew Jackson. At thirteen years of age, he refused to clean the boots of a British cavalryman, who slashed his face, leaving a permanent scar that he would have said was from "a British oppressor." So you have this really deep sense of toughness and hostility that's personal.

The Battle of Cowpens is another example. What was happening with the British in the South is they were just gradually getting ground to pieces, and at Cowpens the American militia turned and decisively defeated a British unit in a way that sent a shock through the entire British system in North America. At King's Mountain, the British repeat Washington's mistake of being down in a valley, surrounded by high hills. And word went out across western Tennessee, Kentucky, and the Carolinas to the Scottish Americans that the people who defeated us at Culloden are now available. And the slaughter at King's Mountain was truly bitter and personal, and it's a fascinating part of this war that the war in the South was much more personal than the war in the North. In the North, you had a much more regular army fight. In the South, what you had is all these folks who had fled the British and hated them and their children and grandchildren; all see this as a moment of personal revenge. And so you have built into our DNA a toughness that is very, very striking.

The American Revolution was an amazing confluence. We had a history that gave people a sense of absolute security that all they were doing is defending their rights. They were not in any way trying to change things; they were trying to sustain things. We had a very clumsy British government that did not realize how much out of sync with the culture it was and that was clumsily forcing people to choose, and with each passing year, more and more people chose independence and chose freedom over subordination to a tyranny. We had very practical leaders who were, on the one hand, very intellectual, but on the other hand, astonishingly pragmatic, and who could weave those two strands together into a system that actually worked, and has continued to work for almost 250 years now.

Finally, we had a period of learning. This is where our similar modern micro-critiquing is just stupid. They didn't get it right. Washington lost a lot of battles. This was a long, hard process. The Articles of Confederation didn't work very well. Many states write three or four constitutions. But what they *did* have is a general sense of direction, a general sense of principle, and a commitment that together, they were going to keep changing things until it worked. The American experience is one of the most remarkable achievements in human history. It is clearly the most remarkable in terms of government and well worth studying. And I think at its heart, it is the definition of American conservatism: the application of principle to the real world in order to effect a better life with the realization that it involves both universal rights and practical, everyday realities.

CHAPTER 4

◆ ◆ ◆

America has always battled the uniquely European notion that it was unsophisticated, a land of hicks and fanatics. Dr. Samuel Johnson, foremost British wit, called Americans "a race of convicts," and added, "I am willing to love all mankind, except an American." French diplomat Charles-Maurice de Talleyrand-Périgord was even more dismissive of America as "a country with thirty-two religions and only one dish."

But of all the critics who have ventured to speak on American politics, none has been so farsighted as Alexis de Tocqueville. His journey in 1831 to the United States began as a trade mission with the stated goal of investigating the American prison system. When he returned to France the following year, he brought back with him the seeds of one of the greatest political works ever written: *Democracy in America*.

Tocqueville illuminated the great freedoms guarded by the American republic in its early period and warned of how they could be lost. His analysis foreshadows the dangers our nation faces now.

Political commentator Michael Barone skillfully revisits the work of Alexis de Tocqueville and reminds us of what the American experiment looked like in its early decades. Barone shows us how Tocqueville accurately captured our unique American spirit and how this spirit continues to be manifest in our nation today.

Michael Barone is the senior political analyst for the *Washington Examiner* and a Resident Fellow at the American Enterprise Institute. Barone is the principal coauthor of *The Almanac of American Politics*, published by *National Journal* every two years. He is also the author of a number of other books, including *Our Country: The Shaping of America from Roosevelt to Reagan* and *Shaping Our Nation: How Surges of Migration Transformed America and Its Politics*. He has written for many major market publications, including the *Economist*, the *Times Literary Supplement*, the *Daily Telegraph*, and the *Sunday Times of London*. He is also a contributor to Fox News Channel. Previously, Barone served as a senior writer for *U.S. News & World Report*, a senior staff editor at *Reader's Digest*, and a member of the editorial page staff for the *Washington Post*. He graduated from Harvard College (1966) and Yale Law School (1969), and was an editor of the *Harvard Crimson* and the *Yale Law Journal*.

THE FRAGILITY OF ORDERED LIBERTY: TOCQUEVILLE AND CONSERVATIVE CONCEPTIONS OF LIBERTY, EQUALITY, AND COMMUNITY

Michael Barone

◆ ◆ ◆

THE JOURNEY OF ALEXIS DE TOCQUEVILLE

On the eleventh of May, 1831, two young French aristocrats, Alexis de Tocqueville and Gustave de Beaumont, arrived from France in Newport, Rhode Island, after sailing for thirty-eight days. They were lawyers with a commission to study American prisons, which they did. But Tocqueville, who was only twenty-five when he landed, did much more. During the course of his 288 days of travels in the young republic, he made the observations and accumulated the material that he fashioned into the two volumes of his *Democracy in America*, which the eminent political scientist and Tocqueville translator

Harvey Mansfield has called "the best book ever written on democracy and the best book ever written on America."

Tocqueville conversed with President Andrew Jackson at a reception in the White House and sat next to former President John Quincy Adams at a dinner in Boston. He was escorted around Washington by Joel Poinsett, the Charleston-born botanist and future secretary of war, and by Edward Everett, the Boston-born lawyer and future secretary of state. He met ninety-five-year-old Charles Carroll, the last surviving signer of the Declaration of Independence, and Sam Houston, the future first president of the Republic of Texas. He attended town meetings in New England and observed slave markets in the South. He visited Indian villages in the Michigan Territory, voyaged on steamboats that blew up shortly after he disembarked, and traveled by stagecoach through Columbia, South Carolina.

Tocqueville was an aristocrat whose family suffered during the French Revolution. His great-grandfather Malesherbes, a distinguished philosopher and lawyer, who was defense counsel in the trial of King Louis XVI, was guillotined months after his client; his father escaped the guillotine only because of the fall of Robespierre three days before he was to be guillotined, and when he left prison at age twenty-two his hair had turned completely white. As a child he met the restored King Louis XVIII after the downfall of Napoleon, and while he and his family thrived under Louis, his brother Charles X, and the new bourgeois King Louis Philippe, the specter of the bloodshed and tumult of the revolution—and the threat of another revolution—was always in their thoughts.

DEMOCRACY: THE WAVE OF THE FUTURE

Tocqueville knew before his arrival that America was different: a *democracy*, the word he used in his title. The young republic had evolved in important respects from the days of the Founders. Eighteenth-century America was still a deferential society, and at the time of the Constitution most states allowed only those with a certain amount of property to vote. It was considered dangerous to allow those without property, without a stake in society, to be in a position to determine the course of government. However, in those first decades of the republic, as historian Gordon Wood has written, "American society became less deferential and more democratic." Tocqueville was struck by the fact that former president Adams was treated as just another guest at dinner and not as a monarch.

By the 1830s, almost all the states had extended the franchise to all white adult males. Some still resisted, as John Randolph of Roanoke did at Virginia's Constitutional Convention, decrying "the all-prevailing principle that Numbers, and Numbers alone are to regulate all things in political society" and the prospect that government "was to divorce property from power." But Randolph's was a minority view in Virginia, as elsewhere. Universal suffrage did not seem dangerous to most legislators in a nation where the large majority of people were farmers who owned their own land and were therefore property holders. On the other hand, for French aristocrats of Tocqueville's time, with their still-vibrant dread of the French Revolution, democracy seemed very dangerous indeed. Tocqueville disagreed, recognizing democracy's dangers but also its opportunities and reasons for hope—and also seeing democracy as the irresistible wave of the future.

THE POWER OF LOCAL GOVERNMENT

One danger Tocqueville perceived in democracy was what he called "individualism," the tendency of citizens, lacking the relations between aristocrats and their inferiors to bind them together, to isolate themselves and withdraw from society. Democracy, he wrote, "threatens to confine [the citizen] wholly in the solitude of his own heart." But the America he observed avoided this danger, he believed, because of two important factors. "The Americans have combated the individualism to which equality gives birth with freedom, and they have defeated it."

One factor was the nature and role of government—specifically, local governments. At the time of his visit, Americans seldom came into contact with the federal government, with the single exception of the post office. But they were of necessity in constant contact with local governments—the New England towns and townships, Southern counties—and, being affected by their decisions, took advantage of the opportunity to participate in its activities. "Thus by charging citizens with the administration of small affairs, much more than by leaving the government of great ones to them," he writes, "one interests them in the public good and makes them see the need they constantly have for one another in order to produce it. . . . Local freedoms . . . constantly bring men closer to one another."

What Tocqueville expresses is an appreciation of the conservative principle that Catholic philosophers refer to as *subsidiarity*. Instead of having a central government superintend local affairs, as was the case in France—where that system long predated the French Revolution, as Tocqueville documented in his later book *The Ancien Régime and the French Revolution*—democracy in America tended to reserve control of all matters that could be handled at that level to local governments, chosen by people who would remain close to their representatives. The Constitution limited the powers of the federal government and reserved other matters to the state governments; state governments in turn delegated to local governments matters that could be addressed locally.

Not every issue could be so delegated, Tocqueville realized. One of the major political events during his visit was the Nullification Crisis, in which the South Carolina legislature, encouraged by Vice President John C. Calhoun, declared that it had the right to nullify a tariff law passed by Congress. President Andrew Jackson reacted furiously, sending federal troops to enforce the law while at the same time moving Congress toward a compromise position on the tariff, thereby addressing some of South Carolina's grievances. Tocqueville's visit also coincided with the success of Jackson's Indian removal policies—the forced movement of the Five Civilized Tribes from the East to what is now Oklahoma over what has come to be called the Trail of Tears. Tocqueville actually witnessed some of the Indians moving west.

These issues foreshadowed crises and illustrated problems that Tocqueville addressed in the last chapters of the first volume of *Democracy in America*, on the fact that blacks and Indians were not considered citizens in this democratic republic. He foresaw the possibility of the rupture of civil war and the tragic fate of many Native Americans even as he saluted the way that democracy bound citizens together through local government. And perhaps he may even be seen as having pointed to the successes of the civil rights movement when he wrote, "To combat the evils that equality can produce there is only one efficacious remedy: it is political freedom."

THE POWER OF NONGOVERNMENTAL SOCIAL INSTITUTIONS

But the "habits of the heart"—another Tocqueville phrase—fostered by involvement in local government also did something else, and here we encounter the second reason Americans avoided the isolation of what Tocqueville calls "individualism." Americans were busy starting thousands of voluntary associations, creating civil society—mediating institutions between individuals and government, institutions through which individuals could affect government or could change society without involving government at all.

Tocqueville paints a picture of a busy people. "Scarcely have you descended on the soil of America when you find yourself in the midst of a sort of turmoil," he writes in Volume 1 of *Democracy in America*:

A confused clamor is raised on all sides; a thousand voices
come to your ears at the same time, each of them expressing some social needs. Around you everything moves:
here, the people of one neighborhood have gathered to
learn if a church ought to be built; there, they are working on the choice of a representative; farther on, the dep-
uties of a district are going to town in all haste in order
to decide about some local improvements; in another
place, the farmers of a village abandon their furrows to
go discuss the plan of a road or school. Citizens assemble
with the sole goal of declaring that they disapprove of the
course of government, whereas others gather to proclaim
that the men in place are the fathers of their country.
Here are others still who, regarding drunkenness as the
principle source of the evils of the state, come solemnly
to pledge themselves to give an example of temperance.

There is a note of astonishment here, particularly in that last
sentence where the wine-drinking French aristocrat contem-
plates the possibility of the prohibition of alcohol.

Tocqueville arrived in America at a time when voluntary associations were championing causes that ultimately transformed the
nation. They were particularly common in New England and upstate New York, which had largely been settled by New England
Yankees, and where he spent much of his visit. The Yankee, as
Orestes Brownson noted, tends to be "restless in body and mind,
always scheming, always in motion, never satisfied with what he
has, and always seeking to make the world like himself, or as uneasy as himself." Tocqueville spent almost half his time in America

in Yankee country (New England, upstate New York, the Upper Midwest), and he admired the reformist Yankee impulse as an example of democratic Americans working together in voluntary associations to improve their society. One of these efforts was the temperance movement, which ultimately persuaded the nation to embark for a dozen years on the "noble experiment" of prohibition of alcohol. That experiment failed, but in Tocqueville's time the temperance movement did vastly reduce alcohol consumption in what one historian called "the alcoholic republic." Another movement that was soon to begin was the women's rights movement, which resulted in an amendment to the Constitution granting women the vote; Tocqueville was astonished to note that "women themselves often go to political assemblies and, by listening to political discourses, take a rest from household tedium."

Another movement that was beginning to gain adherents was abolitionism—the move to abolish slavery—and the corresponding defense of slavery by Southerners. Just a few years before Tocqueville's journey a state Constitutional Convention in Virginia narrowly rejected a provision to gradually abolish slavery, as all the states to the north had done. It's tantalizing to contemplate how history would have unfolded if that decision had gone the other way. Even in the North most Americans considered abolitionists fanatics who would disrupt the Union, but the abolitionist cause had great moral power in a nation whose Declaration of Independence had declared, "We hold these Truths to be self-evident, that all Men . . . are endowed by their Creator with certain unalienable rights, that among these are Life, Liberty, and the Pursuit of Happiness."

There was also a tension between the existence of slavery

and the moral equality inherent in the Christianity professed by almost all Americans. "On my arrival in the country," Tocqueville writes in Volume 1, "it was the religious aspect of the country that first struck my eye." In France and in other European countries with established churches, Tocqueville notes, "the spirit of religion and the spirit of freedom almost always move in contrary directions." Britain's North American colonies had different religious traditions, and immigrants to the colonies and to the young republic brought other religions with them. The Founders, understanding this multivarious religious heritage, provided in the Constitution that there be no religious test for federal office and in the Bill of Rights that "Congress shall make no law respecting an establishment of religion, or prohibiting the free exercise thereof." This did not mean that there was an absolute separation of church and state—during Tocqueville's visit Massachusetts still had an established state church—but as Tocqueville noted, "Diminishing the apparent force of a religion . . . came to increase its real power."

Tocqueville thought that religious belief was more prevalent and stronger in America than in France and that Americans considered "it necessary to the maintenance of republic institutions." "Religion," he writes, "which, among Americans, never mixes directly in the government, should therefore be considered as the first of their political institutions; for if it does not give them the taste for freedom, it singularly facilitates their use of it." Religious belief, he could observe, was the impulse behind the movements for temperance, women's rights, and abolition of slavery; it was an impulse that gave strength to the observation of limits of the power of the state and of temporary voting majorities. "At the same time that the law permits the American people to do everything," Tocqueville continues, "religion prevents them from conceiving everything and forbids them to dare anything." Religion produced movements that could be described as liberal or liberating, but it also fostered a stubborn conservatism that would prevent the excesses and despotism fostered by the antireligious French Revolution.

Religion and law also combined to produce material prosperity. "One is astonished by the growing prosperity of the people," Tocqueville writes at one point. In the two decades before Tocqueville's visit, Americans had been building canals, and just before he arrived the first tracks of the Baltimore & Ohio Railroad were being laid down. Travel times and transportation costs were being hugely reduced and internal trade hugely increased, while American merchants plied the Atlantic and carried on the China trade and American whaling vessels pursued their prey in the South Pacific. Americans were moving westward in vast numbers, creating new New Englands in the Upper Midwest, new Pennsylvanias a little farther south, new slave plantations in the Mississippi Valley lands from which the Indians were being removed, and new communities of Scots-Irish from the Appalachian Mountains to Tennessee and into the technically foreign land of Texas.

UTOPIA, DYSTOPIA, AND WAR

Tocqueville was eerily prescient. He foresaw the possibility of civil war, but thought the North could not subdue a South bent on independence—that was probably true when he wrote, since the North's victory depended on the industrialization and vast population growth that occurred between Tocqueville's time and secession three decades later. Tocqueville mused about the possibility that the world in the twentieth century would be dominated by two great powers, one democratic and one despotic, America and Russia: the Cold War. He also foresaw that a democratic nation could descend into what he called a "soft" despotism. In that respect he anticipated the conservative critique of the growth of the federal government and many of the public policy initiatives of the past hundred years.

Tocqueville's vivid picture of soft despotism appears almost abruptly, at the end of the second volume of *Democracy in America*. Up to that point, his depiction of democratic America is not entirely complimentary. He takes it for granted that democratic America cannot produce the high culture or fine arts fostered by aristocratic nations like France—something that was certainly true during the nineteenth century. He says that a democratic society is less likely than an aristocratic to value excellence and more likely to tolerate mediocrity. He thinks that democracy is more benign in America than it would be in France because it is not the product of a violent revolution that leaves classes divided against one another, but rather springs naturally from a society that was never very aristocratic to begin with.

On the whole, though, his account of the American experiment is positive. He sees Americans overcoming the dangers of individualism through involvement in local self-government and by their propensity to create and work in voluntary associations—the little platoons, as Edmund Burke called them. He sees religion—and the non-privileged place of different churches and sects—in America as tending to produce virtuous behavior and place limits on destructive impulses. He sees an America bursting with prosperity, resourceful in commerce, creative in invention, expanding rapidly over a continent even as it sends out ships to all parts of the world—an America where the ordinary person had a higher standard of living than ordinary people anywhere else on the globe, and one that seemed sure to ascend to greater heights.

He also sees a threat. America's success is the result of things that could in time produce a future much gloomier and could prevent democratic America from achieving its potential. Near the end of the second volume of *Democracy in America* he presents this ominous vision, and conservative thinkers have thought his words presaged developments in American history running up to and including our own time:

> I do not fear that in their chiefs [Americans] will find tyrants, but rather schoolmasters. . . . I think therefore that the kind of oppression with which democratic peoples are threatened will resemble nothing that has preceded it in the world; our contemporaries would not find its image in their memories. I myself seek in vain an expression that exactly reproduces the idea that I form of it for myself and that contains it; the old words despotism and tyranny are not suitable. The thing is new, therefore I must try to define it, since I cannot name it.
>
> I want to imagine with what new features despotism

could be produced in the world: I see an innumerable crowd of like and equal men who revolve on themselves without repose, procuring the small and vulgar pleasures with which they fill their souls. Each of them, withdrawn and apart, is like a stranger to the destiny of all the others: his children and his particular friends form the whole human species for him; as for dwelling with his fellow citizens, he is beside them, but he does not see them; he touches them and does not feel them; he exists only in himself and for himself alone, and if a family still remains for him, one can at least say that he no longer has a native country.

Here Tocqueville foresees a time when the forces he believes have enabled Americans to avoid the perils of individualism will no longer prevail. It is in part a demographic vision: the America in which Tocqueville arrived in 1830 was a country in which more than 90 percent of the people lived on farms. There was no city like Paris, which had 800,000 people and a population density of 59,000 per square mile. America's largest city, New York, had just 200,000, Philadelphia 130,000, Washington 26,000, Charleston 30,000.

THE OVERTHROW OF A DEMOCRATIC PEOPLE

Over the next century, industrialization and immigration transformed the nation's demography. By 1912, one hundred years ago, the United States did have enormous cities with, as Tocqueville put it, "an innumerable crowd": New York had 5 million people, Chicago 2 million, Philadelphia 1.5 million. Vast waves of immigration arrived on American shores, from Ireland and Germany starting in the 1840s, eastern and southern Europe starting in the 1890s, as many as 1,200,000 a year in a nation of 86 million in the single year of 1907. These people worked in garment sweatshops and on auto and steel assembly lines; they owned no property, renting their homes and often not even having bank accounts; they took no part in local government except as voters supporting machine politicians; in some sense they seemed indeed no longer to "have a native country." Or, as Robert Nisbet puts it, Americans increasingly suffered a "loss of community." As Robert Putnam recently discovered, to his dismay, the parts of America that have the greatest ethnic and racial diversity are also the parts with the highest degree of lack of trust in others and lack of participation in voluntary associations: Los Angeles today; the tenements of Manhattan's Lower East Side, then the most densely populated place in the world, a century ago.

The Progressive politicians of that era responded to those conditions, and to their fears that the urban masses would rise in a violent revolution like the Paris Commune of 1871 or the Russian Revolution of 1917, by proclaiming that the Constitution's old limitations on government were obsolete in a time of immigrant tenements and factory assembly lines. Government needed to regulate and control giant corporations and small employers alike and to provide a safety net for them. The result was the policy changes of the Progressive Era and New Deal. Tocqueville anticipated just this development:

Above these an immense tutelary power is elevated, which alone takes charge of assuring their enjoyments and watching over their fate. It is absolute, detailed, regular, far-seeing and mild. It would resemble paternal power if, like that, it had for its object to prepare men for manhood; but on the contrary, it seeks only to keep them fixed irrevocably in childhood; it likes citizens to enjoy themselves. It willingly works for their happiness; but it wants to be the unique agent and sole arbiter of that; it provides for their security, foresees and secures their needs, facilitates their pleasures, conducts their principal affairs, directs their industry, regulates their estates, divides their inheritances; can it not take away from them entirely the trouble of thinking and the pain of living?

So it is that every day it renders the employment of free will less useful and more rare; it confines the action of the will in a smaller space and little by little steals the very use of it from every citizen. Equality has prepared men for all these things: it has disposed them to tolerate them and often even to regard them as a benefit.

Tocqueville in these words provides as trenchant a criticism of the welfare state and the regulatory state as any modern conservative thinker—and managed to do so eighty years before the Progressives, a century before the New Deal, 130 years before the Great Society, and 180 years before the administration of the current president. Local self-government has been in large measure elbowed aside by a centralized bureaucratic apparatus, run by alleged experts, justified by the supposed inability of ordinary people to take care of themselves and navigate the shoals and reefs of an advanced industrial society. This soft despotism—a phrase Tocqueville scholars like Paul Rahe have used, though Tocqueville doesn't use it himself—assumes that people are incompetent children, and in treating them like children encourages them to behave that way.

In an earlier passage Tocqueville proposes the possibility that something far worse could come into existence, a *hard* despotism or tyranny that might try to seize the operation of every institution of society and abolish freedoms of speech and religion—twentieth-century totalitarianism, in a word. If he can be said to have anticipated Woodrow Wilson and Franklin Roosevelt and Lyndon Johnson, he also anticipated Adolf Hitler and Benito Mussolini and Joseph Stalin. He clearly indicates that soft despotism is preferable, but he goes on to insist that soft despotism will have a negative effect on people's character, that it will tend to eradicate the virtue that he saw in democratic Americans in the 1830s. He writes:

> Thus, after taking each individual by turns in its powerful hands and kneading him as it likes, the sovereign extends its arms over society as a whole; it covers its surface with a network of small, complicated, painstaking, uniform rules through which the most original minds and the most vigorous souls cannot clear a way to surpass the crowd; it does not break wills, but it softens them, bends them and directs them; it rarely forces one to act, but it constantly opposes itself to one's acting; it does not destroy, it prevents things from being born; it does

not tyrannize, it hinders, compromises, enervates, extinguishes, dazes and finally reduces each nation to being nothing more than a herd of timid and industrious animals of which the government is the shepherd.

I have always believed that this sort of regulated, mild and peaceful servitude, whose picture I have just painted, could be combined better than one imagines with some external forms of freedom, and that it would not be impossible for it to be established in the very shadow of the sovereignty of the people.

Consider for a moment Tocqueville's description of a democratic people as "a herd of timid and industrious animals." This is the aim, conservatives would argue, of the ideas of progressive education that have dominated American public schools since the 1920s. The "tutelary power" here, to use Tocqueville's phrase, is a huge cadre of professional educators placed in control of the schools by the state and federal governments, replacing the local authorities who superintended public schools for most of the century after Tocqueville wrote and who tended to require a more rigorous course of study and one which emphasized the special character of American life as described by Tocqueville. The aim of progressive education is not to produce excellence, not to enable people to rise in life, but to teach basic reading and arithmetic and to absorb the discipline of the ringing bells and the time clock enough to enable them to make a living on Henry Ford's Model T assembly line. There they could make enough money for food, clothing, and shelter and have enough leisure time for radio or movies or television—facilitating their pleasures, as Tocqueville puts it.

Many conservative thinkers have lamented the extent to which American society has come to resemble Tocqueville's soft despotism—and have lamented even more that American voters seem to have continued to ratify it. In Tocqueville's words, "citizens leave their dependence for a moment to indicate their master, and then reenter it." In this conservative view, we are far along the road to soft despotism and there is no turning around.

A CAUSE FOR OPTIMISM

I want to suggest something different, something that is from my point of view a little more optimistic.

First of all, many of the features of America that Tocqueville describes are still part of American life. America still abounds in voluntary associations, for example, and more so than any other nation in the world. There are some indications that the percentage of people involved in such associations is declining, as Robert Putnam suggested in his book *Bowling Alone*, but there is countervailing evidence as well. The impulse to create and work in voluntary associations is still very much a part of American life. Americans give more money and volunteer more time for charities than any other nation in the world. While it is true that, as American Enterprise Institute president Arthur Brooks has documented, conservatives and religious people tend to give more money to charity than their opposites, many liberals and secular people donate regularly. The American tradition of philanthropy is strong. A century ago, before the income and estate taxes, amassers of great fortunes like Andrew Carnegie and John D. Rockefeller gave enormous sums to charity and changed American life. Carnegie built thousands of libraries in which millions of Americans received their self-education. Rockefeller created the medical research institutions and the advanced medical schools in which America still leads the world, as well as eradicating nutrition deficiency diseases. Currently we see Bill Gates devoting most of his wealth to his charitable foundation, with some creative programs he hopes will transform the lives of countless people for the better. Our "vast tutelary power" of government does not have a monopoly in these areas.

Second, in two important respects America has remained an exceptional nation, in ways that Tocqueville was the first to recognize. One is that we are still by and large a religious people and a people who are respectful of the religions of others. To be sure, there is some increase in the percentage of Americans willing to identify themselves as unbelievers. But, if anything, the number of strong believers has been rising, not declining. The second way America has remained an exceptional nation is that we are once again, as we were in Tocqueville's time but arguably were not in the first half of the twentieth century, a property owners' democracy. Most Americans in the course of their adult working lives accumulate significant amounts—hundreds of thousands of dollars' worth—of property in the form of residential real estate and financial instruments. True, housing values have had a sharp decline, and some of what appeared to be housing wealth has turned out to be a bubble, but by and large the descendants of those unpropertied immigrants and factory workers of one hundred years ago do own property, or soon will, in significant amounts. Religion and property both, as Tocqueville taught, modulate our extreme impulses and make us more likely to work together in government and voluntary associations. They make us less likely to submit to being part of Tocqueville's "herd of timid and industrious animals."

Finally, a strong case can be made that American voters have not supinely ratified the creation of soft despotism. They have tended to resist it. When parties in power have tried to expand vastly the size and scope of government, they have been sharply rebuked by the voters. Woodrow Wilson's New Freedom and attempted abolition of Congress's prerogative of declaring war was rebuked by the record majority cast for Warren G. Harding's "return to normalcy" in 1920. Franklin Roosevelt's plan to pack the Supreme Court and New Dealer governors' refusal to enforce the law against illegal sit-down strikes was rebuked in the elections of 1938 and subsequent years, which produced anti–New Deal Congresses for the next twenty years. Lyndon Johnson's Great Society was soundly rebuked in the elections of 1966 and 1968, and the stagflation that prevailed during Jimmy Carter's presidency produced a forty-four-state landslide for Ronald Reagan in 1980. The two most recent Democratic presidents, after raising taxes and advancing a national health care plan, were both rebuked sharply by record Republican victories in the off-year elections of 1994 and 2010.

Many conservative thinkers would reply that those victories did not change the trajectory of public policy. Creeping socialism, they argue, has continued to creep. There is much to this, but the argument is overstated. In point of fact, there have been some reversals of policies that advance soft despotism. Tax rates were vastly cut and wartime nationalization of the railroads and shipyards was ended after 1920—and the latter policy was not repeated in World War II. The Republican Congress elected in 1946 rejected New Deal policies for national health insurance, federal aid to education, government-built housing; it ended wartime wage and price controls, and it significantly restricted the powers of labor unions. These public policies were enduring—some for a generation, some to this day—and they led to postwar prosperity when almost everyone expected a return to depression. The elections rejecting the Great Society led over the next twenty years, during administrations of both parties, to deregulation of transportation and communications, which squeezed huge costs out of goods and services and made possible the quarter century of robust growth following the tax and spending cuts that resulted from the 1980 election. The 1990s saw a vast decrease in welfare dependency and crime, resulting almost entirely from the pioneering efforts of reformers in state and local government—like Wisconsin governor Tommy Thompson and New York mayor Rudy Giuliani—which were imitated and adapted in other states and cities, and in which the federal government played only a late supporting role. The 2010 elections have not been followed yet by major policy reversals, but it is not difficult to imagine some. The current president's health-care law, which he expected to be popular, has instead become so unpopular that he barely mentioned it in his State of the Union address during his campaign for reelection.

TOCQUEVILLE'S AMERICA

Tocqueville's prescience earns the last word for this man of extraordinarily piercing intelligence, an aristocrat who was so alert to the strengths of democracy even while keenly identifying its weakness. To read even a few of his short paragraphs, densely packed with insight, requires concentration and rereading; to read and absorb whole chapters can take an afternoon or an evening; to appreciate the full scope of his achievement in *Democracy in America* could consume a lifetime. Yet this extraordinary man, one of the great thinkers of the ages, also had a faith in the capacity of ordinary people, given the right circumstances, to govern themselves and contribute to the building of a decent and virtuous society. Those who advocate the course of soft despotism lack this faith; they see ordinary people as incapable of self-governance, in need of a shepherd to guide the herd the right way. Tocqueville sees us ordinary humans as something better. Nobody says it better than Tocqueville himself, and nothing could provide a more fitting conclusion to these reflections than the final passage of *Democracy in America*:

As for myself, having come to the final stage of my course, to discover from afar, but at once, all the diverse objects that I had contemplated separately in advancing, I feel full of fears and full of hopes. I see great perils that it is possible to ward off; great evils that one can avoid or restrain, and I become more and more firm in the belief that to be honest and prosperous, it is still enough for democratic nations to wish it.

I am not unaware that several of my contemporaries have thought that peoples are never masters of themselves here below, and that they necessarily obey I do not know which insurmountable and unintelligent force born of previous events, the race, the soil or the climate.

Those are false and cowardly doctrines that can never produce any but weak men and pusillanimous nations: Providence has not created the human race either entirely independent or perfectly slave. It traces, it is true, a fatal circle around each man that he cannot leave; but within its vast limits man in powerful and free; so are societies.

Nations of our day cannot have it that conditions within them are not equal; but it depends on them whether equality leads to servitude or freedom, to enlightenment or barbarism, to prosperity or misery.

CHAPTER 5

◆ ◆ ◆

While professors routinely place Franklin Delano Roosevelt at the top of their list of "best presidents," conservatives remain highly skeptical of the big government FDR put into place. What was FDR's legacy and what lessons does it have for conservatives?

The story of FDR's presidency shows us the deeply seductive nature of leftism and all it promises. The Left seems to provide easy solutions for the nation's most intractable problems. How to solve the problem of a stagnant economy? The government can borrow to increase its own spending to stimulate the economy. How to solve the problem of the poor? The government can take from the rich and give to the poor. How to solve the problem of high unemployment? The government can increase taxes or borrowing and use these funds to hire more workers. Conservatives, however, understand these "solutions" aren't merely doomed to failure; they are recipes for utter stagnation.

Historian Burton Folsom shows us that eras of government intervention, like FDR's presidency, coincide with eras of technological stagnation. In contrast, eras of economic freedom coincide with eras of technological innovation. Dr. Folsom shows us the spirit of economic liberty that animates modern conservatism and that is needed to revitalize our nation.

Burton W. Folsom Jr. is an economic historian. He holds the Charles F. Kline Chair in History and Management at Hillsdale College. He has published seven books, including *Myth of the Robber Barons*, now in its sixth edition, as well as two volumes on the administration of *Franklin Roosevelt: New Deal or Raw Deal* and *FDR Goes to War* (written with his wife, Anita). He lectures widely on the importance of entrepreneurs and free markets and has been featured on dozens of television and radio programs. Dr. Folsom also serves as senior historian at the Foundation for Economic Education (FEE) and writes a quarterly column for FEE's publication *The Freeman*.

NEW DEAL PROGRESSIVISM, THE JEFFERSONIAN REVIVAL, AND THE AGRARIAN TRADITION

Burton W. Folsom Jr.

◆ ◆ ◆

I'm talking today about President Franklin D. Roosevelt, who attacked the Great Depression in the 1930s with a series of programs called the New Deal. In the classroom and in the textbooks, historians rank him very high among presidents, usually in the top three. In the Arthur Schlesinger poll, the most commonly cited poll, he was rated as "great" by every historian who voted in the poll except for one. And that historian ranked him as "near great."

So we have a top-rated president. And the way FDR's story is told is this: the Great Depression had 20 percent unemployment for several years, all the way up to almost 25 percent in 1933. Roosevelt put people to work with programs such as the Works Progress Administration (WPA) and the Tennessee Valley Authority. And suddenly, jobs were generated! In the case of the WPA, people worked to build roads and other construction projects, or hospitals and schools. That put people to work; and then they spent money, and that got the country out of the Great Depression!

In other words, you have spending and then you get recovery. But here is what Henry Morgenthau, Roosevelt's secretary of the treasury, said about the New Deal, seven years into its implementation. He was looking at the unemployment statistics, and he saw that seven years after Roosevelt was elected, unemployment was at 20.7 percent. Then Morgenthau said this:

> We have tried spending money. We are spending more than we have ever spent before and it does not work. And I have just one interest and if I'm wrong, somebody else can have my job. I want to see this country prosperous. I want to see people get a job. I want to see people get enough to eat. We have never made good on our promises. I say, after eight years of this administration, we have just as much unemployment as when we started, and an enormous debt to boot.

That was spoken by one of President Roosevelt's best friends. The man who made that statement had a photo of himself and Roosevelt side by side. Roosevelt signed it, "From one of two of a kind." The two men often had lunch together, breakfast together. They would pass notes to each other at cabinet meetings. But Morgenthau said in frustration about the New Deal that after seven years, *it had not worked*.

If you ask me, "Are you saying that when you have high unemployment, injecting money into the economy via the WPA and these various programs doesn't work?!" Yes, that's exactly what I'm saying.

I'm going to explain why the New Deal failed to generate recovery, first, by looking at the 1920s; second, by looking at the 1930s; and third, by looking at World War II and its aftermath. After spending—massive, record spending on New Deal programs—the country still had double-digit unemployment every year of the 1930s.

THE 1920s

When World War I ended, there was high unemployment. Four million soldiers came home from the battlefields in Europe and couldn't get a job. We had high taxes in place, thanks to President Wilson's attempts to fund the war. Entrepreneurs were not getting into business very much. In 1921, America faced 12 percent unemployment. That was perhaps *the* major issue in the 1920 campaign. Harding and Coolidge, running for president and vice president, campaigned in 1920 against their opponents with this question on everyone's mind: What are you going to do about this unemployment?

Once they were in office, what did Harding and Coolidge do? Some wanted a gigantic stimulus package, using this logic: "Just about everybody has an automobile, but the roads aren't very good, because they were built for slow-moving horses and buggies. You need different surfacing, of course, for cars. We don't have a lot of paved roads, so why don't we put these soldiers returning home from the war to work building roads? Then they will plow money into the economy, and we'll slash this 12 percent unemployment. So let's do public works!"

Harding said no. Coolidge said no. Their argument was interesting. First, they said, nothing in the Constitution gives the federal government the authority to build roads. There's a reason for that: James Madison even used that rationale for his veto of a public works bill in 1817. Madison and Jefferson, those old-style agrarians, said if you had that power in the federal government for road building, politicians would build roads in their home states where they wanted votes. Therefore, the states themselves should be in charge of road building. Yes, we want roads; we just don't think the federal government ought to be the place where it's done.

That reasoning worked for Jefferson and Madison; it worked for Harding. He also believed that the idea of a federal workforce building roads wouldn't create jobs. Because if you build a road and you put people to work, that's nice, but where do you get the money to do it? That's the key question. What you see is the road being built, and you see former soldiers at work building the road. What you don't see is the money that is taken from taxpayers to build the road. Those taxpayers would have spent the money on other things, and that spending would have helped the economy and created jobs.

And that makes an interesting question: Who better spends money? Government bureaucrats or you? And who is more likely to spend money on things that people really want? We recognize roads have to be built. It should be done at the state and local levels. At the federal level, we keep the government as small as possible, with limited powers. We keep taxation limited. People should be able spend their own money.

Harding's opponents used an argument you might find familiar. They said, in effect, he was engaging in the "politics of no." But Harding responded with a plan: first, to cut federal spending, and second, to cut income tax rates. Now that's interesting. This is the reverse of the stimulus package. You have high unemployment, so what do you do? You cut back federal spending, and you cut the income tax, and in effect more people are going to have money to spend as they see fit. Harding and Coolidge argued *that* would get us out of the depression of 1920 and 1921.

The interesting thing about being a historian is that we get to study what happened. First of all, Harding and Coolidge were true to their word. They did what they promised. Harding died in office, so Coolidge followed him and completed his program. They cut federal spending by about 50 percent in the first two years of Harding's presidency, from roughly $6.5 billion in 1921 to $3.1 billion in 1923. And they cut the federal income tax, the top rate, from 73 percent down to 56 percent, and eventually slashed it to 25 percent. They also cut tax rates for all income-tax payers.

The question is, What was the unemployment rate after this shrinking of the federal government? The answer: 2 percent. I will be technically accurate and use the official figure of the U.S. Census: 2.4 percent. Yes, 2.4 percent unemployment in 1923, after 11.7 percent unemployment in 1921.

Harding and Coolidge, in effect, said, "We're trusting entrepreneurs to make the difference." And what happened was a burst of entrepreneurship. "We get to keep the money we make from the projects we build!" That's exciting. The 1920s: radio is invented and used and becomes a standard household item. It just sweeps in, just as the iPhone has done over the past few years. Six years ago hardly anyone had an iPhone, and four years from now, practically everybody will have one. That was true of the radio in the 1920s.

But I'm not done. Here are some other changes. Sliced bread! Did you ever hear that something is the greatest invention since sliced bread? It was invented in the 1920s. That's the beginning of the peanut butter and jelly sandwich. Then came Scotch tape! Air-conditioning!

Air-conditioning is a fantastic example of how a macroeconomic policy can create entrepreneurship. It was invented by Willis Carrier. He was hired by a firm in Brooklyn, which was a printing company—a printing company!—because it would print items, and the ink smeared when finished products were placed in stacks. Carrier was asked, "Could you invent something to dehumidify the room more quickly? If you dehumidify the room more quickly, we won't get the smearing from the damp ink." And so Carrier began working to develop a machine to pull humidity out of the room, and he noticed that this mechanical process had a cooling effect. He didn't work on air-conditioning further for a while, but said to himself, "You know, this is something that I might want to explore, that I can actually cool a room as well as dehumidify it."

At first, faced with the high taxes, Carrier didn't want to take risks on his invention. But then, when the tax cuts came in 1924, he began to promote his air conditioner. The first industry to buy an air conditioner—now this is interesting—was movie theaters. That's because movie sales would spike in the winter and drop in the summer due to high temperatures in the theater. The Rivoli Theatre in New York City took a chance and bought Carrier's air-conditioning. All of a sudden, it had big attendance. By 1930, there were three hundred movie theaters with air conditioners. These were huge contraptions, multi-ton devices. Next came the factory owners who wanted them. Then, in 1939, I regret to say we put them in Congress, which kept them in session longer. Politicians could then pass more laws. So there are some negative, unintended consequences of air-conditioning.

The 1920s were full of inventions. We had talking movies. In the 1920s we went from movies that were silent movies, like *The Artist*, to talking movies. The studios were ready to take the risk, because the government was telling them, "If you make some money by giving people what they want—and that's how you make money, giving people something that they want—then you get to keep most of the money you make." That generated invention. Risk.

Another product of the 1920s is interesting because we're all still using it. It was called "hookless number 2." Today, we know the invention as the zipper. When Gideon Sundback took his first hookless number 2 to the patent office, the patent guy, and many others, couldn't imagine a use for it.

Nothing happened with hookless number 2 for several years, because tax rates were too high. Then we hit the mid-1920s, and all of a sudden, B. F. Goodrich took a chance and bought 150,000 hookless number 2s to make galoshes for women.

Goodrich advertised it, bringing in Madison Avenue advertisers from New York. The ads featured a picture of a woman with her galoshes, and the caption "Zip 'er up." And calling the device hookless number 2 went by the wayside. "Zipper" was the new name. As an alternative to using only buttons, zippers become increasingly popular.

Another development of the 1920s was the popularizing of the refrigerator. Families used to have an iceman come by and drop a big chunk of ice into the icebox, but a refrigerator was so much easier. Refrigerators became much more popular in the 1920s.

What's interesting about this 1920s phenomenon—all these inventions, the reduction of unemployment, the change in life, the growth in national productivity and prosperity, and low unemployment—is that very little of this could have been anticipated. If you had asked Harding, "Well, what are these people going to invent that's going to make life so much better by the end of the decade?" he couldn't have said, "We're going to invent air-conditioning," or "We're going to invent the zipper, so zip your lip!"

We couldn't have had any of those kinds of conversations because Harding and Coolidge didn't know what was going to work and what wasn't. In a market economy, consumers choose those products that they want to buy, and, lo and behold, some of them are very good. And the 1920s became a decade of incredible inventiveness and remarkable prosperity. Coolidge had more faith in entrepreneurs than in government.

Big changes, like those that occurred in the 1920s, always have detractors. In this case, the detractors were our Southern Agrarians, folks like Donald Davidson and Robert Penn Warren. When they wrote their book *I'll Take My Stand* in 1930, after this great decade, they said, "Industry is breaking down regionalism, and regionalism is wonderful." They didn't want industry, or industrial progress, because it encroached on regional culture. Progress is homogenizing in a way—if everybody has an iPhone, nobody has a rotary telephone, and there may be places where the rotary telephone is a way of life. By the same token, how many of us are willing to give up our iPhones to preserve the agrarian lifestyle? Most Americans weren't willing to give up inventions, either. It's very easy for Professor Donald Davidson at Vanderbilt, in Nashville, to say, "Well, these nationalizing trends are no good!" But what are you supposed to tell the people in Charleston, South Caroline—don't buy an air conditioner? How many would like to go through July and August in Charleston with no air conditioner?

Many of these inventions were wonderful for the South. How big would Atlanta be without air-conditioning? In 1930, before air-conditioning, Atlanta was smaller in size than Akron, Ohio. Now Atlanta is a city of five million. The change and the opportunities that Atlanta is able to offer people in the South are magnificent. True, decades ago the regionalism in the South began to break up, and there were complaints about Yankees coming down and moving in, but economic progress provided tremendous opportunities in the South. Sure enough, we're watching the economy of the South gradually, slowly but surely, surpassing the economy of the North, so much so that we're hearing that Alabama's economy is going to pass Michigan's soon. That was unthinkable forty years ago.

Opportunities are there with industry, but it does break down regional barriers. The Southern Agrarians valued regional barriers. Davidson wrote, in his essay on the Old South and Charleston, that it was too bad when people were motivated solely by money. I think that's right, and the Bible tells us that the love of money is the root of all evil. But I'm not sure that if you're inventing an air conditioner, you necessarily love money. You may be self-interested, but there's an inventiveness, too, a part of you that shouts, "I want to change the world! I want to improve life! I want to help people!" When you invent a product like that, lives are being saved. People are not going to have the kind of overheating and heat stroke that's going to take lives and make people miserable and unproductive. Being cooler in the summer makes it easier to do daily jobs, and I'm grateful for those inventors.

Frankly, I believe that Madison and Jefferson, those old agrarian types, would have been amazed and very pleased to see the South as a center of industrial progress.

1930s

At the end of the 1920s, President Herbert Hoover began to increase the power of the federal government. Even though Hoover was a Republican, like Harding and Coolidge, Hoover was from a different wing of the Republican Party. He favored much more intervention. He thought to himself, "Well, I realize we got unemployment down to 2 percent, but I think we can use government to help make that even better!"

Hoover signed the highest tariff in U.S. history, which in effect said we're not going to buy watches from Switzerland and we're going to put a high tariff on them so we can sell our watches, made in Massachusetts and Connecticut. Not only were American watches, back in the 1920s, more expensive— our watches were roughly four dollars, while a Swiss watch was roughly two to three dollars—but the U.S. watches didn't keep very good time. We had to reset them each morning. The Swiss watches kept better time and were cheaper. So Americans bought the Swiss watches, but American watchmakers lost the business.

Hoover had a solution. He thought, "Let's put a tariff or a tax on imported Swiss watches, and then people will buy American." Well, that was nice, except the people in Switzerland didn't just sit around and say, "Well, we'll just yodel in the hills to the sound of music after losing our watchmaking business." On the contrary, they said, "We're not buying American!"

So now, American automobiles, which were competitive, and American typewriters, and American air-conditioning, saw their market cut off in Switzerland. You might think, "Well, Switzerland. That isn't that big a country." But there was just one problem: this was happening all over Europe. We wouldn't buy British blankets. We wouldn't buy Spanish olives. And so, all over Europe, markets were retaliating against American products. That devastated the U.S. economy. Some of this was reflected, for example, in auto sales. In 1929, the last year of the Roaring Twenties, we sold five million automobiles; in 1933, we sold about a million and a half automobiles.

Now there was more to that decline than just foreign sales, but those were a part of it. We hurt all of American industry through high tariffs.

At the same time, the Federal Reserve raised interest rates, making it harder to borrow money. Milton Friedman won the Nobel Prize writing a book that described how these actions hurt the American economy. Then Hoover raised tax rates. That made it harder for entrepreneurs to make a profit and made them less willing to take risks. Hoover's administration was a failure, and it's not surprising that Franklin Roosevelt beat him.

Franklin Roosevelt ran for office actually promising to *cut* federal spending, because he thought Hoover had gone way too far by taking a good economy and weakening it tremendously.

When Roosevelt came into power, he changed his mind. Roosevelt began pouring federal funds into the American economy, the equivalent of the modern-day stimulus package. One program was called the Triple-A, the Agricultural Adjustment Administration (AAA).

The idea behind the AAA was that farmers would get higher prices for their products. People couldn't afford to buy much, because unemployment was over 20 percent. So Roosevelt came up with an idea so wild it could only have been invented by a college professor: let's pay farmers not to produce! Only a college professor could have thought up this monstrosity. Indeed, one of FDR's advisers who was a college professor suggested that the federal government pay farmers not to produce, and that strategy became part of the Agricultural Adjustment Act: have the farmers set aside as much as a fourth of their land, 25 percent, and they would be paid not to produce on that 25 percent. Farm income would go up, the experts said, and also there won't be a glut of product on the market. The AAA was supposed to reduce the overproduction of corn, wheat, cotton, and other farm products, because farmers would be producing on only three-fourths of their land.

But there was a hitch in this brilliant plan. Roosevelt discovered that there were some farmers taking this money not to produce and then sneaking crops onto that land anyway, to make double the money. The solution? The feds sent inspectors out to everybody's land. They had measuring equipment to ensure that if a farmer had a 160-acre farm, the farmer let forty acres lie fallow. And if those forty acres were growing crops, the farmer would have to dig up what he had planted. Meanwhile, of course, people were starving during the Great Depression.

Ultimately, FDR hired thousands of inspectors and a fleet of airplanes to make sure farmers were not cheating. Soon, the Department of Agriculture became the second-largest department in the federal government, next to the Department of War.

But there was another problem. In 1934, federal experts found that some of the farmers had taken the money that they were paid for not producing and used it to buy fertilizer for the other three-fourths of their land. Many farmers had great production on three-fourths of their acreage. Some crops were actually up in production in 1934.

Thus, the farm crisis persisted.

Now, who paid for all these inspectors and airplanes and photography and all of that? The taxpayer. Taxes rose to a top rate under Roosevelt of 79 percent in the 1930s. The government was telling our super-entrepreneurs that they had to give four out of every five dollars to the U.S. government. Lo and behold, we discovered that very few people were inventing things. If you look at inventions and patents, we find very few in the 1930s, compared with the 1920s.

One of the few inventions was the board game Monopoly. "You're broke, pass 'Go' and get two hundred dollars!" The game excited people, and that's one of the few popular inventions of the 1930s. Fake money.

But we don't find many job-creating inventions in the 1930s.

The Great Depression persisted through Roosevelt's first two terms. So, you ask, "If this was so bad, how did this guy keep getting reelected?" That's a very good question. The easiest way to explain that odd phenomenon is by looking at how people thought at the time—and by looking at FDR's propaganda.

V. G. Coplen was the Democratic Party county chairman in Indiana. He said this about the Works Progress Administration: "What I think will help is to change the WPA management from top to bottom. Put men in there who are in favor of using these Democratic projects to make votes for the Democratic Party." In other words, target WPA projects—everybody has roads they want built—and figure out what states and what districts are going to get those roads. Those who please President Roosevelt, or those who are in swing states that President Roosevelt wants to carry, would get the federal projects (and federal dollars).

For example, the Democrats had not carried Pennsylvania in decades. Pennsylvania was targeted with a heavy amount of WPA spending. David Lawrence, a magazine editor, conducted a survey of Pennsylvania. He found that those counties in Pennsylvania that received no federal funds, or limited federal funds, in 1936 voted Republican. The more money you received, the more likely your county was to vote Democrat. And Roosevelt made sure that a lot of money went into Pennsylvania's big cities, Pittsburgh and Philadelphia.

Here's another quotation, this one from a congressman, Frank Towey, from New Jersey. He said this: "In this county, there are 18,000 people on the WPA. With an average of three in a family, you have 54,000 potential Democratic votes. Can anyone beat that if it is properly mobilized?" Interesting, isn't it? As we went into the 1940 election where Roosevelt ran for a third term, the WPA was very strong.

James Doherty, a New Hampshire Democrat, said this: "It is my personal belief that to the victor belong the spoils, and the Democrats should be holding most of those WPA positions so that we might strengthen our fences for the 1940 election."

Let's conclude with a Southern senator. As you know, Southern senators were a big part of the Democratic Party. Carter Glass, Virginia's senior senator, spoke about the overwhelming reelection of Franklin Roosevelt in 1936, with high unemployment in the United States. He said: "The 1936 election would have been much closer had my party not had a $4.8 billion WPA relief bill as campaign fodder."

Right. He saw it happen, and they all saw it. They saw federal money going out at election time. The Democratic Party was able to win elections even though the policies were not getting us out of the Great Depression. This is a huge change in American history. I wish the Southern Agrarians would have written more on this. But apparently they did not consider this political change quite as threatening as the rise of industry.

A few agrarians did oppose this; I'm not suggesting that Robert Penn Warren was a big fan of Roosevelt. But by writing a big novel against Huey Long, *All the King's Men*, Warren was writing against Roosevelt's main opponent in the Democratic Party.

These people, the Southern Agrarians, were not really as opposed to what was going on in the federal government as they were to industrial development and how it was breaking down regional distinctions in the South.

WAR AND POSTWAR

World War II did not get America out of the Great Depression. Employment during the war was only temporary and often wasteful. For example, during World War II, the United States set up the Office of War Information (OWI). It was designed to give Americans war news and promote enthusiasm for winning the war. Instead, it hyped the benefits of the New Deal and the glories of FDR. In 1943, with Marines fighting in the Pacific, the air force bombing Europe, and a huge shortage in available ships for the war effort, the OWI printed millions of pamphlets on FDR's wonderful administration and planned to ship them to South America. One congressman called OWI's leadership on the carpet and asked how much shipping this project displaced. The response? One shipment alone displaced 800 tons of shipping in the middle of a war. Congress finally cut funding for the OWI and the WPA.

By the time of his death, Roosevelt had dramatically reshaped the income tax structure. The top tax bracket was 94 percent on all income over $200,000. For every dollar you earned over $200,000, you kept six cents. When 1945 came, and the bombs were dropped at Hiroshima and Nagasaki, Roosevelt was already dead, but Harry Truman wanted to continue his policies. Roosevelt had wanted programs to have massive continuation of federal intervention.

But that's when Americans actually resisted. Congress said, "Our people fought this war. Our cadets, civilians who became soldiers, twelve million and more who went overseas, fought that war for freedom. They didn't fight that war so that 94 percent of everybody's earnings could be taken away. That's not the United States. Other people do that. That isn't what we do in this country."

This became the big fight of our time. Roosevelt had wanted big spending and a whole new batch of federal programs after the war. He advocated massive spending in his Economic Bill of Rights, presented in 1944 as a postwar program. FDR wanted a Federal Housing Authority. He said, "Everybody has a right to a 'decent home.'" And this meant that if Mr. Smith had a right to a decent home, then Mr. Jones down the street had an obligation to pay for Mr. Smith's decent home.

That's a different sort of freedom than the freedom of speech. Freedom of speech does not impose obligations on others to sit around and listen. Freedom of religion does not mean you have to pay for anybody's church. But if Mr. Smith has a *right* to a decent home, then all of us have an obligation to finance that home. And by the way, what is a decent home?

Many politicians could see that this was going to be an incredible boondoggle. But those who supported FDR said, "If you don't have government jobs to build people these homes and have more types of WPA projects, we're going to go into huge unemployment." Sidney Hillman, who was head of the CIO (which later became the AFL-CIO), said, "If you don't have a lot of programs, and have them quick, the soldiers are going to come home and you're going to have ten million unemployed in six to ten weeks!" Senator Harley Kilgore, West Virginia, said, "No, it's going to be eighteen million! We're going to have unemployment worse than the Great Depression. Twelve million soldiers are going to come home and there's nothing for them!"

Instead Congress, led by Senator Walter George of Georgia, a Democrat, and Senator Albert Hawkes of New Jersey, a Republican, cut federal tax rates and cut federal spending. They even cited what Harding, Coolidge, and Andrew Mellon (their secretary of the treasury) did in the 1920s.

Federal spending went down by two-thirds after World War II. We cut the corporate income tax from 90 percent to 38 percent! We cut the income tax. We told people, "You're going to get to keep more of what you produce. We're going to trust Americans with the freedom they went overseas to earn and we will take our chances. Rather than empowering government bureaucrats and czars with power to allocate federal funds taken from taxpayers, we're going to cut the tax rates and turn people loose."

Unemployment in 1946 and 1947, the two years after the war, was the same: 3.9 percent. We assimilated twelve million people back into the workforce with an incredible expansion by American entrepreneurs. Inventions began cropping up again. Television had been invented before the war, but it became increasingly popular after the war. Xerox machines, fast food, McDonald's, Holiday Inns. We saw a renewal of the inventive spirit of the 1920s.

That is what ended the Great Depression: giving people more freedom, not empowering government bureaucrats. That is the story of overcoming the New Deal and Franklin Roosevelt.

That is our choice today. Either we can follow Roosevelt, or we can follow those who came before and after him. We can prosper, or we can increase government and lose our liberty and prosperity.

CHAPTER 6

◆ ◆ ◆

Libertarianism is understood by many to mean simply "Leave us alone!" This message has great appeal among economic conservatives, foreign policy isolationists, social liberals—and the young. Libertarians generally believe that government does not have the right to tell us how to conduct our personal lives, so long as we are not injuring anyone else. In the social realm, libertarians fall out of line with many other conservatives who fear this approach may be slouching toward libertinism. But in the economic realm, the libertarian movement has defined conservatism for much of the twentieth century.

In his essay, economist Dr. Yaron Brook reviews the important twentieth-century libertarian economists, who are central to the larger conservative tradition. These economists are strong advocates of limited government, low taxes, and free markets, and their views are widely endorsed by conservatives in general.

And then there is Ayn Rand. Standing somewhat apart from conservatism and libertarianism, Ayn Rand and her philosophy, objectivism, developed as a very distinctive modern strand of philosophy and ethics. Brook explains that Rand challenged conventional morality and altruism, which she associated with the traditional virtue of self-sacrifice on behalf of others or one's group. Rand believed that altruism leads to statism: liberals and socialists using altruism to call on us to sacrifice ourselves for the good of the collective. Rand's message resonates in this era in which the Left increasingly takes the labor of some and hands it to others, in the name of altruism.

Dr. Yaron Brook is the executive director of the Ayn Rand Institute. Dr. Brook received his M.B.A. and Ph.D. in finance from the University of Texas at Austin. He is a columnist at Forbes.com, and his articles have been featured in the *Wall Street Journal, USA Today, Investor's Business Daily*, and many other publications. He is a frequent guest on national radio and television programs and is a coauthor of *Neoconservatism: An Obituary for an Idea* and a contributing author to *Winning the Unwinnable War: America's Self-Crippled Response to Islamic Totalitarianism.* Dr. Brook is coauthor with ARI fellow Don Watkins of the national best seller *Free Market Revolution: How Ayn Rand's Ideas Can End Big Government.* A former finance professor, he speaks internationally on such topics as the causes of the financial crisis, the morality of capitalism, ending the growth of the state, and U.S. foreign policy.

THE EMERGENCE OF
LIBERTARIANISM

Yaron Brook

◆ ◆ ◆

My goal in this chapter is to evaluate three prominent economists who influenced conservative and libertarian views on
economic liberty, highlighting their successes and failures as
advocates of free markets from the perspective of Ayn Rand's
philosophy of objectivism. This is by no means a comprehensive presentation of the libertarian movement and its impact on
conservatives, or of Ayn Rand's thought; I want to focus only
on a few essentials.

To understand the growth of modern conservatism in
America and its relationship to modern libertarianism, you
have to go back to the end of World War II. The Allies had
just defeated Hitler and the Japanese, two fascist empires with
ideas of world domination—two ideologically collectivist regimes. But at the same time, communism was an ideology
on the rise, stronger than ever in the Soviet Union and just
taking hold in China. The United States and its allies had
surrendered virtually the whole of Eastern Europe to communism, and Korea would become a battleground for com-

munist control. To all appearances in the late 1940s and early 1950s, the nations of the world were falling under the spell of communism, which was enthralling people, especially Western intellectuals.

At the same time, the United States was emerging from the Great Depression era, when collectivism—the idea of sacrificing individual liberty for the sake of the state, for the sake of the economy, for the sake of the group—had been dominant. For more than fifteen years, the United States had significantly increased the size and role of government, on collectivist rationales such as reducing unemployment.

These twin collectivist threats—communism abroad and statism at home—aroused fear among those who admired liberty, venerated the Founding Fathers, and cherished the spirit of individualism that characterized America in the nineteenth and early twentieth centuries. A number of prominent thinkers were discussing these issues and arguing against collectivism, Ayn Rand among them. She had published a semi-autobiographical novel in 1936 called *We the Living*, based on her experience under Soviet communism before she escaped to America in 1926. In terms of sales, the book was a complete failure, thanks in large part to an American intelligentsia enamored of collectivism and therefore unwilling to take seriously or recommend an author who described Russian communism accurately. Not until the 1950s and '60s, when it became impossible to evade the evidence of Stalin's misdeeds, did some American leftists and intellectuals begin to acknowledge the evils of communism.

THE GREAT FREE MARKET
ECONOMICS

Friedrich Hayek

One voice that resonated powerfully with conservatives and others who worried about the rise of communism was Friedrich A. Hayek (1899–1992), whose *The Road to Serfdom* was first published in the U.K. in 1944. Hayek is probably the most influential libertarian thinker of modern times; he is certainly the libertarian thinker with the most influence on conservatism.

Hayek was a brilliant Austrian economist, one of the great economists of the twentieth century and an advocate for minimal government intervention in the marketplace. The thesis of *The Road to Serfdom* is this: if you plant the seed of collectivism and allow government to grow, what you get in the end is authoritarianism. Hayek argued that Nazism did not arise spontaneously from nothing—it sprang from the seed of collectivism that was cultivated for years in Germany and matured into fascism. His account of communism's growth was similar: it did not arise spontaneously but grew slowly from the seed of collectivism.

Hayek powerfully and prophetically described what was happening in the West in the 1940s. As hard as it is to imagine, the West was moving left so fast that even the war hero Winston Churchill couldn't maintain his leadership. Despite his historic success in helping lead the Allies to victory over fascism in World War II, Churchill had to vacate the prime minister's office in 1945 when his Conservative Party lost to the socialists in Britain, the Labour Party. Hayek warned the British that this was going to happen.

Unlike Rand's 1936 novel, Hayek's book was a publishing sensation when it came to America later in 1944, and it spurred many thinkers to come forward in support of anti-collectivist ideas. The problem is that Hayek, though he supported the free market overall, was also a compromiser who acknowledged the state's legitimate role in such areas as "facilitating competition" and "helping markets along." Hayek was not a purist when it came to markets—he allowed for significantly more government intervention than many free market thinkers did, at that time and since. This is why many conservatives like him, precisely because he is not a purist. Conservatives are not purists when it comes to free markets—they don't believe in limiting government's economic role to setting up property rights and leaving the markets alone. Conservatives want to tinker with the economy.

Hayek was a thinker who is associated with and adopted by both conservatives and libertarians; however, he never considered himself a conservative. He actually wrote an essay entitled "Why I Am Not a Conservative," in which he criticized conservatives and the term *conservatism* itself. What, exactly, are they trying to conserve? Hayek asked. To adopt conservation as a principle means preserving a lot of undesirable things. So Hayek considered himself a liberal—not a modern liberal, mind you, but a nineteenth-century liberal. Those liberals considered themselves Progressives, because they were for genuine progress. They were not leftist Progressives who advocate that government move things forward. Hayek's type of liberal wants to leave markets and individuals alone for the most part so they can achieve progress. Such liberals are revolutionaries and radicals, not conservatives who cling to tradition. If you look at the way many libertarians write about their history, they trace their roots to these early liberal thinkers. But twentieth-century liberals in America reversed the word's meaning, and what was a pro-capitalist term became a pro-government term.

As a side note, Hayek ultimately taught in London at the Institute of Economic Affairs and had great influence on Margaret Thatcher. Thatcher completely changed the British economy and the U.K., revolutionizing it toward more freedom. She will go down as one of the great political figures of the twentieth century—greater than Ronald Reagan, because she had a more profound impact in the U.K. than Reagan had in America, and because the U.K. was in much worse shape in the late 1970s. Thatcher studied Hayek. So through Thatcher, Hayek had a profound impact on the politics of the U.K.

Ludwig von Mises

Hayek's teacher was Ludwig von Mises (1881–1973), probably the greatest economist of the twentieth century. Mises advocated a pure form of capitalism, real free markets. The school of thought that combines the thinking of Mises and Hayek is called the Austrian school of economics, and in my view it's the best school of economics in the world today.

Hayek was a socialist when he came to study with Mises, and Mises turned him into a capitalist—so Mises is responsible in a certain sense for the economist that Hayek became. Mises believed that government has only one role in the economic sphere, and that is the protection of property rights. Government sets up rules for property rights, and then catches the criminals who violate those rules. Mises advocated no regulations, no incentives, no manipulation of the market, and no role for any of the regulatory agencies that we have today. It is hard to imagine, but he wanted to eliminate government involvement in the economy, meaning no Food and Drug Administration, no Securities and Exchange Commission, no Department of Commerce, no Department of Labor, no special rules for unions (which should be free to organize, but without government privileges).

Mises had, and still has, a huge influence on free market economists and libertarian thinkers. These economists provided us with a deep and unique economic understanding of the world. Mises said, in essence: "Markets work. We need government to protect our property rights but otherwise leave us alone." In his view, economics teaches this: if you leave people alone, lots of good things happen. And if you look at history, when we leave markets alone, boom!—the standard of living goes up, quality of life goes up, we get industrialization, we get technology, we get iPhones and iPads—we get good stuff. But when government regulates and controls the economy, the result is a distorted marketplace, and you get crises, declines, recessions, depressions, poverty.

In a purely economic analysis, the market provides solutions to problems that are supposedly government concerns. For example, in the absence of an FDA, private entities will emerge to test drugs and food, and to investigate risk factors. Not only will free market incentives lead people to do what is required, but the results will be more trustworthy overall than those generated by bureaucrats. For every important question, Mises and the Austrians indicated how things would work out better in a free market, under true capitalism.

Mises was probably the most influential of the economists within the libertarian movement. He taught at New York University, but it is interesting that both he and Hayek (who taught at the University of Chicago) couldn't get regular tenured positions from their universities because the schools, even then, were dominated by collectivist, anti–free market, anticapitalist forces. So the free market economists had to rely on external funding from foundations and other institutions.

Milton Friedman

Probably the best-known libertarian economist is Milton Friedman (1912–2006). Along with Frank Knight at the University of Chicago, Friedman started the so-called Chicago School of economics. Friedman made many arguments on behalf of free markets. But when comparing Friedman to Mises, it is important to remember that Mises was part of the Austrian School of economics, which occupied a position outside of mainstream economics and rarely published in the prestigious academic journals. By contrast, Friedman employed the tools of conventional, mainstream economics to advocate on behalf of free markets, and as a consequence, he became more well known than the Austrians did—certainly within the field of economics. Even Friedman's opponents held him in high regard as an economist.

Friedman was a strong advocate for free markets on grounds

of both efficiency and principle. He held that leaving individuals alone to seek their own ends is right, and it works. This recalls Adam Smith, writing in *The Wealth of Nations* (1776), who showed that when you leave individuals alone, the economy grows.

Friedman had a very successful career at the University of Chicago. At universities all over America today, in the field of economics, Chicago-trained faculty wield a disproportionate influence compared with those educated at other schools. This is partly due to the fact that Friedman, like Hayek, was willing to compromise on matters of principle when it came to practice and policy. For example, there is a hotly contested debate among free market advocates about the need for a central bank. Pure and uncompromising advocates of free markets reject the idea that a central bank is required. They advocate free banking without government intervention in money or banking. But Milton Friedman supported the idea of a central bank, although toward the end of his life he changed his mind. As for Hayek, it is less clear what his position was: sometimes he's for a central bank, and sometimes he's against one. Mises, however, never supported a central bank, and many of today's Austrian economists agree with him.

What did these three prominent economists have in common? Clearly they were united by a certain respect for the marketplace, a respect for capitalism, a respect for the idea that if markets are left alone, they create enormous amounts of wealth. Free markets allow the poor to rise up from poverty. They allow technological innovation. They allow creativity. Not only do they allow for everything we want materially, but the wealth produced on free markets makes possible much of what we want spiritually.

The Anarchists

I don't want to be accused of not including the anarchists, so I will briefly mention that part of the libertarian movement. These are the libertarians who believe that there should be no government (by contrast, Mises, Hayek, and Friedman all believed there should be government). The leader of this influential part of libertarianism was an economist named Murray Rothbard, who ended his career at the University of Las Vegas. Libertarian anarchy emerges from this approach: "Why stop at privatizing the post office and privatizing schools? Let's privatize the police force and the military, and let's have competing governments in the sense of competing police forces and so on."

Today, a significant portion of the libertarian movement believes in anarchy. This belief manifests itself not only in direct arguments for no government, but also in a hatred of government, a resentment of all government functions. Anarchists view government as the biggest initiator of force, as the biggest violator of our rights, and therefore hate and resent the very institution of government. Of course, there's an element of truth to this, because the biggest violator of individual rights today, the biggest imposer of force on our lives today, is indeed government. But does this mean one should hate all government on principle? I would rather fight as the Founders did, to confine government to its proper and necessary function: the protection of individual rights.

Libertarian Influence

What impact have these libertarians had on the American conservatives? Not much. I think they have had an impact on what some people say, maybe even on what some people think. But I'd say they've had almost no impact on what conservatives actually do when they rise to positions of power. Many people in the Reagan administration, for example, would have considered themselves economic libertarians in the sense of believing in a very, very minor role for government. But they didn't do much toward that end. The fact is that under Reagan, the government didn't shrink—it grew. It grew perhaps at a slower rate, and it was somewhat deregulated, but deregulation had already started under Jimmy Carter. Conservatives don't like to admit it, but the fact is that many of the benefits Reagan got credit for resulted from deregulation that occurred under Jimmy Carter's administration. Indeed, Gerald Ford really started it, and then came Carter. For example, government used to control the price of airplane tickets; Jimmy Carter deregulated that market. And the government used to control prices in the trucking industry; Jimmy Carter deregulated that market. Broker fees used to be regulated, and interest payments on savings accounts used to be controlled under Regulation Q. All of that was freed up in the 1970s under Gerald Ford and Jimmy Carter, not under Reagan.

So Ronald Reagan benefited from the fact that there was already some momentum toward deregulation. During his tenure, there was certainly some deregulation and tax cutting—but there was no shrinkage of government. For instance, Reagan came into office saying he was going to do away with the Department of Education. But by the end of his second term, that agency was far bigger than when he started. So the rhetoric of the pro—free market economists was there, but the actions—not so much.

You'll hear similar rhetoric from modern presidential candidates. In 2012, Mitt Romney talked about the need to shrink government dramatically, and about the importance of individual rights to life, liberty, and the pursuit of happiness. Then moments later he was discussing which industries he wanted to subsidize or penalize, which programs he wanted to increase, and how he was going to boost the American economy by going after the Chinese. Rick Santorum wanted to give special privileges to manufacturers, claiming that manufacturing is somehow superior to service industries. Newt Gingrich wanted to provide tax favors to industries he favored. These candidates opposed free trade and supported expansion of regulatory state power. Each wanted to manipulate the market in a different way, based on his agenda. That is typical of conservatives— they don't advocate markets free of government intervention.

And then there's George W. Bush. I saved him for last because where do you end if you start there? Consider this: during the first six of his eight years in office, Bush's Republican Party had majorities in both houses of Congress, including a lot of conservative senators. Yet in 2002, Congress enacted Sarbanes-Oxley, one of the biggest regulatory bills since the 1930s, and one of the costliest. Sarbanes-Oxley probably shaved $1.5 trillion off the nation's GDP. It is a horrific, stupid law that impedes innovation and growth, causes a huge misallocation of capital, and—not surprisingly—catches no crooks. Bernie Madoff happened anyway. The housing crisis and Wall Street shenanigans happened anyway. Sarbanes-Oxley accomplished nothing.

This wasn't all George Bush's fault. The conservatives in the U.S. Senate didn't help—exactly none of them voted against Sarbanes-Oxley (the vote was 99–0). The bottom line is that conservatives may talk the talk, but they don't walk the walk when it comes to economic liberty. That's what history shows, and it's true no matter who's in Congress or who occupies the White House. Government has grown for more than a century—that is, government has *only* grown, never shrunk. Regardless of whatever deregulation occurred, there were always other areas that were very quickly reregulated or regulated anew—along with new taxes, new regulations, and new schemes for redistribution of wealth. We saw all that under George W. Bush, who was the biggest regulator and expander of government programs since Lyndon B. Johnson.

In this quick overview of three economists associated with the libertarian movement, we see two things. On the one hand, these economists have defended free markets from an economic perspective. They have shown brilliantly that, indeed, markets do work. Yet on the other hand, as we see in the conservative movement, these arguments don't seem to have had real effects on policy, or on the perceptions of the American people. The drift away from free markets continues, without effective opposition.

AYN RAND AND THE MORAL DEFENSE
OF CAPITALISM

In her lifetime, Ayn Rand observed all these trends and arrived at a diagnosis of why the free market economists keep losing the fight. It comes down to this: most people don't care about economics because economics is not what life's about. Life is not just about wealth, or how much GDP we can create, or what kind of iPhone we can buy. There are much more important values involved in politics. *People don't vote their pocketbook.* If they voted their pocketbook, we would have laissez-faire capitalism in America today, because capitalism is clearly better for your pocketbook than statism. We have great economists— both Hayek and Friedman won Nobel Prizes—who have demonstrated beyond any reasonable doubt the relationship between economic freedom and wealth creation. But the fact is that people want to believe what they're doing is right, just, fair, good. People care most about *moral* values, which means the ultimate driver of politics is not economics—it's morality.

On Rand's view, collectivism will keep winning in the political arena until people come to understand why it's morally wrong to view people fundamentally in groups. But I would argue—and Rand would argue—that most conservatives are collectivists. Again, I'll give you Rick Santorum. What is the basic unit—the unit of morality, the unit of politics, the unit of economics—for Rick Santorum? It's the family, not the individual. In an interview, Santorum once said individual happiness is not the goal—the family is the goal, the solidity of the family. That's collectivism, and a dramatic departure from the

Founders' view. And if the basic political unit is the family, then policy prescriptions will be concerned not with individual freedom but with what's "good" for the family. And so if I think outlawing divorce would be good for the family, then I'll outlaw divorce. This illustrates the basic problem conservatives face: because they are themselves collectivists in one form or another, they can't attack collectivism on a moral level, much less offer a moral defense of individualism.

Libertarians face this same problem, even when they deny allegiance to collectivism in any form. Rand's insight here is key: neither conservatives nor libertarians challenge collectivism at its root—because what's at the root of collectivism is the morality of *altruism*. What is altruism? Altruism doesn't mean being nice to other people, or holding the door for a senior citizen. Altruism is the idea in ethics that the well-being of other people is your primary moral responsibility. So when you think about "the good," the good is "what I can do for other people," not "what I can do for myself." Altruism is about self-sacrifice—the sacrifice of your values for the sake of others. The choice comes down to altruism versus egoism (self-interest).

For altruism, the fundamental unit is other people, not the individual or the self—and so it's not about pursuing your own happiness. But the Declaration of Independence doesn't say you have a right to be your brother's keeper, or to go and help your fellow man, or to become a Mother Teresa. Instead, the Declaration affirms your right to "the pursuit of happiness." The Founding Fathers were being profoundly selfish in that document. They declared that you have inalienable rights—rights that can't be taken away by anybody—to pursue your *own* life and happiness.

At the root of collectivism, Rand tells us, is the notion that virtue comes from self-sacrifice. How does that play out in real life? Consider the businessman turned philanthropist Bill Gates. This man made billions of dollars during the 1990s and 2000s by heading up the Microsoft Corporation. But what did we think of him morally when he was making all that money? Morally, we didn't think well of him at all. Okay, so he's a great businessman—but that's not the moral life, like Mother Teresa lived. We think of Mother Teresa as a saint, while Gates was just out to make money. But then look what happened next: Gates retired from business and set up a charitable foundation, to give his money away—and now he's a good guy, he's a moral example for others. And if he wanted to make the push for sainthood, all he would have to do is give away everything and move into a hut or a tent—and if he bled a little bit and showed some suffering, that would pretty much guarantee sainthood.

In short, we don't ethically admire the creation of wealth—we admire people when they give it away. I once gave a talk in Charleston, South Carolina, at a luncheon sponsored by The Citadel's business school to honor local business leaders. I was the keynote speaker, and so I watched as everybody went before me and introduced the businessmen who were receiving awards. It was fascinating, because it all fitted perfectly into the thesis that I hadn't even delivered yet. The introductions began by describing the honorees' business achievements, the wealth they created, the employment they created, the great standard of living they had provided for their family and for themselves—all that crammed into about two minutes. And then, for the next fifteen minutes or so, they described the honoree's philanthropy and community service. I regard that as bizarre, for reasons that will become clear as we proceed.

When Bill Gates made his billions of dollars, how much did he help us? We all bought his products, which made us hugely better off, by an amount many multiples of the money he made. Microsoft helped standardize software on computers all over the world, making networking possible, ultimately making the Internet possible in the form that we have today, benefiting billions of people all across the world, including the poor. I believe he helped many, many more people in a much more profound way by running Microsoft than by giving away his money philanthropically. There's no question about that. And there's no question that through Microsoft, Gates helped many more people in more profound ways than Mother Teresa ever did. But what's the difference, morally speaking? It's this: as Microsoft CEO, Gates earned a return on helping people. He made money for himself in the process. He helped himself by helping other people. That is morally unacceptable by an altruist standard—which explains why, when he stopped making money and started giving it away, his moral standing improved even though he was helping fewer people. That's what altruism demands: it demands that you give without expectation of getting. That's what sacrifice is: sacrifice is giving and not getting. Sacrifice is lose/win—you lose, and somebody else wins (on this earth, at least).

As Microsoft CEO, Bill Gates engaged in *trade*. When I

trade something with you—let's say I sell you a car and you pay me $20,000—which of us has lost? Nobody has. I won, because the car was worth less than $20,000 to me, so I made a little bit of profit. And you won, because the car was worth more than $20,000 to you—that's why you were willing to give up the money. All voluntary trades are win/win in this sense—both sides intend to benefit (although in any given case, for various reasons, the actual result might fall below expectations). Now what's the moral status of win/win transactions in our culture? They earn you no moral credit. But as soon as we're talking win/lose, then it must be morally good, because somebody lost a value. It's bizarre, but that's what altruism demands.

The flip side of altruism is self-interest. What do we think of self-interested people, morally speaking? If I say, "That person is selfish," what do we think, immediately? Without even a pause to think, what comes to mind is: he's got to be bad. Why? Because he's probably lying, cheating, and stealing—or he would be if the government weren't watching him like a hawk. If he's selfish, he's in the same camp with Bernie Madoff.

But in reality, what is business all about? It's about making money. It's about making great products, the products you want to make. I love the example of the iPhone, because Steve Jobs made a lot of money on it. The profit margin was about 60 percent. If Jobs had cared about me in an altruist sense, he would have sold it cheaper or given it away, but he didn't. He wanted to make money by creating a product he enjoyed. How many customer surveys did Jobs do before designing the iPhone? Zero. None. He created what he wanted to create, based on what he thought we should like. Steve Jobs was a self-interested—call him "selfish"—businessman. All business-men are. That's why we're so embarrassed by them. That's why we spend only two minutes describing their business activities at an awards dinner, because they're selfish. We all know it. We know capitalism is about a bunch of people pursuing self-interest.

Adam Smith understood that in 1776. The baker doesn't bake bread to make you better off. He doesn't care about you in an altruistic, self-sacrificial sense. He makes the bread to make a living, and he gives you good customer service—not because he loves you above himself, but because that's how he sells more bread. That's the reality: we all, in the business world, are after self-interest. And yet we are taught that self-interest involves lying, stealing, cheating—so of course we want reg-ulations. We want government bureaucrats overseeing what selfish businessmen do, because the bureaucrat is *not* acting out of self-interest.

The conflict here is between self-interested capitalism and the morality of altruism. If the epitome of virtue is to sacrifice, then how can we complain when our taxes go up? All the gov-ernment is trying to do is help somebody. It wants us to give up some of our wealth, so that somebody else is supposedly better off.

The key to understanding our political world is that people vote their morality, not their pocketbooks—which typically means taking an altruist path, even if it conflicts with their economic understanding of markets. They want to be good, morally good—and President Obama understands this really, really well. For Obama, every election is about fairness, about the kind of economy and the kind of world we want for our future. He is about the "vision thing." He frames the election in terms of morality, not economics, because in economics he loses, and he knows it. But he has a chance of winning when the choice is between altruism and self-interest.

This is what Rand challenges. She says, in effect, "Yes, you economists are all correct, especially Mises, in the way you've described the economy. You've shown that everybody who's willing to work is better off under capitalism. But that's not the reason to adopt capitalism, or to be an individualist, or to advocate freedom. The reason is that capitalism is *moral*." Rand can say that persuasively only because she rejects altruism. She can say that only because she is willing to challenge every secular philosopher of the last two thousand years—every thinker since Aristotle (with a few exceptions here and there)—who basically said that your purpose in life is to sacrifice for others. She is willing to challenge the Judeo-Christian tradition of morality, which is altruism. Rand advocates a different morality: the morality of self-interest. She says that your proper purpose is to pursue your own life, to make your life the best it can be, to live the most flourishing, successful, happy life you can. If you think about it carefully and look around at the world, you will discover that this doesn't involve lying, cheating, and stealing, because those things turn out to be incredibly self-destructive. The moral life is a rational, long-term life of honesty and a sense of justice and integrity. It's not easy to be rationally selfish, because it involves discovering what *in fact* leads to happiness—but it is possible.

Rand believed this to be the only morality consistent with

America's founding: my life is the standard—I don't want to live for somebody else—I'm not your servant—I don't owe you anything (unless we're trading)—I don't owe my life to any group, to any other individual—I am here for me. And yes, I want to trade with other people in all kinds of ways—some of them material, some of them spiritual—but I don't want you to sacrifice for me. I don't want you to give me stuff that I haven't earned. And I don't want to give you stuff you haven't earned. I want all our interactions to be win/win. This is the only morality consistent with that part of the Declaration that affirms the inalienable right to life and liberty. The Founders were talking about individual lives: they weren't talking about "the American life" or "the family's life." They were talking about individuals' liberty—your ability to think what you want to think, do what you want to do, and pursue the values you choose, not what somebody else chooses for you—not what the group decides is in the common good, but what *you* decide is for *your* good. Finally, the Declaration contains the most selfish political statement in human history, recognizing your right to pursue your own happiness. And that's the essence of Rand's morality.

Now think about a rational, productive individual who's concerned only about the pursuit of his own happiness. What kind of government does he want? Does he want a government that looks over his shoulder like a paternalistic mother and says, "Don't do that! Don't eat that! Oh, no, trans fats, that's not good for you! Don't go into that elevator! An inspector wasn't there. Don't go west, young man—don't take risks. Don't invent an iPhone—do this instead." Does he want that? No. Individuals who want to pursue their own life, pursue their own interests, pursue their own passions, pursue their own values, to make of themselves the best they can be—those individuals want just one thing from government: to be left alone—to have their freedom protected from crooks and that is it. They don't want government telling them what to do, because government doesn't just make suggestions, it issues orders. Government puts a gun to your head and says, "Don't eat trans fats or you go to jail."

Rand held that the morality of self-interest is a core, foundational idea for the establishment of limited government. On her view, you're not going to achieve or sustain the limited government envisioned by the Founders without a new morality, and that means rejecting altruism. Of course, there's more to it than that. Rand was a philosopher who appreciated the need of a philosophic foundation for politics. Ayn Rand said she was an advocate of capitalism because she was an advocate of individualism—and she was an advocate of individualism because she was an advocate of self-interest—and she was an advocate of self-interest because she was an advocate of *reason*, and unless we understand that reason is the standard for knowledge and guide to action, we'll never get the rest. This is what differentiates her from libertarian thinkers—her view that a philosophical approach was needed to defend capitalism. And her philosophical ideas are still rejected by most libertarians and clearly contradict the tenets of conservatism.

But what Rand provides, that the libertarians or conservatives cannot, is the answer to an important question we should all care about: What makes America special?

Everywhere in the world, before the founding of this country, the individual belonged to someone else. Your life as an individual, your body as an individual, your soul as an individual, belonged to the tribe—it belonged to the king—it belonged to the pope—it belonged to society. The world was always a collectivistic world, without exception. What's unique about this country is that for the first time in history, a nation was founded on a truly radical, revolutionary, *moral* principle. This is what the American Revolution was all about: your life does not belong to anybody—it is yours to live on your own terms.

This is the greatest country in the history of mankind because of that founding principle, because of that founding idea. And that's the founding principle we need to recapture, explain, and defend. If only we can grasp that idea—that our lives are ours to live, to pursue our own happiness, as the Founders put it—then the future is ours. But if we lose that idea, then the future is lost, and we will go down the road that *Atlas Shrugged* lays out in chilling detail, the road to collectivistic destruction.

CHAPTER 7

◆ ◆ ◆

The importance of William F. Buckley Jr. to conservative thought in the second half of the twentieth century cannot be overstated. Before Buckley burst onto the scene in the 1950s, American conservatism was almost completely moribund. Conservatism at that time wasn't a movement at all—it was a frayed rope, with strands of anti-communism, religious morality, and libertarianism protruding out from an unwinding center.

That's where William F. Buckley came in. Buckley was a true intellectual in the classical sense: he was a man of ideas. He was a thinker who shaped his world and brought others to conservatism through his writings and his example. By the end of his life in 2008, the *New York Times* proclaimed that Buckley's "greatest achievement was making conservatism—not just electoral Republicanism but conservatism as a system of ideas—respectable in liberal post–World War II America." Buckley made conservatism respectable, but he also helped move conservatism from the realm of ideas into a viable political movement.

In this essay, David Keene, one of the chief spokesmen for conservative principles and politics, lays out his friend Bill Buckley's key philosophies—the philosophies that undergird the three-legged stool of conservatism and continue to animate conservatism today. Keene was a personal friend of both Buckley and his brother, and an eyewitness to the development of the postwar movement at whose center Buckley stood. Keene is vital to the history of the conservative movement; his personal experience provides a unifying field theory of modern conservatism.

David A. Keene is the opinion editor of the *Washington Times*. From 2011 to 2013, he served as president of the National Rifle Association, and remains on the board and executive council. He also serves on the boards of the Constitution Project and the Center for the National Interest and is a founding member of Right on Crime, a conservative criminal justice reform organization. From 1982 to 2011, Keene was the elected chairman of the American Conservative Union, and remains on the board. Keene also served as the national chairman of Young Americans for Freedom, editor of the oldest conservative student journal in the country, a John F. Kennedy Fellow at Harvard University's Institute of Politics, a First Amendment Fellow at Vanderbilt University's Freedom Forum, and on the board of visitors at Duke University's Public Policy School. Keene is married to Donna Wiesner Keene, a Senior Fellow at the Independent Women's Forum, and has five conservative children.

WILLIAM F. BUCKLEY JR., FUSIONISM, AND THE THREE-LEGGED STOOL OF CONSERVATISM

David A. Keene

◆ ◆ ◆

William F. Buckley edited *National Review* for nearly four decades and churned out an estimated 350,000 published words a year during that period. He traveled the country giving speeches and debating liberals on more than 500 American campuses. He published more than fifty books and hosted nearly 1,500 episodes of his public television show, *Firing Line.* George Nash, author of the most thorough history of the post–World War II conservative movement, said Buckley was "arguably the most important public intellectual in the United States in the past half century. . . . [F]or an entire generation, he was the preeminent voice of conservatism." And, perhaps his greatest achievement, Buckley brought the disparate wings of an emerging new conservatism together to create a politically viable movement where none had existed.

HOW I BECAME A CONSERVATIVE

Like many who joined the conservative movement early, I began life as a Democrat. My story is worth the telling because it is so much like what was happening to many others just like me in the late 1950s and early 1960s. At fifteen, I stood in the snows of Wisconsin during the 1960 Democratic primary passing out literature for John F. Kennedy. I would later learn that the early conservative movement included many disillusioned former Democrats or the sons and daughters of former Democrats, liberals, dissidents, and worse.

Not only was I from a Democrat family, but I was from a working-class labor family. My father was a workingman and a union activist. He spent ten years as the president of the Labor Council of Rockford, Illinois. My mother was elected president of the Women's Auxiliary of the United Auto Workers.

My parents were what many called "yellow dog" Democrats in those days, except that my father had actually once run for office in Rockford as a Republican. He did it for tactical reasons, but when a reporter for the local newspaper asked the famous labor union leader and socialist Walter Reuther as he passed through Rockford whether he realized that my father was a Republican, he said, "A Republican? I always thought he was a communist."

Despite his strategic switch of party, my father lost his race and returned to being a staunch Democrat. For many of my generation, however, loyalty to the Democratic Party and the policies it represented began to change for good—thanks in large measure to Bill Buckley and *National Review*. Buckley's magazine began popularizing ideas that just seemed to make sense to us and drew us away from the Democratic Party.

My own conversion came about while I was still in high school, only a year after I had stood on that street corner passing out Kennedy campaign literature. I was interested in politics and, more important, in ideas. Our high school librarian, perhaps a closet conservative herself, called me over to her desk one day and told me that she had ordered a copy of a book published in 1944 in Britain, by an economist named Friedrich Hayek, which she had been told could not be put on the library shelves.

In April 1945, *Reader's Digest* released a condensed version of *The Road to Serfdom* by Hayek, an Austrian economist in residence at the University of Chicago. Daniel Yergin, in his book *Commanding Heights*, which chronicles the development of conservative free market thinking after World War II, has suggested that the *Digest*'s decision to popularize Hayek may have been the most important single publishing decision of the mid-twentieth century.

The book that had been banned from our school, however, was not *The Road to Serfdom*, but Hayek's *The Constitution of Liberty*. Our high school librarian wasn't about to throw it out, so she told me I could have it if I wanted it. I took it home and read it, and it remains on my bookshelf to this day.

From Hayek to Buckley was an easy and natural step. I started to read *National Review*, and like thousands of budding young conservatives, I began eagerly devouring each new issue as it came out.

THE POWER OF BUCKLEY'S IDEAS

Political power and influence come ultimately from the power of ideas. Back in 1936, the economist John Kenneth Galbraith wrote that ideas "are more powerful than is commonly understood. Indeed, the world is ruled by little else. Madmen in authority, who hear voices in the air, are distilling their frenzy from some academic scribblers of a few years back. . . . Sooner or later it is ideas, not vested interests, which are dangerous for good or evil." Galbraith was referring to the scribblings of Marx and other philosophers who together produced the monsters of the twentieth century: Lenin, Stalin, Hitler, and Mao. But he could have been talking about William F. Buckley.

Buckley was all about ideas. In today's world, he would be described as a public intellectual. He gave voice to the ideas that were to culminate in the modern political movement that he more than anyone called into being.

He burst onto the scene at the age of twenty-six with *God and Man at Yale*. This book was a powerful critique of the educational homogenization to which he was subjected as an undergraduate at that esteemed university. Four years later he founded *National Review*, a journal of opinion that would change the world.

To grasp the enormity of all this, one has to remember just what the political and intellectual landscape looked like in the years following World War II. Yergin describes the postwar period as a time in which collectivist faith in government dominated the world. Britain had become socialist and nationalized its industry. Country after country developed five- and ten-year plans under which the state would direct the national economy. History seemed to be not just on the side of collectivism and socialism, but on the side of communism. One has to remember that when Whittaker Chambers abandoned communism and penned *Witness*, he was convinced that he was leaving the winning side for the losing side. In this country, establishment intellectuals like Lionel Trilling dismissed the very idea of an American conservative tradition as silly at best and pathological at worst.

This was the world that young Bill Buckley set out in 1955 to challenge and to change with his magazine, *National Review*. The mission statement for its November 1955 maiden issue stated that *National Review* "stands athwart history, yelling stop, at a time when no one is inclined to do so, or to have much patience with those who so urge it." Buckley didn't know if he, or ultimately we, would prevail, but he knew that we had to give it a try, against formidable odds.

Buckley was the catalyst for popularizing and shaping the intellectual landscape and bringing about political change. As Buckley and his colleagues set about building the new movement, they spent a great deal of time recruiting and mentoring young conservative intellectuals, writers, and activists around the country. Buckley himself was always available to young people with advice, encouragement, and assistance. The same was true of many of those around him.

Frank Meyer, then the highest-ranking U.S. communist to defect, became both book review editor of *National Review* and the conscience of the growing movement. He also became my mentor and friend. Frank lived on top of a mountain in Woodstock, New York, wrote at night, and slept during the day. Young people like me made pilgrimages to see Frank, drink his whiskey, argue issues with him, and open ourselves to harassment from the great man when he didn't think we were doing enough to advance the cause.

Like Buckley, Meyer was striving to turn the intellectual movement of the late 1950s into a political movement that might turn their ideas into reality. But to do this, different strains of conservatism would need to come together, and the movement would need to be purged of its fringe elements.

THE ORIGINS OF FUSIONISM

Buckley was determined to streamline the tiny but growing movement. Like most nascent intellectual movements, conservatism consisted mainly of academics, students, and writers. These intellectuals spent inordinate amounts of time and energy arguing about minor, as well as major, doctrinal differences. Included among them were the remnants of the old anti-Roosevelt coalition, isolationists, states' rightists, a smattering of racists, the objectivist followers of the newly famous Ayn Rand, religious extremists, conspiracy theorists, and even a few monarchists. The mix was very interesting, but it was hard to imagine it as a viable political movement.

Buckley and his band of merry men and women at *National Review* decided that their immediate mission was to get rid of the crazies, the racists, and those who couldn't get along with others. At the same time, they wanted to mold the remaining conservatives into a coalition that could give voice to a new intellectually vibrant conservatism capable of influencing the nation's culture and politics. Through *National Review*, Buckley began knitting together the different strains of thought that he and his followers believed legitimate and capable of working together to form a viable conservative movement.

In those days, there were three main camps that had overlapping but occasionally conflicting views. These were: (1) the anti-communists who, like Buckley, Chambers, Burnham, and Frank Meyer, saw Marxism-Leninism as an existential threat to everything they held dear; (2) the libertarians, animated by a commitment to limited government, free markets, and individual liberty; and (3) the traditionalists who believed that free men must act morally to preserve those rights they cherished.

Buckley and Meyer were persuaded that these camps faced the very same threats and could be united in a larger movement. Free markets, individual autonomy, and religious freedom were all threatened by communism and its American agents and sympathizers. The United States was a fortress of freedom in a dangerous world and all who valued freedom and tradition were in the same boat. What's more, none could afford to push the others overboard lest they all perish.

A coalition of these groups, Buckley and Meyer believed, could form the basis of a viable and long-lasting political conservatism that just might change the world. The emerging coalition was the product of what Meyer termed *fusionism*.

Before that movement could grow and attract others to their cause, though, they would first have to jettison those who made it difficult, if not impossible, for others to join. Some who were considered by outsiders at least to be part of this movement were unacceptable to the rest and had to be excised if the coalition was to hold together and grow.

I once told Frank Meyer that what they were doing was in fact following advice that my father had once given me. He had bought a tavern in the small Wisconsin town in which we lived and spent the first few weeks not attracting new customers, but throwing out some who seemed to have come with the place. "When you buy a tavern," he told me, "you have to throw out those who've been tossed out of every other tavern in town or you will never attract any new customers." It remains sound advice.

Buckley purged the mainstream conservative movement of what he considered fringe philosophies. The first to go were the Birchers. The John Birch Society was the brainchild of Belmont, Massachusetts, businessman Robert Welch and was named for a soldier killed in Korea by communist Chinese soldiers shortly after World War II ended. Welch considered John Birch the first casualty of the Cold War. The John Birch Society attracted tens of thousands of followers, but it quickly became apparent that Welch was a conspiracy theorist of the first order. Welch had suggested that President Eisenhower was a conscious agent of the communist conspiracy—to which Russell Kirk (a Buckleyite if there ever was one) responded, "Ike isn't a communist; he's a golfer." John Birch Society's bizarre theories were easily caricatured by a hostile establishment and used to tar conservatives like Buckley as part of what the press liked to call "the lunatic fringe."

Buckley famously read the Birchers out of the movement. I

was an undergraduate at the University of Wisconsin by then and a board member of Young Americans for Freedom, a national group founded by some young conservatives at Buckley's Sharon, Connecticut, estate. Later, I would chair the organization. Soon after Buckley's decision, the YAF board passed a resolution at our national convention denouncing the Birchers. It wasn't easy at the time, but political necessity demanded it.

Next to go were the followers of Ayn Rand, the objectivists, who Buckley saw as too doctrinaire and whose militant atheism offended him and many other conservatives. According to Buckley, Rand's atheistic philosophy of anti-altruism "risked, in fact, giving to capitalism that bad name that its enemies have done so well in giving it."

Finally, Buckley could find no room in the movement for the racists and for the extreme libertarians who seemed most interested at the time in selling off the public highways and legalizing drugs. This group of libertarians agreed with the so-called new left that the United States rather than the communist world was mainly responsible for the Cold War.

Buckley ejected these groups from the movement, but not simply because he found their beliefs objectionable. Rather, he was carefully and deliberately attempting to assemble a conservative coalition that could present an appealing and consistent philosophical message to those fed up with the direction in which the United States seemed to be heading in the 1950s.

After the cleansing of these fringe elements, what remained was the traditional three-legged stool of conservatism: traditional conservatives, libertarians, and social conservatives united by a common hatred of communism and a fear that our nation might be sliding into socialism.

Buckley didn't oppose diversity nor would he countenance future "purges" just to force ideological homogeneity. He believed conservatives needed to distance themselves from elements he saw were making it impossible to forge a politically effective movement from the philosophical and ideological jumble of the time. His stance in the context of the times was practical in that he believed strongly (and correctly) that if conservatives were ever to win the political power to achieve their policy ends, they would have to appeal to a broader sector of the electorate than they would be able to reach absent some retooling.

GOLDWATER TO REAGAN

Buckley and his followers succeeded beyond his wildest dreams. By 1964, the new conservatives would nominate Barry Goldwater as the Republican candidate for president, send the Eastern establishment packing, and effectively seize control of one of the nation's major political parties.

After Goldwater was defeated in the general election, Buckley urged conservatives to begin putting together the infrastructure needed to train men and women not just to run for office but to win and govern. Buckley was instrumental in the formation of the American Conservative Union (ACU) in late 1964. The ACU is now best known for its main conference, the Conservative Political Action Conference (CPAC), started before PAC meant political action committee, a fund-raising vehicle created by campaign finance reforms in the seventies. He was deeply involved in the launching of the Philadelphia Society, which was also founded in 1964 "to sponsor the interchange of ideas through discussion and writing, in the interest of deepening the intellectual foundation of a free and ordered society, and of broadening the understanding of its basic principles and traditions."

In 1965, Buckley decided to run for mayor of New York. He ran to show conservatives that it was possible to mount an offensive against the liberal establishment, but he didn't expect to win. Asked at the time what he would do if by some miracle he did win, Buckley replied famously, "Demand a recount."

During those turbulent 1960s, conservatives around the country paid attention to Buckley's campaign. If Bill Buckley could run for mayor in the very belly of the liberal beast, many believed, they could get into politics themselves. They came out of the closet, stood up for their ideas, and ran for office. They even began to win.

Buckley quickly became the face of the emerging conservatism. He seemed to be everywhere. He was on television, in the bookstores, and in newspapers, and his magazine was becoming more and more influential. He was not just bright but engaging and entertaining. He was an implacable but happy warrior who fought on the battlefield of ideas rather than personalities. His friends included liberals as well as conservatives; he and John Kenneth Galbraith seemed to meet up every year in Switzerland to ski, and one was as likely to find him in the company of actor David Niven as conservative politician Barry Goldwater.

When Goldwater ran and captured the Republican presidential nomination in 1964, Buckley and his colleagues at *National Review* were torn. The "practical" Buckley wondered if Goldwater was the candidate most capable of vanquishing the Democrats, but the "ideological" Buckley saw the need for a conservative standard-bearer and eventually he and his magazine opted to strongly support the Arizona senator.

The Goldwater campaign gave Buckley what he'd been seeking. Just as he had called a philosophical movement into being and worked mightily to give it a political voice, Goldwater and his followers seized control of one of the nation's major parties in answer to Buckley's call.

Four years earlier, the senator from Arizona had been nominated for the vice presidency and in withdrawing his name from consideration had famously challenged conservatives to "grow up." In nominating him, they did just that.

That campaign also produced Ronald Reagan, who, after delivering a nationwide address considered one of the high points of the 1964 campaign, went on to be elected governor of California in 1966. As governor, he was preparing for the day when a movement conservative in the Buckley mold would actually win the presidency. He made a last-minute attempt at securing the GOP nomination in 1968, but though the conservatives who nominated Goldwater four years before were in the ascendancy, that year's nomination went to Richard Nixon as the candidate most thought had the best chance of winning.

I came to Washington two years later to work for President Nixon's first vice president, Spiro Agnew. I had just graduated from law school, packed everything I owned into a U-Haul trailer, hooked it up to the bumper of my ten-year-old station wagon, and headed east at twenty-four years old.

In D.C. I was given a very nice office in what was then called the Executive Office Building next to the White House. I rearranged the furniture, hung my pictures, shelved my books, and began working.

A few days later, the vice president wandered into my office and observed that I had done a bang-up job of decorating. He then asked if I knew who had my office when Hubert Humphrey was vice president just a couple of years before. I said I had no idea, and he remarked, "No one else does, either."

I've often thought that everyone who arrives in Washington would benefit from a similar bit of advice because, sadly, too many who come here to change the world conclude that the key is being here rather than the mission that brought them to Washington in the first place. The perks and apparent power that come with a job in the executive or legislative branch of the federal government are heady stuff for a young conservative, and the allure is hard to resist.

The problem is that those who allow their ambition to trump principle eventually become a part of the very problems they came to Washington to solve. Before I took the job with Vice President Agnew, I had been warned of this danger by one of the men I admired most. Dr. Walter Judd had been a Minnesota congressman and a champion of the early conservative movement. He was a mentor who advised me on politics and counseled me on personal decisions. In his view, people should not come to Washington "unless they were independently wealthy or had a profession or business to which they could return." Otherwise, there was a good chance of being compromised, seduced, and forced to abandon principle to get ahead. I was neither wealthy nor established, so the one major decision I was to make I made without consulting Dr. Judd. I knew he would urge me to wait, make a life for myself, and jump in when I could walk away if I had to. He was upset by my decision, but although I didn't consult him, I always kept his warning in mind.

The early movement was small, and those who joined were socialized and educated by the Buckley family and other leading conservatives. By the time we entered the fray, we knew why we were conservatives and what that meant. It made a real difference. Buckley and those of us who made up that early band witnessed what happened when conservatives actually took up the reins of power. But no one has come up with a real solution to the socialization problem, other than counseling people to pay attention to what my wife calls "your personal gyroscope" that knows where your truth lies.

Frank Meyer warned back in the 1960s that different constituencies within the movement might want very different things if they ever managed to come to power. Meyer even acknowledged that some conservatives might be willing to use the power of the state in ways others would find less than appealing. He urged, however, that rather than dealing with hypothetical situations, conservatives dedicate themselves to winning elections. Then they could "fight out their differences in the basement of the White House."

When conservatives did end up in the White House, first in small numbers under Nixon and Ford, then in a theoretical majority in the Reagan days, those differences began to emerge—in part because many of the generation that inherited a movement in triumph had not been sufficiently socialized into the ethos of the movement Buckley had formed.

In 1980, Ronald Reagan delivered the triumph that had begun as a gleam in the eye of young Bill Buckley. The Reagan years changed the way in which people looked at government programs. After Roosevelt, there was an assumption that if there was a problem, the solution was to spend taxpayer money on it. Anyone who questioned that assumption obviously didn't want to solve the problem. Reagan changed all that. After Reagan, there was a presumption—a still-dominant presumption—that if you have a problem and you want to spend money on it, you first need evidence that government is the solution, and that it won't actually make the problem worse.

THE DISINTEGRATION OF THE FUSIONIST IDEAL

By the end of the Reagan administration, Buckley was convinced that the balance among the movement's various constituencies was off-kilter. It seemed to him that some, including people in powerful positions, just did not grasp the nature and spirit of the movement. Many conservatives who had come to Washington to do good had stayed to do well; sectarianism and hubris were leading the movement down the road to foreseeable disaster.

This tendency was exemplified shortly after George H. W. Bush was elected president in 1988. Asked by a reporter if he considered himself a conservative, candidate Bush had said, "I am a conservative, but I'm not a nut about it." His brother Prescott Bush called me around that time and said that he was thinking of running against Senator Lowell Weicker in the Connecticut primary. Weicker was still a Republican, but acted as an Independent. Prescott told me, "I need your help because we conservatives have to stick together." I replied, "Prescott, you have never been a conservative, and you will never be one. If you want my help because I don't like Lowell Weicker, that's one thing, but don't try that one." He responded, "No, you don't understand. Now that Reagan's been elected, we're all conservatives." To Prescott and many others, "conservatism" was more of a party moniker than an idea-based philosophy.

In 1991, when President George H. W. Bush presented Bill Buckley with the Medal of Freedom at a White House ceremony honoring his life and work, it might have seemed that the movement he founded had triumphed. By that time, however, Buckley sensed that the movement was fraying around the edges.

Buckley had never been doctrinaire in his conservatism and opposed those who wanted to fit the movement with an ideological straitjacket. Over the years, he had differed with fellow conservatives on all manner of important issues. For example, he favored the legalization of marijuana for both libertarian and empirical reasons. The war on drugs, he was persuaded, would never be won and was far too costly to continue. He also favored a National Service mandate. He looked back at how earlier generations had been socialized through military service and believed young people had benefited greatly from the experience of service to their country.

Buckley had never been a follower, and he spoke up when he sensed that a new generation of conservatives was leading the movement in directions he considered politically and phil-osophically unsound. Like all movements that become popu-lar, the fusionist achievement was threatening to come apart at the seams.

One can tell that an idea-driven movement is on the verge of great political success when the rats begin to board the ship. The new recruits that streamed into the conservative move-ment added to our numbers and were certainly well inten-tioned. There were too many, however, to be individually socialized into the core mission and spirit of the movement. Before long, they were becoming conservatives not because of Hayek or Buckley or Kirk, but because of Reagan, Bush, and Gingrich.

The tendency to attract new members who may not share or understand a movement's core principles happens in many different settings. Think of the communists. At the end of the Soviet era, philosophical communists were hard to find. In-stead, the Communist Party was like the Rotary Club—albeit a dangerous Rotary Club. People joined the party because that was how you got a patronage job. Membership was the key to professional success. Whereas Marx and Lenin had wanted to change the world, the communists of the late 1980s wanted job security, good salaries, and pensions. They were a bunch of thugs, but they weren't Marxists or Leninists anymore.

A classic example of this trend occurred in Romania. As his regime began to collapse in 1989, the dictator Nicolae Ceaușescu ordered troops to fire on his citizens, and they did. In order to perpetrate this type of inhumanity, the troops had to believe that they were doing it for a purpose. They had to believe they weren't just killing people; they were called to a higher good, much like today's suicide bombers. The general who ordered the shooting later committed suicide, showing that communism had by that time lost the quasi-religious appeal that motivated true believers. The general couldn't live with himself because he didn't believe in the principles anymore. It was a sign that communism in Europe was on the verge of total collapse.

When I was a young conservative, you did not join the movement because it was the road to success. It was just as likely to be the road to political and professional oblivion. If you joined the movement, you did so because you believed in its core principles. By the 1980s, many people were joining the movement in hopes of getting a job in Washington. And for conservatives of this stripe, it seemed reasonable to compromise on principles a little here and there to remain in a position of influence and to achieve larger goals down the road.

Shortly after being elected Speaker of the House in 1995, Newt Gingrich brought his Republican colleagues together for a meeting. He told them that the single most important thing

ly told an interviewer, "but he is not *a* conservative." In other

to remember was that it was vital that they be reelected. He told them the House Appropriations Committee was willing to give them whatever they might need to enhance their re-election chances, including supporting earmarks to bring pork spending to their districts. By that time, doing well had replaced doing good as a primary objective for many who had been elected as outspoken conservatives.

While many new conservatives managed to grasp the core values of the movement, fewer and fewer studied or read the philosophical texts. The result was a superficial brand of conservatism that was more political and situational than philosophical. This has led in recent years to a simplified conservatism whose adherents sound as if they're reading from a sheet of "talking points" rather than reflecting the values that animated Buckley, Hayek, and the Founders.

The distinction is important, as Buckley's description of President George W. Bush attests: "He is conservative," Buckley told an interviewer, "but he is not *a* conservative." In other words, he didn't fully embrace the movement's core principles. George W. Bush had neither devoured *National Review* nor understood the philosophical underpinnings of the movement that made it possible for him to become president.

The challenge for conservatism today, in which many conservatives are engaged, is to reeducate and resocialize the core of the movement, and remind new recruits of just what it means to be *a* conservative rather than simply "conservative."

A few years ago, a CPAC banquet honored former conservative senator James Buckley—Bill's brother—and former liberal senator Eugene McCarthy for their 1974 challenge to that era's campaign finance reforms. At the banquet, McCarthy remarked, "You conservatives have had a good run, but you are in trouble because I keep hearing talk of hyphenated conservatives. That's what happened to liberals in the 1960s, and when it happens you are headed for a crack-up." In recent years there have emerged paleoconservatives, national defense conservatives, social and religious conservatives, constitutional conservatives, Tea Party conservatives, and neoconservatives—all vying for the right to redefine and lead the movement Buckley had called into being. It reminds one of the time Al Gore in Milwaukee mistranslated *E pluribus unum* as "out of one, many."

As Bill looks down on conservatives today, he is no doubt hoping that we will be wiser than McCarthy's liberals and will work as hard to preserve the conservative movement as he did to build it.

CHAPTER 8

◆ ◆ ◆

At the same time Bill Buckley was founding *National Review*, Henry Regnery was publishing Kirk's *The Conservative Mind*, and Ronald Reagan was still doing television commercials for General Electric, a postwar conservative grassroots movement was developing in parallel with the intellectual movement. Phyllis Schlafly, our next author, tells the compelling story of this grassroots movement.

As Mrs. Schlafly explains, the tension between the grassroots citizens at the base of the party and the Republican Party leadership stemmed from the widespread interest by the base in Christianity and the family—the social issues. The heart and soul of grassroots conservatism came from the social conservatives who felt the heavy foot of secularism treading on tradition.

In the 1970s to early 1980s, the Equal Rights Amendment (ERA) was a flash point for conflict between establishment Republicans and the grass roots. The establishment believed that unless it embraced the ERA, women would forever abandon the ranks of the GOP for the Democratic Party. The grass roots believed that if they told the truth about the ERA, the American people would stand against it. They did, and ERA was defeated.

Through her own compelling personal story, Phyllis Schlafly explains the growth of grassroots conservatism, how she led the pro-family movement to defeat the ERA, and how social conservatives enabled the Reagan Revolution.

Phyllis Schlafly has been a national leader of the conservative movement since the publication of her best-selling 1964 book, *A Choice Not an Echo*. She has been a leader of the pro-family movement since 1972, when she started her national volunteer organization called Eagle Forum. In a ten-year battle, Mrs. Schlafly led the successful movement to prevent the Equal Rights Amendment from being adopted. An articulate and successful opponent of the radical feminist movement, she appears in debate on college campuses more frequently than any other conservative. Mrs. Schlafly is a Phi Beta Kappa graduate of Washington University, received her J.D. from Washington University Law School, and received her master's degree in political science from Harvard University. She is the author and editor of twenty books. She has played an active role in every Republican National Convention since 1952. Mrs. Schlafly was named one of the one hundred most important women of the twentieth century by the *Ladies' Home Journal*.

CULTURAL CONSERVATISM AND THE RELIGIOUS RIGHT

Phyllis Schlafly

◆ ◆ ◆

In 1775, the people who were meeting and talking about their gripes against the British crown were all trying to make the king shape up and be a good fellow and recognize their rights. All of their entreaties were addressed to the king; the idea of not having a king really hadn't occurred to them. When they had their convention in July of 1775, they submitted the Olive Branch Petition. They were continuing to make entreaties to the king to give them their Englishman's rights.

In January of 1776, a little book was published; you could call it a pamphlet. It was called *Common Sense* by Thomas Paine. It was only forty-six pages. It wasn't written in the scholarly method of the other writers who wrote at that time. It was written for the guys who went to the coffee shop, the guys who went to the pub. It was in plain language for plain people, and it basically said, "We've got to get rid of the king." It was published January 10. By July 4, we had the Declaration of Independence. *Common Sense* is one of the most amazing literary accomplishments in history, and considering the population we had at that time, it probably is the best-selling book in history.

The pamphlet gripped people. It created the movement for independence. It was a different technology. It was something like moving from the horse and buggy to the automobile, or from the typewriter to the Internet. That's what the pamphleteer did. He made the pamphlet the new technology, the language of ordinary people. He didn't have his piece decorated with Latin phrases; it was just direct political language that anybody could understand.

Now let's fast-forward to the 1930s, the time of the Great Depression. High unemployment, even worse than today. But even then, Americans were not looking to government to solve their problems. Franklin Roosevelt, who was expected to be elected president in 1932, supposedly to end the Depression, ran on the Democratic platform. Let me tell you what that 1932 Democratic platform said: "We advocate an immediate and drastic reduction of government expenditures, by abolishing useless commissions and offices, consolidating departments and bureaus, and eliminating extravagance to accomplish a saving of not less than 25 percent in the cost of the federal government. We favor a federal budget annually balanced."

Well, that sounds like the Tea Party, doesn't it? It certainly doesn't sound like the New Deal. FDR knew that was what the American people wanted to hear. However, once he was elected, he embarked on a big spending program, expanded the bureaucracy, and used the Commerce Clause to do all kinds of things that we still think are unconstitutional—the same arguments that were used in the ObamaCare case that was argued before the Supreme Court.

By the time FDR ran for his third term, prominent Democrats had left him. The American people really hated FDR, very much like the significant number of people who really hate Obama today. Nevertheless, they elected him four times. That does not mean that people approved of his spending programs and what he was doing; he certainly did not solve the unemployment problem. But he spent the money in states where it would get him votes to be reelected and continued to use spending to be reelected.

Then something happened, which brought another little book to the fore. It was written by an Austrian named Friedrich Hayek, who had become a British citizen. It's a short book in which he directly attacked collectivism, the planned economy, and the whole idea that central planning was the way to run an economy. He took the position that in order to preserve liberty, we had to make a choice: Do we want the government to plan everything? Or do we want the rule of law?

The initial printing was only two thousand books. And then something happened to bring it to the grass roots: the *Reader's Digest* reprinted it. It's hard to imagine or believe today, but the *Reader's Digest* then had five million subscribers, and everybody read the *Reader's Digest* in those years. So this reached the plain people, the grass roots. They believed it, and it had a tremendous impact on our country in explaining what was wrong with the New Deal, and how we did not want central planning of our economy.

I happened to be at the Harvard Graduate School that year—

don't let anybody tell you that opportunities for education for women started only when the feminists came along, because I was getting my degree at the Harvard Graduate School in 1945, before all these feminists were born. Hayek came there to speak on his cross-country tour. I remember how the professors gathered us to explain to us how we were not supposed to believe what Hayek was saying. They were preparing us for his coming, and how to refute him and to answer him. They were all New Dealers, my professors at Harvard. I remember one whose favorite saying was, "We shouldn't talk about balancing the budget. We should talk about budgeting the balance." We had another professor who devoted one whole lecture in his constitutional law class to telling us that Henry Wallace was the greatest political thinker of the twentieth century. Now, if you study your history, you know he was the closest thing we ever had to a communist anywhere near the White House. He was too far left even for Franklin D. Roosevelt, who dumped Wallace as vice president when he ran for his fourth term in 1944 and replaced him with Harry Truman.

In any event, the conventional wisdom in America then was that the planned economy was the wave of the future. There was a lot of opposition to Roosevelt that was building. There were a number of organizations organized by the grass roots to oppose him. There are only two that I know have survived to this day. One is the Association of American Physicians and Surgeons, founded in the mid-1940s, which represents conservative doctors. They filed three briefs against ObamaCare. The other is America's Future, which still publishes a newsletter. Most of the others died out.

So where was the political opposition to Roosevelt? The Republican Party in those years was pretty well run by what we call the kingmakers, headquartered in New York, and particularly in the Chase Manhattan Bank. They thought they were divinely appointed to select the Republican nominee, who would not very much challenge what Roosevelt was doing. In 1940, they forced on the Republicans a man named Wendell Willkie, who wasn't even a Republican; he was a Democrat. He was sort of a ninety-day wonder. The kingmakers lined up all the media, did a lot of crooked things, and put Willkie over as the nominee. He ran for president on the Republican ticket and lost to Roosevelt.

Then in 1944, the kingmakers tried New York governor Tom Dewey, the one whom Teddy Roosevelt's daughter described as "looking like the little man on the wedding cake." Dewey didn't do very well in '44. And then came 1948, and they had the gall to nominate Tom Dewey again, and we, the grass roots, were very much opposed to that nomination.

There were all kinds of wonderful issues that Dewey could have talked about: the Truman scandals, the Korean War, the communist infiltration of our government, the Alger Hiss case. But Tom Dewey waged a "me-too" campaign, and he lost again.

Then came 1946, the off-year election. By this time, the grass roots were really getting angry, and they went out and carried on a campaign under the slogan "Had enough." They elected the biggest Republican majority in Congress in the twentieth century.

As we approached the Republican National Convention of

1952, everybody expected a Republican year. The contestants were Senator Bob Taft, who had the support of the grass roots and was, I think, the first authentic conservative. However, I can tell you: in those days, people never called themselves "conservatives." It was not a word that we used. Taft was just a run-of-the-mill, garden-variety Republican. The kingmakers put up Dwight Eisenhower, a military hero, whom they had installed as a university president to keep him safe until the time of the convention so he wouldn't have to take any stands on controversial issues. The grass roots wanted Bob Taft, because he spoke up for typical American values, foreign and domestic. His book, *A Foreign Policy for Americans*, was another short book that we liked and we distributed. And he was the guy we hoped to nominate in 1952.

In 1952 there was another crooked convention. The kingmakers succeeded in nominating Eisenhower, after they went to the governor of California, who was then Earl Warren, and promised him the next vacancy on the Supreme Court if he would deliver the big California delegation for the vote on the Credentials Committee and the vote on the Rules Committee, both of which were crucial to whether Taft or Eisenhower would be nominated by the convention. And Warren delivered the California votes. Eisenhower was not part of the deal, but he was persuaded to fulfill that part of the commitment that his handlers had made, and it was a terrible, terrible mistake, because the Eisenhower court became the infamous Warren Court. Later on, Eisenhower was asked one day, "Did you make any mistakes while you were president?" He said, "Yes, two, and they're both sitting on the Supreme Court."

Eisenhower was nominated and we all supported him and he won. But after that, we began to realize the enormity of the communist threat, both the Soviet missile threat and the infiltration of our government by communist spies and people who were sending our secret information to the Soviet Union. There was also infiltration in the universities and in Hollywood. We had investigations of communism by the various congressional committees and reports that were widely read by the American people. In those days, everybody could read. They read the congressional reports, and the grass roots understood what communism was and why we wanted to get rid of the infiltration in our government. The grass roots took up the study of communism from the congressional reports.

In 1956, a man named Dr. Fred Schwarz suddenly rose to prominence. He had an enormous impact in building the start of the conservative movement. He brought thousands of people into what we referred to as the anti-communist movement, so that we had a grass roots that was well informed. I assisted him in putting on his first educational event in 1956 at the Tower Grove Baptist Church in St. Louis, where he realized what he could do by training people with a five-day class. So he then had these classes all over the country, and to this day, I meet people who came into the conservative movement attending one of the Schwarz schools. It was such a big thing that when he got to California, he filled the Los Angeles sports arena with 16,000 people for one of his schools.

He ultimately wrote a book called *You Can Trust the Communists (to Be Communists)*. Unlike some of our enemies today, the communists told us exactly what they were going to do.

"We are going to bury you!" they said, and they told us exactly how they were going to do it. Schwarz called his organization the Christian Anti-Communism Crusade, so it had a certain evangelical aspect to it. At the end of this first school, I said, "Well, we've got to bring the Catholics in, too, and have them join." And he said, "No, you can't put the Catholics and the Protestants in the same room. It just isn't going to work—the Catholics will have to have their own organization." So we got the Catholics to start their own organization called the Cardinal Mindszenty Foundation. We promoted study groups all over the country, and at one time, we had five thousand of these study groups.

People were learning: learning about government, learning about our enemies, learning about communism. This had a major impact. I looked up some of the resolutions passed by the Illinois Federation of Republican Women from the 1950s and '60s; these were just ordinary women, Republican volunteers who liked to be supportive and support their candidates in politics. And they had resolutions against the centralization of power in Washington, against UN treaties and UNESCO, against the drive for disarmament. They had resolutions that demanded victory over communism, full support of the House Committee on Un-American Activities. They had a resolution to stop all federal aid to education, to wipe it out. They had resolutions that condemned the Supreme Court decisions that were siding with the communists. They had resolutions that condemned the accumulated power in the executive branch and the president, the sprawling bureaucracy, the weakening of constitutional restraints that permitted advocates of socialism and communism to make inroads in national security, and resolutions against the further centralization of power in the federal government. Again, nobody used the word *conservative*; they were just garden-variety Republicans. That's just the way people thought, especially in the Midwest. Nobody called them extremists. Our files have a whole file of letters from congressmen saying, "Thank you for sending us this resolution; we agree one hundred percent with it." That was the thinking of people in those days.

It was a different time. Even the American Bar Association was on our side in the fight against Supreme Court decisions siding with the communists. The American Bar Association had a committee that put out a report on communist tactics, strategy, and objectives, which set forth ten of the worst pro-communist decisions of the Supreme Court. This was put in the congressional record first by Senator Bridges and then later, by Senator Dirksen, and I'll bet millions of copies went out. It became a major vehicle to educate the grass roots about how the court was favoring communism.

In those years, one of the most popular speakers was Dean Clarence Manion of the Notre Dame Law School. He wrote a book, less than a hundred pages, called *The Key to Peace* and talked about the religious foundation of our country, a lot of the conservative ideas that we hear today. Again, we're not using the term *conservative*, but conservative was just the way people believed and thought in those days.

Then we looked around for a president. Who were we going to run for president? Somebody suggested a senator from Arizona. Well, nobody from Arizona had ever been elected president before. Arizona? At that time, we didn't have any baseball team that was farther west or south than St. Louis. Nobody went to Arizona in those days. You had to come from Ohio, Pennsylvania, or New York to be president. But we all picked Barry Goldwater as the guy we wanted, so he had to have a book, too. His book *The Conscience of a Conservative* soon came out in paperback too. Actually, the book was written by Brent Bozell, who's the father of the guy who runs the Media Research Center. But Dean Clarence Manion gave it the title. And that was the first time people began to call themselves "conservative," because after *The Conscience of a Conservative* came out, it was proof that conservatives were not heartless people. They really had a conscience. And we began, proudly, to call ourselves "conservatives."

We made a try for Goldwater in Chicago in 1960, but we didn't have enough votes. That's when Goldwater came out on the stage and said, "Conservatives, this isn't our year. Go home and I'll see you in four years." So that's what we did, and we distributed his book and did some more studying. One of the major factors in building the ranks of the conservatives was a paperback called *None Dare Call It Treason* by John Stormer. It was a little longer than some of these other paperbacks, but it really set forth what had happened to our country and the dangers of communism, central planning, an overgrown bureaucracy, and high taxation. He published it himself and he sold seven million copies, and it was a major educational tool of the grass roots, who were now beginning to come alive.

We approached the 1964 convention of the Republican Party, which was in San Francisco. I had been to all of them beginning in 1952. Most of the people who go to Republican conventions as delegates are first-timers. The majority of them have never been before, and they don't know what to expect and don't know how it really operates. I figured they ought to know what went before, so I wrote my little book called *A Choice Not an Echo*, and I plunged in with a printing of 25,000. I thought that would be it. I ended up selling three million out of my garage, and they went to all the people who were delegates who were interested in the next nomination. Every week, I still meet some public official who says, "I came into the conservative movement reading *A Choice Not an Echo* in 1964." Most political literature just simply revs up your juices for your prejudices, but my book persuaded people.

Goldwater's opponent was Nelson Rockefeller, a former New York governor. My book persuaded Rockefeller people to switch and support Goldwater, and persuaded Lyndon Johnson people to switch and support Goldwater. So we had the 1964 convention and we nominated Goldwater; the conservatives took over the Republican Party. And then, as you know, Goldwater went down to a smashing defeat.

But twenty-seven million people voted for Goldwater, and they never regretted it, and that was really the start of the coming together of the conservative movement. Because of his defeat, however, we thought, "Well, I guess we can't really elect a real conservative president," and that's why we went for Richard Nixon on the next round. We thought he was the best we could do, which turned out to be a mistake.

In any event, the conservative movement was there, and the anti–communist movement was there, but that wasn't enough.

THE EQUAL RIGHTS AMENDMENT

Then something else happened. Congress voted for a new constitutional amendment, supported by the feminists, called the Equal Rights Amendment. Everybody was for it. There were only a couple of dozen people in the House who voted against it. There were only eight in the Senate who voted against it. President Nixon, President Ford, and President Carter were all enthusiastic supporters of it. All the governors. The media were 99 percent in favor of it. Everybody was for it; everybody who was anybody in politics, from left to right, from Ted Kennedy to George Wallace, endorsed it.

I was asked to speak about it and made a speech about it, which then turned up in my Phyllis Schlafly Report, which I'd started a few years before. I wrote one called "What's Wrong with 'Equal Rights' for Women?" and sent it out to my friends. I sold the report by subscription for five dollars a year, mostly to women I had worked with in the Republican Party. And one day the next month, an Oklahoma friend called up and said, "Phyllis, we took your report to the legislature, and they voted down the Equal Rights Amendment."

So I invited one hundred women from thirty states to meet me in St. Louis. I put them on a bus and took them down to the riverfront, and we boarded one of the showboats and I climbed up on the stage, where they do all these melodramas, and I told them, "We're going to go out and beat the Equal Rights Amendment." At that point, nobody thought it was possible. They thought we were crazy, because in the first year, the ERA-ers got thirty states; they only needed thirty-eight, three-fourths of the country.

We had big fights in state after state. Illinois was the front line. Illinois voted on it every year for ten years, and we kept beating them and they kept coming back. Five states that had previously voted for it rescinded. We kept beating ERA.

We won because the ERA was bad law. You've read the Constitution: you know men are not in the Constitution. It's a completely sex-neutral document. It only talks about "citizens, persons, electors, presidents, and we the people." ERA did not offer any benefit to women. I testified in forty-one state legislative hearings, and in only one state did one of its people come in and say, "Our state has a law that discriminates that ERA will remedy." What was the law? It said that wives could not make homemade wine without their husbands' consent. For this we needed a constitutional amendment? You've got to be kidding.

When the feminists went on TV, however, they made women think ERA was going to give them a raise. But ERA would have nothing to do with employment, because the employment laws were already sex-neutral. What ERA would do would be to make every law sex-neutral, and the classic discriminatory law was the draft law. We were then in the Vietnam War; we had a draft. My daughters—I had daughters and sons that age—they thought it was the craziest thing anybody said. You're going to give women a constitutional amendment, and the first thing they'll do is sign up for the draft like their brothers? It was unsalable.

But the battle continued.

When ERA came out of Congress, the advocates were given a time limit of seven years. They realized they might not win before the deadline. Bella Abzug was then in Congress (you remember, she's the woman with the funny hats) and she got Congress to give her $5 million to have a special convention in Houston, which was supposed to be used to ratify the Equal Rights Amendment. They had their meeting, and it was an enormous media event. Three thousand media people went to Houston to cover this. The feminists passed their resolution saying they wanted the Equal Rights Amendment, but that didn't satisfy them. They began to tell the rest of their agenda. They said they wanted abortion funded by the taxpayers. They said they wanted a whole list of gay rights. They wanted universal, government-supported day care. For all these resolutions, they were letting off balloons and they were prancing around. We're talking about 1977; this was not agreeable to the American people, but all this was on television.

The feminists believe that women are victims of the patriarchy, and it's up to new laws and the Constitution to remedy the second-class citizenship of women. Absolutely false. American women are the most fortunate class of people who ever lived on the face of the earth. We can do anything we want to do. But at any rate, that's the line they're putting out, and their prime example of the "oppression" of women by the patriarchy is that society expects mothers to look after their babies, and that burden has got to be lifted from them by the taxpayers.

Every important and well-known feminist was in Houston. Betty Friedan was making an impassioned plea to invite the lesbians to come and join them. They passed all the radical resolutions.

While the ERA forces had their big shindig, financed by the taxpayers, we took another hall across town, in Houston, and invited people to come at their own expense and to attend our pro-family rally. We packed 20,000 people into a hall that was supposed to hold only 18,000, and they all came at their own expense. I think that's the day "pro-family movement" went into the political vocabulary, because that's what we called ourselves.

I remember, after that was over, somebody asked the Missouri governor, "Governor, are you for the Equal Rights Amendment?" "Well," he said, "do you mean the old ERA or the new ERA? I was for equal pay for equal work, but after they went down to Houston and got tangled up with all those abortionists and lesbians, I can tell you, ERA will never pass in Missouri." Of course, he was absolutely right. After that convention, ERA never won another vote. ERA's probably been voted on twenty-five times in various committees or legislatures or even referenda, but it's never won anywhere else. Their own $5 million conference, which they were so proud of, simply destroyed them.

But the fight went on, because then ERA advocates ran to Jimmy Carter and got him to give them a three-year extension. The cartoonists had a field day with this; this was like giving a baseball game three more innings when the game was not tied up. But they did not get any more states. A court finally held that the extension was illegal. We had a victory party in 1979, which was the end of the original seven years, and we proclaimed victory. Then we had another victory party in 1982, the end of the crooked extension.

The press was so angry with me; they could hardly stand it. But it was important for all of the conservatives left over from the Goldwater campaign to realize that it is possible for conservatives to win.

THE BIRTH OF THE PRO-FAMILY MOVEMENT

When I started out, I was holding my finger in the dike with a handful of my Republican women friends. We'd go to the state legislature and we would be successful. Then I realized, about 1976, that we were going to need more help. That's when I went to the churches, and asked, "Please come and join us." I prayed that we could bring a thousand people to Springfield, Illinois, for a demonstration. That was the day, on April 26, 1976, that a thousand people did come to Springfield, Illinois. Our legislature had never seen anything like this before. Our people came and showed legislators that we were opposed to ERA. So that is the day we invented the pro-family movement.

In building my organization—first of all "Stop ERA" and then morphing into Eagle Forum—I was very ecumenical. I didn't let them talk about religion. I combined the Catholics, the Protestants, all the denominations, the evangelicals, the Jews, the Mormons. I had them all. The message was, "I don't care what your church is. We're all going to work together to beat the Equal Rights Amendment." And I made them all get along. This was the first time a lot of Catholics and Baptists were in the same room together, and they just had to get along. That was my policy.

But I didn't have help from the establishment. In ten years, *National Review* never had a single article about the Equal Rights Amendment. They were no help at all. I think *Human Events* had one article. There were only two newspapers that had one friendly editorial—one was in St. Louis and one was in Tampa, Florida. What I did was not an outgrowth of the conservative movement or of the Republican Party. The Republican presidents had all signed on to ERA. As for the rest of the people, they didn't believe I could win. Nobody believed I could win. You know, "This is just Phyllis's plaything. She can't possibly win."

The cultural conservative movement I founded is the base of the GOP today.

We really swelled our ranks when the Baptists joined us; that's when Jerry Falwell started his Moral Majority. We actually had ten thousand people at another demonstration at the Springfield capitol. We were realizing that people of faith and people who had similar values could work together for a goal they shared.

Initially, *Roe v. Wade* and abortion did not actually galvanize that movement. When *Roe v. Wade* was handed down by the court in 1973, the Catholic bishops jumped in to fight it. Well, the Protestants were not going to join up with something the Catholic bishops were running, so they hung back. But eventually, we all got on the same page. It was about 1976 that we realized that one of the reasons the feminists wanted

ERA was they felt it was the key to locking abortion funding into the Constitution. The Supreme Court had handed down a decision, *Harris v. McRae*, which said you did not have a constitutional right to have your abortion paid for. The feminists, however, wanted it paid for, and they thought they could get funding through ERA because they could charge that it was sex discriminatory to deny this money.

That was the start of what we now call the pro-family movement that has played such a big part. After we proclaimed victory over ERA in 1979, the next big thing coming up was the election of Ronald Reagan in 1980. A lot of us were not sure we could win. You know, we didn't have a vision of victory in the conservative movement in those days. There were not enough people left over from the Goldwater voters to elect a president. But Reagan successfully and skillfully combined the fiscal conservatives left over from the Goldwater campaign, the people who had been brought into the anti-communist movement who cared about national defense, and the people who'd been brought in to the pro-family movement through Stop ERA and the fight for life. And he won a great victory in 1980 and '84.

You need those three legs in order to win. You really can't win with only one of them. Reagan proved that that is the key to success.

When candidates now say, "We're going to put the social issues or the moral issues in the deep freeze or the back burner," they're making a terrible mistake, because they're kicking away large blocks of voters who are important to any Republican victory. The pro-family movement has played a tremendous role; there are so many people who came into the Republican Party through these social and moral issues. The people who care about the moral issues are extremely important to the conservative constituency, and they have to be kept part of it. Human motivation is very complex, and the decline in marriage rates is the chief reason for the enormous amount of welfare and enormous numbers of people who are being supported at taxpayer expense.

We don't want to build a nation of dependent people. We want a nation of people who can make their own way. I grew up during the Great Depression; we didn't look to government; government wasn't any help at all. And now we've got more than forty programs that funnel cash or benefits to people who are not married. They say it's for the children, but it's encouraging women to have children without getting married. It's a terrible mistake; they're going to be poor. They ought to tell them, "You're going to be poor all your life if you do that."

The welfare part of our budget is the fastest growing and the biggest segment of federal spending. It's far more money than we're spending on national defense. Obama knows that. That's why they're trying to increase the number of single moms; most of them vote for Obama because that's where they're getting their support. Look at the figures on how marriage has declined and the numbers of people who think it's okay to do without marriage. That's extremely unfortunate; a happy marriage is the best thing you can hope for a happy life. To tell young people that it really doesn't matter whether you get married or not is a terrible thing. Just look at the figures: we had a 41 percent illegitimacy rate in this country last year.

Of course, the feminists have promoted the idea that kids don't need fathers, and the family courts have almost adopted that, too. Fathers are necessary, and I do worry about the deterioration of morals in the whole culture. I don't think it's making people happier or making a better country.

Social issues and fiscal issues are intertwined. Social issues and foreign policy are intertwined. You cannot remove the beating heart and soul of conservatism and hope to save the philosophy or the movement.

CHAPTER 9

◆ ◆ ◆

There is no more unifying figure in the history of the modern conservative movement than President Ronald Reagan. Virtually every conservative attempts to claim the mantle of Reagan, from isolationists to interventionists, from debt hawks to tax cutters, from libertarians to religious traditionalists. Everyone finds something to love about the most successful president of the last half century.

Our next author, former attorney general Edwin Meese, explains the legacy of the greatest president of the twentieth century. He tells Reagan's story from close observation, having worked with him for many years and eventually serving in his presidential cabinet.

Meese tells of Reagan's extensive reading of the canons of conservatism—Hayek's *The Road to Serfdom*, Chambers's *Witness*, *Human Events*, and *National Review*. Through his reading and studying, Reagan gradually formed the core of a philosophy that would carry him to the presidency. He also believed that our founding philosophy provided a path toward prosperity, growth, and individual happiness.

Standing up to communism was central to Reagan's administration and its legacy. Reagan began calling the Soviet Union "an evil empire" and "the focus of evil in the modern world," which focused America on the importance of containing and defeating communism. Russian author and dissident Natan Sharansky, imprisoned by the Soviets for his political opposition, would later tell of how he and his fellow prisoners in the gulag rejoiced when they heard of Reagan's speech.

Reagan's discourse and decisive policy changes revived the American economy and spirit, and he gave hope to people around the world. Even years after his death, Reagan's legacy lives on in the continuing debate between the various wings of conservatism—wings that he united and forged into a victorious coalition.

Edwin Meese III, the prominent conservative leader, thinker, and elder statesman, serves as the Heritage Foundation's Ronald Reagan Distinguished Fellow Emeritus. He spent much of his adult life working for Ronald Reagan, first when Reagan was elected California governor in 1966 and then when he sought and won the presidency in 1980. From 1981 to 1985, General Meese served as counselor to the president and functioned as Reagan's chief policy adviser. He then served as the seventy-fifth attorney general of the United States from 1985 to 1988. From 2001 to 2013, General Meese was chairman of Heritage's Center for Legal and Judicial Studies, which now bears his name in recognition of his contributions to the rule of law and the nation's understanding of constitutional law.

THE REAGAN REVOLUTION

Edwin Meese III

◆ ◆ ◆

BEFORE REAGAN

It has become common to speak of the "Reagan Revolution," which rightly recognizes the remarkable transformation in American politics ushered in by President Ronald Reagan. But it is easy to miss what an unusual revolution it was. Interestingly, it was not a revolution achieved by force of arms, but a revolution accomplished by ideas. This revolution of ideas resulted from four different factors coming together: first, a movement; second, a message; third, a leader; and finally, a crisis. It was the confluence of those elements that enabled conservatives to reshape the American political landscape by bringing about what we now call the Reagan Revolution.

The remarkable success of the Reagan Revolution was the culmination of the modern conservative movement in America, itself a phenomenon of over half a century. Those of us who have thought a lot about the history of the conservative movement look at it unfolding in three phases. The first phase, which started immediately after the end of World War II, was its period as an intellectual movement. At that time many prominent scholars, here and abroad, became concerned about the drift toward socialism in the United States and around the world. Their thinking was that although the West had defeated the threat of the Axis powers, it confronted a new threat—an intellectual threat—to our material well-being and even our civilization itself. These scholars produced written works that were fundamental to the movement's beginning. At the popular level, though, there was really only one regular conservative publication, *Human Events*, which started in the late 1940s.

Following this beginning of intellectual foment, the next important episode in the conservative movement was the advent of a new leader, Bill Buckley. Unlike the older scholars, Buckley introduced a new vigor and a new enthusiasm. He had just graduated from Yale, after having first served in the army. At Yale, he was the leader of almost everything: chairman of the *Daily News*, the most prominent position on campus; active in the political union; and chairman of the debating association. He was truly "a big man on campus."

Buckley was also a genuine scholar. Right after he graduated from Yale, he wrote the book *God and Man at Yale*. If you were to pick it up now, you would find it remarkably applicable to academia today, particularly in respect to diagnosing its pathologies. He was prescient in detecting a drift in economics and political science toward socialism. Similarly, in religious matters, he anticipated a trajectory toward an antireligious disposition long before it was obvious to others who were at Yale at the time. Needless to say, his book did not receive enthusiastic agreement from the people running the institution at the time, particularly the Yale faculty and administration. It did, however, bring Buckley attention and prominence across the country—especially in the burgeoning conservative intellectual community.

Buckley accomplished many things that were important to the growing conservative movement. Perhaps most significantly, he started *National Review,* which has been the biweekly chronicle of the conservative movement from its inception to this very day. Among other things, it has engaged many top writers and provides an invaluable archive for those interested in conservatism.

Buckley was pivotal in the transition from conservatism's first phase as an intellectual movement to conservatism's next phase as a political movement. In 1960, he gathered a group of young conservatives, many of whom were involved with Young Americans for Freedom, at his home in Sharon, Connecticut. There they wrote the Sharon Statement, an exposition of basic principles and a manifesto of what modern conservatism should aspire to accomplish. This was a singular event; it went beyond simply thinking, talking, and writing about conservatism to outlining actual political action to guide a new breed of young activists.

Not too many years later, Barry Goldwater confirmed the conservative movement as a political movement when he ran for president in 1964. Though he didn't win, his successful recruiting of young people for his campaign made him one of the most influential figures in the history of conservatism. Goldwater's campaign coalesced and launched a cadre of movement conservatives, which endures today. These people worked on the Goldwater campaign and then continued to work together, staying involved in politics and in any number of small organizations. The principal national conservative political organization at the time was Young Americans for Freedom, but additional thousands of young people were all active in the conservative movement in their own way, in their own areas. It was this cadre that was absolutely critical to Ronald Reagan's success when he ran for the presidency.

THE NASCENT REAGAN REVOLUTION

The third phase of conservatism in this country saw its transformation from a political movement into a governing movement. It started with Ronald Reagan in 1967 when he became governor of California. Conservatism was not talked about much in professional political circles at that time. There had been a number of other movements on the left in the early and mid-twentieth century—the Progressive movement, the New Deal, the Great Society—but it was uncommon to pair philosophy with actual governance from a conservative standpoint.

That is precisely what Ronald Reagan did as governor, and it was precisely what was needed: to show that conservative ideas worked in practice. Reagan inherited a government in California that was virtually bankrupt. His predecessor had, through a trick, which changed the method of accounting, enabled him in his final years to spend fifteen months of revenue during twelve months of spending. So the first challenge Governor Reagan faced was literally a half-empty treasury, lacking the funds to finish the fiscal year without borrowing. California, like most states, does not permit deficit spending, so Reagan was forced to raise taxes in his first year in office.

Now, for someone who had campaigned as a conservative and showcased the importance of keeping government within its budget, to have to raise taxes was a terrible blow. True to his conservative ideals, Reagan insisted that he was going to "cut, squeeze, and trim the government," and if he was able to cut enough government spending to get it back within its revenues, he would refund any excess taxes. In other words, he would not sustain the tax increase as an instrument for government growth. And that is just what he did; in the course of his eight years in office, he administered three different tax rebates.

One reason Reagan was able to "cut, squeeze, and trim" was that he recruited top executives from leading businesses to serve for six months in the state government, finding economies and savings in every department and agency of the California government. Executives from the telephone company, for example, discovered ways to organize the state telephone system more efficiently and save considerable money. It cost the telephone company revenue, but its leaders were willing to do it for the common good. Other businesses, likewise, in their particular fields of specialty, were able to recommend similar savings.

One example illustrates the innovation and creativity that were so much a feature of Reagan's governing. At the end of 1967, his first year in office, the Department of Motor Vehicles mailed out automobile license renewal forms—some three months in advance. The news media ridiculed the department, implying incompetence because license renewals were not due until March of the next year. Actually, the Finance Department had discovered that there was going to be an increase in the postage in January, so mailing the renewals early saved hundreds of thousands of dollars. When you consider the population of California, and the number of cars, you end up with a lot of stamp money.

Those kinds of practical steps revealed how a philosophy of thrift and responsibility could be transformed into a governing movement. Reagan proved that conservative ideas make sense, and that they actually work in practice. That is why his political career was so important in launching this new phase of conservatism.

The second major factor in Reagan's success was his message, which was derived from the best conservative and classical liberal thinking throughout history.

He based his ideas on lessons from the Magna Carta, English common law, the writings of the Founders, the work of Tocqueville, and other documents from the early days of the American republic. Reagan synthesized all of this, and articulated a conservative message that shaped what we now call the Reagan Revolution.

In other words, ideas were very important. One remarkable thing about the Reagan Revolution is the way in which differing ideas—or differing ideas about conservatism—were brought together into a comprehensive philosophy and shaped a viable strategy. In *Reappraising the Right*, George Nash describes the conservative movement that came to power with

Ronald Reagan in terms of having five distinct parts, five different "idea clusters" that came together under his leadership.

One idea cluster was made up of classical liberals and libertarians, who were very much concerned about the threat posed by the growth of the state. They were prepared to revisit the very idea of the welfare state, seeing it as a threat to individual liberty, free enterprise, and prosperity. Another idea cluster was what George Nash called the traditionalist conservatives; they were worried about the fact that the ethical norms and the institutional foundations of American life were being weakened at the hands of secular and relativistic liberals. They harked back to the basic principles that Bill Buckley had described in *God and Man at Yale.* A third group was made up of the anti-communist Cold Warriors, who were convinced that our country was increasingly imperiled by Marxism, and particularly by the Soviet Union. The fourth group was the neoconservatives, those former "liberals [who had been] mugged by reality." They generally embraced idealistic goals but recognized that liberalism was not working and gravitated toward something else. One of the things that the Reagan Revolution did was to give them a place where they could find respectability, as neoconservatives. Finally, the fifth group was the religious right, principally interested in the moral life of the country, animated by the culture wars of the 1960s and '70s. The Reagan Revolution succeeded in bringing all five of these strains together, and incorporated them into a common conservative message.

The third factor, of course, was the leader himself. You cannot have a movement without a leader—at least not one that is likely to succeed. The late Rufus Fears, a very insightful professor at the University of Oklahoma, has written a great deal about leadership, tracing it all the way back to the Greeks and Romans. He writes that the difference between a statesman and a mere politician is the possession of four qualities: a bedrock of principle; a moral compass; a vision of where that leader wants to go; and the ability to communicate that vision and gain adherents.

As a leader, Ronald Reagan, had all of these qualities. His principles really were those of the Founders, and they informed the way he served in office, as both governor and president. His belief in and commitment to free enterprise and individual freedom, as well as an insistent dedication to limited government, were the principles that characterized his governing of both California and the United States. His moral compass was clear; he was a man of great integrity, a man of great courage— both physical and moral courage—and also a man of great perseverance. Once he had set his goals, he would not give up; he would continue to work for them against all odds. He had an unmistakable vision for where the country ought to be going, a vision that emphasized a return to the foundational principles and ideas of the Founders. He espoused the view that a president must govern in accordance with that key concept in the Declaration of Independence, that the only legitimate government is one that governs with the consent of the governed. His distinctly American vision of a free society offered a powerful alternative to the great threat of communism and, particularly, the Soviet Union.

It is important to remember that Ronald Reagan was a man

of ideas. He had read extensively; he had thought deeply about history and political philosophy. He was able to bring these intellectual and political strains together into a comprehensive conservative message because he had thought through them. The result of this theoretical synthesis was what George Nash described as a "grand coalition." It provided a message, a philosophical foundation, to go along with the movement.

Reagan's unique ability to communicate that vision and to engender confidence in the people of the United States was central to his leadership. He talked directly to the people, in language that was understandable and resonated with his listeners. He spoke as one of them, who shared the view of their problems and their aspirations.

He avoided political jargon or academic phraseology. Instead, he used down-to-earth examples and humorous anecdotes. He both informed and inspired, appealing to the heart as well as the mind. As a result, Reagan became known as the "great communicator"—one of the foremost political speakers in modern history. Nevertheless, in his characteristic self-deprecating way, he said it was not his ability, but the ideas he was expressing, that motivated his audiences.

THE CONVERSION OF REAGAN

It is important to keep in mind that in his early adult life, Reagan was a self-proclaimed liberal. On occasion he would even describe himself as a former "bleeding-heart liberal." It may have been the result of his strong religious background;

his mother was extremely devout, the kind of lady who would visit the jails, take food to prisoners, and help neighbors, and was constantly engaged in charitable works. Reagan followed that path as a young man. He was inspired by the idea that everyone should be his brother's keeper. It took him a while to realize that when government is involved, far from helping you be your brother's keeper, the government often strays outside its own realm, more likely to become your brother's master and yours, too. That change in his approach to government and politics began to take place in the 1950s.

Even before that, however, his experience in Hollywood started him thinking about the contradictions of liberal philosophy. It began with his election as president of the Screen Actors Guild during the late 1940s. The Screen Actors Guild is one of several unions in Hollywood, including those representing cameramen, stage managers, grips, and other workers in the motion picture industry. Reagan was the leader of SAG at a time when the Communist Party USA, the internal Marxist party in this country, tried to take over the unions as a means of controlling the movies for propaganda purposes. Ronald Reagan led the actors and other union leaders in resisting the communists. It was a bitter conflict, with strikes, intimidation, and violence. But eventually the communist threat was defeated and industrial peace was restored to Hollywood.

That was how Reagan came to appreciate the reality of the threat of communism and began his thinking of how to overcome that threat. That education was invaluable; at the same time that he was encountering communism as a domestic threat, he was reading about the international aspects of communism. It happened that the lawyer for the Screen Actors Guild, a friend of Reagan's, was an avid researcher and writer on international communism. He would pass along books like *The Treaty Trap* to Reagan, who would devour this information. Both his reading and his experience were seen to contradict his former liberal views.

In the 1950s, Ronald Reagan became the host of a popular television program called *General Electric Theater*. Part of his contract required that he visit General Electric plants during the week. Being a movie star—he'd starred by that time in fifty-one movies and was now a television star—he was quite popular. Over the course of ten years, he visited 137 GE plants, and during that period he talked with both workers and managers about their problems and concerns. He also read much of the material that GE was providing to its employees, including educational material on politics and free enterprise. This continued Reagan's education about communism, socialism, the market system, and the threats to our political and economic systems. It was an important time for him, and had much to do with his transformation from a liberal to a conservative.

Reagan's high public profile resulted in his becoming a very popular speaker. After he had given talks to the workers, he would be invited to service clubs and civic groups, to give talks on free enterprise. Soon various political figures, particularly conservatives, would ask him to speak on their behalf. Once when speaking in 1962, in the course of his speech, he remarked that he had been a lifelong Democrat but now was favoring this particular Republican candidate. During the questions that followed, one of the ladies in the back of the room raised her hand and said, "Mr. Reagan, you sound more like a Republican than you do a Democrat." And he said, "Well, I guess my views have really gone in that direction. One of these days, if I find a registrar, I'll reregister." The lady said, "I'm a registrar, and I'll see you after the meeting." And so Ronald Reagan became a registered Republican.

I've indicated that Reagan read deeply, but it is difficult to overstate the extent of his intellectual preparation for governing. He read Bastiat's *The Law* and Hayek's *The Road to Serfdom*, and he was fascinated with Whittaker Chambers's *Witness*, in which Chambers described both the appeal of communism and communism's failure. He even memorized parts of Chambers's book that he felt were particularly poignant, and he would cite them by heart in his speeches. He read *Human Events* and *National Review* regularly, keeping up to date on the latest ideas in the conservative movement. His extensive reading was a very important preparation for governing.

Reagan always had a particular interest in the founding of this country. He was tremendously impressed by the biographies of the leading figures of the era. He was fascinated with what they did and how they thought, particularly their self-sacrifice for the cause, and their willingness to put aside personal interests—or even the interests of the states they represented—in order to create a new united nation, a United States of America. He was inspired by the kind of leadership that could produce the Declaration of Independence, the creed of freedom for our country, and the Constitution as the vehicle for implementing those principles.

In 1964, having been a fairly prominent speaker for some time, Reagan was asked by a group of businessmen if he would agree to speak on a national telecast on behalf of Barry Goldwater. He agreed; they raised the money so that it was funded separately from the Goldwater campaign, and he was given a prime spot on television. His speech was entitled "A Time for Choosing," and in it he explained the principled conflict between liberalism and conservatism, and the implications of the outcome of that conflict for the country. He insisted that we had to choose, one way or another, between the freedoms and principles of the Declaration of Independence and our Constitution or endure a more powerful, more centralized government that would be a danger to our liberty.

The broadcast was a great hit. The group of business leaders were so impressed with Reagan's remarkable ability to promulgate a vision persuasively that they asked him to run for governor of California. Reagan was initially dismissive: "They don't want an actor for governor." When they persisted, he told them that he would think about it, talk to people throughout the state, and see if their idea was valid. For about six months, he traveled around California, gave presentations, and took questions—in part, to demonstrate that he was capable of more than simply delivering scripted lines.

GOVERNOR REAGAN

The tremendous response he received from the people of California persuaded him to run for governor in 1966, even though it was against a very popular incumbent who was running for his third term. It turned out to be a nasty election—as a matter of fact, his opponent even ran a rather vicious ad showing a teacher talking to a little girl, remarking, "You know, it was an actor that shot Lincoln."

Ronald Reagan defeated Pat Brown by nearly a million votes in 1966, and that started him on his political career. He had an impressive record as governor, erasing the deficit and putting sound fiscal policies into place. It was a period of great stress, but Reagan handled the upheaval of the late 1960s and early 1970s with good planning, good preparation, and effective personal involvement with average people, even including students. On one occasion he arranged a meeting in the state capital of the student body presidents of all the colleges in California. He used the opportunity to explain to the students the importance of the philosophical and political foundations of the country as well as the principles of freedom and individual responsibility. One of the student body presidents suggested that someone of Reagan's generation could not understand the younger generation with so many remarkable innovations transforming life as they knew it. After all, the student pointed out, Mr. Reagan did not grow up with television, coast-to-coast air travel, or man walking on the moon. He implied that because Reagan and his generation didn't have these new things in their youth, they were incapable of understanding young people today. Governor Reagan was unflappable. "You're right," he said, "my generation didn't have those things. *We invented them!*"

When Reagan left the governorship in 1975, there was a

groundswell of support for him to run for president in 1976, even though the incumbent, Gerald Ford, was running for re-election. Reagan took the unusual step of running against an incumbent president of his own party because of his dissatisfaction with two issues: the growth of the federal government, even under Republican presidents, and our flawed policy of détente with the Soviet Union. Reagan knew that the Soviet Union was cheating on the terms of international agreements and was continuing to pursue its expansionist ambitions while our leaders were complacent and allowed it to do so.

Reagan, of course, did not win the nomination. He came close, even to the point of contesting the nomination at the convention. But in many ways, it was probably a good thing that he wasn't the Republican nominee. The country was probably not as ready for his ideas in 1976 as it would be in 1980. But he had sought the nomination by running explicitly to the right of the incumbent; as a result, he enlarged the cadre of conservative support that had started with Goldwater. The people who had worked in his 1976 campaign, particularly those who would become engaged in electoral politics, continued as conservative activists and expanded the conservative movement.

PRESIDENT REAGAN

How does one man stand out so much that even now, nearly a quarter of a century after he left office, he's still the former president most talked about, even above more recent holders of that office? Clearly, part of it was his personal character. I am often asked what Ronald Reagan was really like as a person. I always answer that his most significant characteristic was his optimism and his cheerfulness. He was always upbeat; as he would say, he believed the glass was half full rather than half empty. He exuded that confidence and invigorated others with his optimism. As a result, he was able to inspire people to achieve more than they initially thought they were able to do. He was genuinely an inspirational leader as well as an intellectual leader and a very good executive.

This ability to inspire and motivate is most important in dealing with the last element involved in leadership—*crisis*. An aide to President Obama, Rahm Emanuel, was quoted as saying, "Never let a good crisis go to waste." In other words, a president has more opportunity to accomplish things in the midst of a crisis. Ronald Reagan was sworn into office at the height of arguably the greatest crisis facing the country in many years. Inflation in those days was 12.5 percent. Interest rates were 21 percent. This nation had a serious energy shortage; a person had to get up early in the morning to get a car into line at the local gas station because by 8:30 all the gas it had for that day would have been sold. The country had a serious unemployment rate, at one point as high as 10 percent.

We also had a crisis in foreign affairs and national security. There was the threat of communism; the Soviets' potential for aggression was great. Two years before Reagan was inaugurated, they had marched with impunity into Afghanistan. They were using Cuban troops in Angola to subvert the government. They had a Marxist bastion in our own hemisphere, in Nicaragua, and they were trying to bring down the government of El Salvador. In addition, Reagan was very disturbed about the captive nations of Eastern and Central Europe that were under the heel of the Soviet Union. There was sustained oppression of the people in Poland and other countries, where the people were suffering under martial law and military dictatorships.

Compounding the problem was the fact that our military capability had deteriorated following the end of the Vietnam War, and we were at one of our weakest points militarily since before World War II. As was said at the time, there were planes that couldn't fly for lack of spare parts, ships that couldn't sail for lack of trained crews, and tanks and artillery that couldn't maneuver for lack of ammunition or fuel. In the midst of increasing global instability, our military situation was extremely dire.

Further compromising national security was the country's leadership position on the world stage. We were no longer as respected as we had been since the end of World War II, and the pundits were saying that capitalism had peaked, that democracy was as widespread as it was ever going to be, and that the wave of the future was socialism. Looking at what was happening in Africa, Asia, and even in Latin America, some commentators predicted that the United States also would be moving in a socialist and less democratic direction. Moral equivalence—the notion that freedom and democracy on one side and totalitarianism on the other were morally equal ways of governing—was an increasingly common posture among those postulating on foreign affairs. Not only had other countries lost confidence in the United States, but also many people here had lost confidence in ourselves and our institutions. Too many people felt that America's best days were behind us and that we were a country in decline.

Whether or not the time was right for a conservative leader with a conservative message to mobilize the conservative movement, it was clear that the country was at a crossroads and needed what Reagan had promised. When he took office, he put into practice the principles that shaped his conservative message. They came straight from the best of the American political experience, particularly the founding, and they revolved around six major ideas: first, the importance of constitutionalism and the rule of law; second, preserving individual liberty; third, limited government (in accord with what the Founders had in mind when they wrote Article I, Section VIII, of the U.S. Constitution, where they identified specific enumerated powers for the federal government, beyond which it should not go); fourth, free market economics; fifth, traditional American moral values, with emphasis on religion and family as the moral foundations of a nation; and sixth, a strong national defense.

From these principles came policy. Reagan's first act, for example, even before he left the Capitol at his swearing in, was to sign his first executive order, which abolished the price controls that had been hobbling our energy resources. In response to the economic crisis, he obtained through Congress tax rate reductions. When he took office, the top marginal tax rate was 70 percent. He cut that back as he implemented tax rate reductions across the board. He advanced regulatory reform, discarding unnecessary and burdensome regulations that were stifling business and industry. He worked with the Federal Reserve for stable monetary policies. He slowed the growth of federal spending. For the eight years he was president, the country saw the slowest increase in federal spending of any presidency since World War II.

He rebuilt the American military. The all-volunteer program of the armed forces was in jeopardy in 1980, and talk of resuming the draft was widespread. Reagan increased salaries, improved the budget, and raised the living standards of our military personnel. He gave priority attention to the people in the military and personally showed pride in our men and women in uniform. He rebuilt and expanded our strategic weaponry. He increased and improved our conventional weapons, modernizing our tanks, artillery, planes, and ships—eventually moving toward the goal of a six-hundred-ship navy. He invested in our intelligence system, developed our industrial mobilization capabilities, and launched an unprecedented initiative that was very important to him: finding a defense against strategic nuclear weapons. The Strategic Defense Initiative, which was an antiballistic missile program, is, of course, still going today.

Reagan dramatically revised our posture toward the Soviet Union. He did not shy away from the moral dimension of the conflict. He forcefully and confidently labeled those who live by oppressing others as "the epitome of evil in the world." He called the Soviet Union an "evil empire," and excited quite a reaction. Many editorialists at places like the *New York Times* and so-called experts in the field of national security thought Reagan's saying that was terrible and unnecessarily provocative. Much of the "striped-pants set" at the State Department was very upset. Reagan's response was, "Look, they know they're evil. The people that they're oppressing know they're evil. Why don't we admit that they're evil?" Reagan's statement was more important than even many who supported him realized. More than irritating liberals who disagreed with him, it gave hope to those held captive behind the Iron Curtain that there was an American president who knew what the situation was, and was willing to speak the truth about it.

Reagan let it be known through Soviet ambassadors that any further Soviet aggression would be met by the free nations of the West—with military action, if necessary. What's more, he worked with and encouraged freedom fighters in Angola, Nicaragua, Poland, and elsewhere to roll back prior Soviet aggression.

In this way, forthrightly defending the American commitment to freedom, and working with allied leaders like Margaret Thatcher, Reagan reestablished our position of world leadership as the United States regained the respect of other countries. At the same time, he revived the domestic American spirit through his powerful and persuasive addresses on television. He helped Americans to believe that our best days were yet to come, and revived that signature American can-do spirit.

Of course, as President Reagan's attorney general, I would be remiss if I did not point out his work to rehabilitate American jurisprudence: the principle of constitutionalism and the rule of law. He took great pains to state the importance of judges ruling not on the basis of politics or their own personal convictions, but rather strictly on the basis of what the Constitution and the laws passed by Congress actually say.

Separation of powers simply demands that judges not arrogate unto themselves the responsibilities of legislators or attempt to rewrite the Constitution. This became an inflammatory subject because the courts had strayed far from a constitutionally faithful path in the 1950s, '60s, and '70s. President Reagan's careful appointment of constitutionally faithful judges was extremely important and he buttressed his appointments with his arguments on behalf of judicial integrity and the rule of law. His personal advocacy provided the inspiration for those in the Justice Department who were committed to recovering a constitutional republic.

One of the axioms of the Reagan administration was that "personnel is policy." The Reagan Revolution was embodied by the people who put President Reagan's vision into effect. The kind of people a president appoints—their philosophy, their beliefs, their fidelity—determines how an administration will act. Moreover, Reagan believed that we should be a team. People could express differences of opinion, but once a decision was made, he expected them all to work together, carrying out and implementing those decisions. He invested a lot of time personally in crafting policy and didn't allow people to come in and get a snap decision out of him in the Oval Office. He used the eighteen of us who were members of the cabinet as his primary forum for decision making. That way he benefited from many different points of view before making a decision.

Despite the fact that Reagan had a responsibility to govern, he did not give short shrift to conservatives in favor of bureaucrats. He involved conservatives in his administration, and he let members of the conservative movement know that he was one of them and that he appreciated what they were doing. Each of the eight years that he was president, he attended or gave a speech by television to the Conservative Political Action Conference so that these several thousand conservatives would know that he supported them and thought that what they were doing was important. Likewise, he awarded the Medal of Freedom and other presidential honors to conservative leaders for what they had done in service to the country.

Finally, he made it a point to get his views across to the country as a whole. He believed in the ideas he had read as a young man and was always eager to show that conservatism works, that it was something that people could embrace, and that it was the right course for the country. His speeches invariably communicated his conservative vision. He was a marvelously gifted speaker, but his speeches were inspirational to the country in large part because of the substance of that conservative vision. It was an essential part of his success.

In short, what Ronald Reagan did was best described by George Nash in his book *Reappraising the Right* when he said, "[Reagan] transmuted American conservatism from theory to practice. He gave conservatives a successful presidency to defend and a statesman to honor, and shifted the paradigm of political discourse for at least a generation." We now know that the impact of the Reagan Revolution will be for much more than a generation. It is a vital part of our nation's history.

CHAPTER 10

◆ ◆ ◆

We have seen how diverse strands of conservatism came together in the modern conservative movement following World War II. The postwar movement had traditional conservative intellectuals like Bill Buckley and Russell Kirk, and it had grassroots activists like Phyllis Schlafly, all of whom had grown up with conservative ideology. The identity of traditional and grassroots conservatives came into sharper focus with the rise of yet another strand of conservatism in the middle of the twentieth century: *neo*conservatism.

Foreign policy expert Douglas Feith gives a very personal history of neoconservatism and explains how former liberals like him became conservatives. Unlike other strands of conservatism rooted in tradition, neoconservatism is a newer approach, springing from the minds of former liberals who were, as a famous remark put it, mugged by reality just as much of the Democratic Party was abandoning traditional liberalism in favor of the counterculture and a weak foreign policy.

Neoconservatism, which arose in opposition to domestic policy failures of the 1960s, is best known now for its influence on conservative foreign policy. Feith argues that one of the key contributions of the neoconservatives was applying traditional conservative arguments about morality to issues of foreign policy as well as domestic policy.

Feith explains how the Left hijacked the term *neocon* during the George W. Bush administration and recast it as a pejorative, leaving the term with little descriptive meaning at this point. Because many of Bush's advisers agreed with neoconservatives, critics in the press labeled them as neoconservatives, too. Bush's enemies then began twisting the term *neocon* to mean anyone associated with Bush's foreign policy, particularly Jewish conservatives.

Feith's thoughtful essay makes clear what neoconservatism is, and what it is not—and he shines a light on the most controversial foreign policy decisions of the Bush administration, which still divide conservatives today.

Douglas J. Feith is Senior Fellow at the Hudson Institute, where he heads the Center for National Security Strategies. He is the author of *War and Decision: Inside the Pentagon at the Dawn of the War on Terrorism*. From July 2001 to August 2005, he served as undersecretary of defense for policy. In the Reagan administration, Mr. Feith worked as a Middle East specialist for the National Security Council and as deputy assistant secretary of defense for negotiations policy. Mr. Feith holds a J.D. (magna cum laude) from the Georgetown University Law Center and an A.B. (magna cum laude) from Harvard College. He was a professor of national security policy at Georgetown University, a Visiting Scholar at Harvard's Kennedy School of Government, and a Distinguished Visiting Fellow at Stanford's Hoover Institution.

THE COLD WAR, ANTI-COMMUNISM, AND NEOCONSERVATISM

Douglas J. Feith

◆ ◆ ◆

Some years ago, a candidate for mayor of New York City visited a senior-citizen center in the Bronx and spoke about what he said was *the* issue of the day: crime. He roused his audience by telling them: "A judge I know was recently mugged, and do you know what he did? He called a press conference and said to the reporters, 'This mugging of me will in no way affect my decisions in matters of this kind.' An elderly woman then stood up and, with a heavy European accent, shouted, 'Then mug him again!'"[1]

In discussing neoconservatism, the story is apt because it brings to mind that famous quip by Irving Kristol in which he defined a neoconservative as a liberal who was mugged by reality. Kristol, the founding editor of a journal called *The Public Interest*, was one of the two men commonly recognized as the fathers, or perhaps godfathers, of neoconservatism. The other is Norman Podhoretz, who edited *Commentary* magazine for thirty-five years.

Historians debate neoconservatism's birth date. Some say it was in the 1930s, when Kristol was a college student dabbling in left-wing (but anti-Stalinist) ideology. Kristol himself pegs 1965 as the start of the neoconservative "current of thought," because that was when he founded *The Public Interest.*

Who are the neoconservatives and what are their main ideas? They are men and women who started their political lives left of center, as liberals or, in the case of Kristol and some others, as Trotskyites. By the mid-1960s, however, they were questioning prevailing liberal thought, especially the premises of President Lyndon Johnson's Great Society programs for fighting poverty. They were skeptical about social engineering projects. They warned that the premises of such projects were often simplistic and overly optimistic and the results were often unintended and negative. Though national security is a prominent feature of neoconservative thought, from the beginning, neoconservatives devoted a great deal of attention also to domestic policy issues.

Kristol wrote that neoconservatism "describes the erosion of liberal faith among a relatively small but talented and articulate group of scholars and intellectuals, and the movement of this group (which gradually gained many new recruits) toward a more conservative point of view: conservative, but different in certain important respects from the traditional conservatism of the Republican party."

Kristol says that most neoconservatives were "from lower-middle-class or working-class families, children of the Great Depression, veterans (literal or not) of World War II, who accepted the New Deal in principle, and had little affection for the kind of isolationism that then permeated American conservatism." His account of the original neoconservatives is that they regarded themselves "as dissident liberals—dissident because we were skeptical of many of Lyndon Johnson's Great Society initiatives and increasingly disbelieving of the liberal metaphysics, the view of human nature and of social and economic realities on which those programs were based."[2]

Further, the neoconservatives took arguments of cultural conservatives that relied on morality, and gave them intellectual heft and compelling articulation that delighted the cultural conservatives. Before the neoconservatives, cultural and Bible Belt conservatives were often dismissed as intellectually non-serious, because many intellectuals dismissed anything religious as nonserious. The neoconservatives were able to explain that moral considerations are actually not only intellectually respectable but crucial to the functioning of a healthy society.

If I had to capture the essence of neoconservative thinking in a phrase, it would be "skepticism toward all 'isms.'" Neoconservatives are not a political party. They don't have an agreed-upon set of policy prescriptions for domestic or foreign affairs. What they do have is a common perspective on how to analyze public policy. Kristol rejected the idea that neoconservatism is an ideology; he described it is a "persuasion" or a "current of thought."

The neoconservatives criticized ideological orthodoxies of the Left and Right. They set themselves up as opponents of political ideologues of all stripes. Different people use the term *ideologue* differently. It usually has a negative connotation, and generally refers to a set of ideas premised on assumptions that people hold as a matter of faith, not reason. Though dictionaries generally define *ideologue* neutrally, as a person interested in ideas, it's clearly not a compliment to call a person an "ideologue."

I define an ideologue as a person indifferent to the facts. When an ideologue has theories or preconceptions that are contradicted by facts, the ideologue does not modify his assumptions; he ignores or suppresses the facts. As the saying goes: you can't reason a man out of something he didn't reason himself into.

Kristol and his fellow neoconservatives in the mid-1960s soured on Great Society political liberalism not because they became indifferent to the poor or decided that the poor did not deserve help from the government. Rather, they examined the actual effects of Great Society programs and concluded that many were bringing about the opposite of what they were intended to do. The programs produced public housing projects for the poor that gave tenants no stake in their property and turned into breeding grounds for drug abuse and violence. Efforts to improve public safety were accompanied by large public expenditures for additional social services despite a lack of evidence that such services reduced crime. The neoconservatives were more concerned with results than intentions, which is another way of saying they were anti-ideological.

A NEOCONSERVATIVE TRANSFORMATION

My own personal experience is not in domestic policy issues but in national security issues, so I will devote most of my reflections to neoconservatism's contribution to that area of policy. I'll talk about the neoconservative movement in the first person, from my own experience, because my political evolution toward neoconservatism was similar to that of many others of my generation.

Let me share with you some family background.

My father was a Jew born in Europe in 1914. The Nazis killed both of his parents, four of his sisters, and his three brothers. As a sailor on British merchant vessels when World War II started, he managed to come to the United States during that war and join the U.S. Merchant Marine. In the course of his American wartime service, he survived the loss of three ships to enemy fire.

My mother was born in the United States, and she and my dad created together a rather typical, politically liberal Jewish suburban home. The *New York Times* was delivered every day, and we read it and believed it. My mother thought Alger Hiss was innocent and the Rosenbergs probably were, too. My parents voted for Adlai Stevenson, John Kennedy, and Lyndon Johnson. I remember once sitting beside my father on the edge of his bed, looking through papers on his night table. He had cards showing he was a member or contributor to the American Civil Liberties Union, the NAACP, and the Democratic Party.

I grew up with liberal ideas on the major political issues of the day. At the same time, our home had important bourgeois features that were not in any way in tension with our liberal politics. My parents were patriotic. They gave their children religious instruction, a strong sense of family, and a commitment to principles of hard work and personal responsibility.

When I was a kid in the early 1960s, being a liberal meant supporting color-blind government, free speech, a strong American defense, and friendly relations with Israel. If one supports all those things nowadays, one will generally be considered a conservative.

When I was a kid, liberals like us readily accepted the idea that America was an exceptional country in that it was founded with a mission not only to safeguard its own people's liberty but to demonstrate to the world the possibility of popular self-government. Liberals today tend to ridicule or belittle the concept of American exceptionalism, arguing that it is arrogant.

I was in high school in the late 1960s and in college in the early 1970s. Those years were dominated by the remarkably bitter controversy about the Vietnam War. Though America's involvement in the war was the work of Presidents Kennedy and Johnson, both of whom were liberal Democrats, liberals turned against the war and the antiwar movement became increasingly strident and radical. Antiwar demonstrations routinely featured speakers who denounced President Johnson as a war criminal, condemned America as an imperialist aggressor, and sympathized with America's communist enemies. Not everyone in the antiwar movement struck such notes, but over time they grew more and more pronounced.

In high school, I was prepared to enter the army if drafted, but my views on the war were negative, generally in line with those of the liberal editorial page of the *New York Times*. I considered myself a Democrat, and I don't think I had a single friend who was a Republican. In fact, I wasn't aware that any of my parents' friends were Republicans. Nevertheless, I found myself increasingly uneasy about what I was hearing from the Democratic Party, which was adopting the rhetoric and ideas of the antiwar movement, of the New Left, and of the 1960s counterculture. In his 1976 essay "What Is a 'Neoconservative'?" Irving Kristol observed: "If there is any one thing that neoconservatives are unanimous about, it is their dislike of the 'counterculture' that has played so remarkable a role in American life over these past fifteen years."[3]

In 1968, support in the Democratic primaries for "peace candidate" Eugene McCarthy was strong enough to dissuade President Lyndon Johnson from even running for reelection. By 1972, the strength of the party's New Left wing was sufficient to bring about the nomination of George McGovern to run against Richard Nixon.

When I entered college, I knew very little history and had not thought deeply about foreign affairs, but like everyone else, I participated in many discussions of the Vietnam War. Much of the antiwar argumentation sounded persuasive to me. I didn't see how that remote war could meaningfully affect us at home. The famous domino theory was so widely ridiculed that I wouldn't credit it. President Nixon, who became the focus of the antiwar effort, struck me as an unappealing character who lacked credibility even before the Watergate scandal broke.

Two things in particular, however, caused me to move away from the antiwar cause. First, I was repelled by the prevalence of extremist anti-American rhetoric: the condemnations of U.S. officials as fascists and the spelling of *Amerika* with a *K* to make the whole country appear fascist, the attacks on capitalism and on the "bourgeoisie," and the sympathy expressed toward the Soviet Union, which I knew to be an inhumane, totalitarian state.

Second, and of critical importance, I came to realize that pacifist notions underlay much of the argumentation of the antiwar Left. The pacifism was asserted through slogans such as "Nothing ever gets resolved by force" and "War is not the answer."

As limited as was my knowledge of history, I was certain that there were forces for evil in the world that could not be contained, much less eliminated, through diplomacy. The Nazi regime and the Soviet regime each had its own totalitarian, revolutionary ideology and a record of murdering millions. I knew that diplomacy, though tried far beyond the point of reasonableness, could not have solved the Hitler problem. I knew that the Nazi threat was in fact resolved by force. I knew that the Soviet Union was a serious enemy, too—able and willing to use military force to spread its influence. I knew, therefore, that whether or not war was the answer depended on what the question was. When someone asserted that war was never the answer, it struck me as the proverbial thirteenth chime of a clock, which calls into doubt the integrity of all the previous chimes.

Many types of theories can be very seductive when one knows very few facts; an impressive teacher can easily make a complex theory sound compelling to a student who has no substantial knowledge in the field. I had started college as a physics major and was trained in the scientific method. I had absorbed the lesson that theories are nothing more than hypotheses until they are rigorously tested against the facts. There were few historical points I felt confident I knew to be facts, but the idea that Hitler had to be resisted with force was one of them.

The pacifism of so much antiwar argumentation was the flaw that caused me to look with skepticism at the key arguments of the antiwar movement. Those arguments began to unravel in my mind, and I became open to rethink everything I thought I knew about foreign policy and government. I expanded my reading beyond the *New York Times* and other liberal publications. Of greatest significance, I became a regular reader of *Commentary* magazine, which brought me intellectually into neoconservative circles. My physical entrance, as it were, into those circles in Washington, D.C., is another story.

When I was a student at Harvard College, I learned that Leslie Gelb, the diplomatic correspondent of the *New York Times*, was going to be giving a guest lecture on U.S.–Soviet relations at Wellesley, the nearby women's college. One never passed up an opportunity to visit with the women of Wellesley, of course, so I accepted an invitation to attend and to join a dinner with Mr. Gelb afterward. At the dinner I suggested that the Nixon administration's posture toward the Soviet Union was too accommodating on arms control, human rights, and other issues. After a while, Mr. Gelb offered that, given my views, perhaps I should be working for Senator Henry Jackson. He told me that if I sent him my résumé, he would send it along to Jackson's aide Richard Perle. I did so, and he did so, and Perle hired me for a summer internship in Senator Jackson's subcommittee office immediately after I graduated from college.

Jackson was an impeccably credentialed liberal Democrat with a purity rating in the 90 percent range from the liberal Americans for Democratic Action. He was also a defense hawk and the Senate's leading voice of opposition to the Soviet Union. Jackson was deeply skeptical of the Nixon-Kissinger détente policy. He brilliantly dissected the Nixon administration's arms control treaties with the Soviet Union and laid open their flaws. He publicized the Soviet regime's failures and brutalities, especially its mistreatment of pro-democracy dissidents and its refusal to allow its oppressed Jewish citizens to emigrate to Israel. He successfully pushed for enactment of a law called the Jackson-Vanik Amendment, which made most-favored-nation trade status for the Soviet Union conditional on Moscow's granting emigration rights to Soviet Jews. Jackson showed how highlighting human rights can be used to galvanize popular American support for an assertive foreign policy and to undermine the standing of America's anti-democratic enemies.

As the Vietnam War wound down and then ended in 1975 with the North Vietnamese conquest of South Vietnam, the main national security debates in the United States were about our policy toward the Soviet Union. Having broken with the Democrats over their lurch leftward under the leadership of George McGovern and others, the neoconservatives were by no means comfortable with the Republican administration's policy toward the Soviet Union.

RISE OF THE NEOCONSERVATIVES

You'll recall that I identified Norman Podhoretz, the editor of *Commentary* magazine, as one of the leading neoconservatives. In light of the strong popular opposition to the Vietnam War and the U.S. withdrawal from Vietnam, Podhoretz wrote, the United States "had to find a way to restrain Soviet expansionism that did not depend entirely or even largely on the use or the threatened use of American military power." Accordingly, Nixon and Kissinger developed détente, the essence of which was "to offer incentives (mainly consisting of economic benefits) for Soviet moderation and restraint, and to threaten penalties (mainly consisting of the withdrawal of those benefits) for aggressive or adventurist activity."[4]

Podhoretz was the key neoconservative intellectual critic of the Nixon administration's strategy toward the Soviet Union. "[O]ne might say of this strategy," Podhoretz wrote, "what Edmund Burke said of Lord North's treatment of the American colonies: 'This fine-spun scheme had the usual fate of all exquisite policy.' Brilliant though it was in achieving perfect internal coherence, it failed because it misjudged the nature of the Soviet threat on the one side and the nature of American public opinion on the other."[5]

Podhoretz noted that neither Nixon nor Kissinger "had any sympathy for the Soviets." Nor did they "ever doubt that the Soviet Union had expansionist aims or that it was capable of great ruthlessness in the pursuit of those aims." While both men always make their obeisances to the role of ideology in determining Soviet behavior on the international scene, for the most part they saw the Soviet Union as a nation-state like any other, motivated by the same range of interests that define and shape the foreign policies of all nation-states. From this perspective—the perspective of *Realpolitik*—Communist Russia was not all that different from Czarist Russia, the facts of geography, history, and ancestral culture being far more decisive than the ideas of Marx and Lenin.[6]

Here is the essence of the neoconservative critique of the Nixon-Kissinger foreign policy. The neoconservatives believed that the so-called Realist School of international relations, which argued that nations act on the basis of objective material interests in promoting their military and economic power and that their respective ideologies and forms of government have little to do with determining their actions, was altogether inadequate to explain the behavior of ideological regimes like that of the Nazis or the Soviets. Podhoretz wrote that if the Soviet leaders behaved in accordance with *Realpolitik*—not in accordance with communist ideology—then

> it would certainly be possible to make a deal of the kind contemplated by the policy of détente. If, in other words, the aims of the Soviet Union were limited, they could be respected and even to a certain extent satisfied through negotiation and compromise, with the resultant settlement policed by means other than, and short of, actual military force.[7]

"But," Podhoretz asked:

what if the Soviet Union is not a "normal" nation-state? What if in this case ideology overrides interest in the traditional sense? What if Soviet aims are unlimited? In short (and to bring up the by-now familiar contending comparisons), what if the Soviet Union bears a closer resemblance to the Germany of Hitler than to the Germany of Kaiser Wilhelm?

Podhoretz answered that Wilhelmine Germany was "an expansionist power seeking a place in the imperial sun and nothing more than that." Hitler, however, was more than an assertive *Realpolitiker*. The Nazi führer, Podhoretz explained,

was a revolutionary seeking to overturn the going international system and to replace it with a new order dominated by Germany (which also meant the political culture of Nazism). For tactical reasons and in order to mislead, Hitler sometimes pretended that all he wanted was the satisfaction of specific grievances, and those who were taken in by this pretense not unreasonably thought they could "do business" with him. But there was no way of doing business—that is, negotiating a peaceful settlement—with Hitler. As a revolutionary with unlimited aims, he offered only two choices: resistance or submission.

Podhoretz argued that the Soviet Union posed the same kind of threat to the West.

Neoconservatives recognized the importance of ideas—not just of military and economic interests—in world affairs. This neoconservative perspective dates back to the American Founding Fathers, who believed not only that they owed it to their own community to create self-government to protect the liberties of their people, but that they were doing something that would demonstrate to the world the possibility of popular self-government.

One of the main contributions of modern neoconservatives to the field of national security was an emphasis on the role of ideas in international affairs. This emphasis helped explain the motivations of ideological regimes in the world and also gave attention to the moral dimension of national security policy. Whereas the so-called realists spoke of the Cold War as essentially a clash of great powers—often referring to the Soviet Union simply as Russia, as a way of deemphasizing the ideological nature of its regime—the neoconservatives saw the Cold War as a battle between liberal democracy and totalitarian communism.

Podhoretz argued that the Soviet regime "has committed itself by word and deed to the creation of a 'socialist' world." He went on: "There is no reason to think that it can be talked out of this commitment or even (as, at bottom, détente assumes) bribed out of it." Even if the Soviet leaders had become cynical and no longer believed Communist Party ideology, Podhoretz wrote,

they are (to borrow from their own vocabulary) *objectively* the prisoners of Marxian and Leninist doctrines.

Without these doctrines, which mandate steady international advances in the cause of "socialism," they have no
way to legitimize their monopoly of power within the
Soviet Union itself. Hence even if they wanted to limit
their aims and become a "status-quo power," they would
be unable to do so without committing political suicide.

Podhoretz concluded that

the conflict between the Soviet Union and the West is
not subject to resolution by the traditional tools of diplomacy. Or, to put the point another way, given the
nature of the Soviet threat, détente is not possible. Certain agreements may be possible from time to time, but
they will invariably cover ground (cultural exchanges,
arrangements for travel and communications, and the
like) that is peripheral or even trivial from the point of
view of the central issue. Where really important ground
is touched upon, the agreement will invariably result in
a Soviet advantage.

This was the case, Podhoretz noted,

not because the Soviets are necessarily better at negotiating than we are or because they will necessarily cheat.
They may or may not be better and they may or may not
cheat. It is, rather, because in any negotiation between a
party with limited aims and a party with unlimited aims,
the party with limited aims is bound to lose in the very

nature of things. Even a deal that on the surface promises mutual benefits will work out to the advantage of the side pursuing a strategy of victory over the side pursuing a strategy of accommodation and peace.[8]

It's hard to overstate the importance of this neoconservative critique of the Nixon administration's Cold War strategy. It brought together practical political leaders like Senator Jackson with intellectuals like Podhoretz, Professor Jeane Kirkpatrick of Georgetown University, and Professor Eugene V. Rostow of Yale Law School.

THE NEOCONSERVATIVE BEDROCK: REAGAN VS. CARTER

Neoconservatives in the 1970s were guided by two basic points about national security. First, *ideas have consequences*. Ideas matter. So-called realists are not being realistic when they overemphasize the importance of guns and money and deemphasize the importance of ideas in world affairs, ignoring or downplaying America's practical as well as moral interest in supporting individual rights and democracy abroad.

The second point is captured by the slogan: "Peace through strength." This provides not only an answer to pacifists who deny the relationship between peace and military power, but also an observation about the limits of diplomacy. In stressing "peace through strength," neoconservatives were not rejecting the value of diplomacy, but they were warning that diplomacy unsupported by military power cannot be expected to produce or sustain peace.

After Nixon resigned in 1974, Kissinger remained secretary of state throughout Gerald Ford's presidency. When Ronald Reagan challenged Ford for the Republican nomination for president in 1976, he drew heavily on the critique of the Nixon-Kissinger détente policies. Reagan often sounded both of these major neoconservative themes: "Ideas matter" and "Peace through strength."

During the Carter administration, neoconservatives criticized President Carter for failures relating to both of these themes. Carter did not appear to understand the Soviet Union and the ideological nature of the Cold War. He warned against Americans' "inordinate fear of communism." He famously kissed Soviet leader Leonid Brezhnev at one of their summit meetings. Admitting to being shocked by the Soviet invasion of Afghanistan on Christmas Day in 1979, he said: "This action of the Soviets has made a more dramatic change in my own opinion of what the Soviets' ultimate goals are than anything they've done in the previous time I've been in office."[9] That did not inspire confidence.

President Carter also lacked appreciation for the concept of peace through strength. His diplomacy was naive, as was especially evident in his efforts to involve the Soviet Union in Arab-Israeli peace talks. Although Carter became famous for hosting the Israeli–Egyptian negotiations that produced the Camp David Accords and the Egyptian-Israeli peace treaty, attentive students of the subject remember that Carter administration officials initially opposed Egyptian President Sadat's peace initiative on the grounds that a separate bilateral deal would impede negotiation of a comprehensive Arab-Israel peace. The crowning example of Carter's weakness was the Iranian hostage crisis, when Iranian followers of the Ayatollah Khomeini broke into the U.S. embassy in Teheran and held a large group of diplomats and embassy officers hostage for more than fourteen months.

Neoconservatives were important voices of opposition to the Carter administration's national security policies. Former military and civilian officials, many who served formally or informally as advisers to Democratic senators Henry Jackson, Hubert Humphrey, and Daniel Patrick Moynihan, formed organizations such as the Committee on the Present Danger and the Jewish Institute for National Security Affairs that used neoconservative argumentation against what they saw as the naïveté, weakness, and anti-Israel inclinations of the Carter administration.

In the 1980 presidential election, because of the still-unresolved Iran hostage crisis, foreign policy was a prominent concern. Ronald Reagan deployed against Jimmy Carter a critique that drew heavily on the themes that neoconservatives had developed to oppose the policies of Carter and Nixon.

Reagan appointed many neoconservatives to prominent positions in his administration: Jeane Kirkpatrick became U.S. ambassador to the United Nations; William Bennett became drug czar and then secretary of education; Eugene Rostow became director of the U.S. Arms Control and Disarmament Agency; Elliott Abrams and Paul Wolfowitz became assistant secretaries of state; Richard Perle became an assistant secretary of defense; and I, still a junior member of the neoconservative community, became a member of the National Security Council staff and eventually a deputy assistant secretary of defense. There were quite a few others as well.

After Ronald Reagan became president, the term *neocon* came into widespread use. It helpfully shed light on the sociology of the Reagan administration. Reagan supporters and advisers could be divided into neoconservatives, a fairly small group of intellectuals whose important writings resulted in disproportionate intellectual influence, and the lifelong conservatives, sometimes laughingly called "paleoconservatives."

The neocons and the ordinary conservatives had different backgrounds but generally got along well in the Reagan administration. The neocons started life as liberals or far leftists, not members of Young Americans for Freedom, and they were disproportionately Jewish. The neocons read and sometimes wrote for *Commentary*, as opposed to *National Review*. Politically, neoconservatives believed they could help Reagan attract support from traditionally Democratic constituencies because the neocons had no connection with the history of support for isolationism or opposition to civil rights. Each of these Reagan-supporting groups identified with the president; the neocons thought of him as a fellow neocon, given that Reagan began his political life as a liberal Democrat and a labor union leader.

President Reagan's strategy against the Soviet Union was the approach proposed by Podhoretz, Richard Perle, Admiral Elmo Zumwalt, Senator Jackson, and others throughout the 1970s. It repudiated the Nixon administration's goals of stabilizing U.S. relations with the Soviet Union and relaxing tensions. Reagan's goal was victory. Once when asked to describe his strategy, he famously responded that it's simple: we win, they lose. It sounded flip but it was serious. It was based on the conviction that Soviet communism and the Marxist ideology on which it was based were rife with "internal contradictions" and doomed to collapse.

Like the neoconservatives, Reagan believed that Marxism-Leninism was premised on a flawed view of human nature. It aimed to create "the new Soviet man," an unnatural being who could be brought into existence only through gross coercion. Reagan rejected the idea that the communists could, even by coercion, change the nature of the human being, who is a self-serving creature though capable of virtuous action. Reagan further believed that coercion was ultimately unsustainable and the natural desire of people for freedom would defeat the communists' efforts to reshape the public through social engineering. He was confident in his bold comment that "the march of freedom and democracy will leave Marxism and Leninism on the ash heap of history" (borrowing another good communist phrase).[10]

This integration of philosophical insight into strategic thinking is a hallmark of neoconservatism, distinguishing it from the so-called Realist School.

Reflect for a moment on the magnitude of the accomplishment of Reagan's Soviet strategy. It helped destroy the Soviet Union utterly, ending the nuclear balance of terror. It released the nations of Central and Eastern Europe from the Soviets' imperial grip. It created opportunities for freedom and independence for the peoples of the fifteen republics of the former Soviet Union. The Soviet Union's disintegration was arguably the greatest strategic victory in history. Under President Reagan's leadership, the West not only defeated its enemy, which possessed an enormous arsenal of nuclear weapons, but destroyed the Soviet Union as a state, and did so *without war*.

President Reagan implemented this strategy through multiple means: imposing trade restrictions, opposing the Soviet gas pipeline to Western Europe, tightening export controls, arming the anti-Soviet forces in Afghanistan, getting NATO to support deployment of intermediate-range nuclear missiles in Europe, developing missile defense, exposing Soviet human rights violations, embarrassing the Soviets politically before the world, and encouraging Soviet dissidents who were demanding democracy and respect for individual liberties.[11]

These means reinforced one another. Economic and military pressure helped persuade Gorbachev and his politburo colleagues that the Soviet Union needed radical reform or it would fall hopelessly behind the Western powers technologically. Gorbachev embraced the idea that only greater liberality regarding thought and speech could remedy this problem. Thus, the themes of human rights and democracy played a role in inducing Gorbachev to launch experiments in glasnost (openness) and perestroika (reconstruction) that brought about the crumbling of the authority of the Soviet leadership and the disintegration of the Soviet Union. Gorbachev evidently did not understand his own political system well enough to realize that such liberalization would so undermine the system's foundation of lies that the whole edifice would fall. Reagan recognized that vulnerability. His encouragement of dissent, democracy, and freedom was not only a tribute to American principles; it was strategic. It was neoconservatism in action.

In the Reagan years, conservative and neoconservative generally melded to the point that neoconservatism could reasonably be called simply "Reaganite thinking." By the mid-1990s, Kristol could write: "It is clear that what can fairly be described as the neoconservative impulse (or, at most, the neoconservative persuasion) was a generational phenomenon and has now been pretty much absorbed into a larger, more comprehensive conservatism." [12]

NEOCONS DURING THE BUSH YEARS

The term *neocon* came back into popular use after George W. Bush's election. It became a useful handle for journalists and others because they wanted to understand the philosophical makeup of the new administration and were wondering who would predominate. Would it be the Reaganites? Or would it be the traditional conservatives of the Realist School, people aligned with George H. W. Bush, James Baker, and Brent Scowcroft?

It turns out that George W. Bush was, in many ways, a Reaganite. He believed in an active U.S. national security policy, especially after 9/11. He believed in peace through strength and saw military power as necessary, a crucial component of effective diplomacy. In confronting America's enemies he was willing to pursue victory and not just stability.

That said, the term *neocon* quickly lost its integrity during the George W. Bush years. First of all, it began to acquire a bigoted connotation. George W. Bush was strongly pro-Israel and, because the neoconservatives were disproportionately (though by no means exclusively) Jewish, critics of the president and his friendly-to-Israel advisers used *neocon* as a term of contempt. The implication was that the person in question was a Jew with loyalty to Israel rather than to the United States. Satirizing the bigots, the *New York Times* columnist David Brooks wrote an article in President Bush's first term that defined *neocon* as follows: "'Con' is short for conservative and 'neo' is short for Jewish." [13]

The term became an epithet, a verbal piece of nastiness used to smear officials considered too hard-line or too militaristic, not unlike the word *fascist*, commonly used by leftists to attack someone simply by voicing opposition and vicious contempt. So it is now with the word *neocon*, when used by opponents of the George W. Bush administration.

It became common to attribute to neocons—especially to neocon officials—positions we did not hold, intentions we never had, and actions we never took. Neocon officials have been falsely accused of advocating war without considering alternatives. It is widely but falsely believed that neocon officials proposed to spread democracy by the sword and favored war against Saddam Hussein to democratize the Arab world or to advance Israel's interests rather than America's. It has also been widely but falsely reported that the neocons in the Bush administration argued that the Iraq War would be easy and that there was no need to plan for its aftermath. All of these notions are false and my book *War and Decision: Inside the Pentagon at the Dawn of the War on Terrorism* presents the official documents that demonstrate their inaccuracy.

Of the many books that inaccurately depict the subject, one is especially noteworthy: *America at the Crossroads* by Francis Fukuyama. Fukuyama is a prominent, impressive scholar, himself a neoconservative before he recanted. In his book, he inaccurately attributes the aforementioned ideas and actions to neocon officials (other than the accusation that the neocons supported war in Iraq for Israel's sake, which he refutes). His thesis is that sound neoconservative thinking and experience over the years were ignored or misapplied by the neocon officials in the Bush administration. Remarkably, he fails to quote so much as a sentence, even a word, from any of the Bush administration's neocon officials. The only neocons he cites to support his thesis are journalists and non-government commentators. This is unworthy of the scholarship of Fukuyama's other work. He was unable to find comments from neocon officials to support his allegations because, when we spoke or wrote about the points at issue, we didn't make the points he attributes to us. In fact, we didn't agree with them.

The term *neocon* was further abused by its application to people like Donald Rumsfeld, Vice President Dick Cheney, and George W. Bush, though there is nothing "neo" about them. If they are neocons, then who are the traditional conservatives?

The term *neoconservative*—and with it *neocon*—is no longer useful. It has been distorted, besmirched by calumny and bigotry, and misapplied to the point that it has lost the philosophical and sociological meaning it once had. This is a cautionary tale about political labels, which often change their connotations and even their meanings over time. Labels can be useful—it is hard to have philosophical and political discussions without using them—but they must be used with care and caution, with knowledge of their origins and evolution, and with skepticism.

All of which reminds me of a riddle Abraham Lincoln liked to pose: If you call a dog's tail a leg, how many legs does a dog have? The answer is four, because calling a dog's tail a leg doesn't make it a leg.

What, then, to do with *neocon*? The term, unfortunately, is ruined, but the neoconservative philosophical persuasion endures. In the 1960s, '70s, and '80s, neoconservatives played a distinctive role in challenging many long-unchallenged assumptions of both liberals and conservatives. Neoconservatives highlighted the practical significance of the moral dimension of social welfare programs, U.S.–Soviet relations, and other topics. They brought a grateful, patriotic sensibility into public policy debates. Their contributions were valuable; their "current of thought" merged so thoroughly into the conservative mainstream that it is no longer distinctive. Neoconservatives always contemplated the United States with gratitude; attentive students of the conservative intellectual tradition in America will understand that America should reciprocate that appreciation.

CHAPTER 11

◆ ◆ ◆

The economic principles of conservatism are perhaps the least controversial principles in the conservative movement. Almost all conservatives agree on preserving free market capitalism, limiting government regulation, and holding tax rates low. Conservatives call on government to maintain the rule of law, protect property rights, and preserve the value of our currency in order to support economic growth and sustain our economic well-being as a nation.

Government cannot defend our nation's economic welfare, however, if it is captured by special interest groups determined to use the levers of government for their own ends. When interest groups champion government spending that benefits themselves but not the nation, when they demand regulation that burdens commerce, and when they write themselves benefits into the tax code, basic precepts of economic freedom are violated. Conservatives understand this as a violation of the principles of the free market.

For "fiscal conservatives," economic freedom is their core issue. Fiscal conservatives are often grouped together with libertarians, but not all fiscal conservatives hold libertarian views on non-economic issues. The Left often tries to portray the conservative focus on economic issues as a form of greed, but it is really about individual freedom.

Economist Daniel Mitchell lays out the principles of free market economics that are central to the conservative tradition and which conservatives generally uphold. The economic principles that Dr. Mitchell identifies as necessary for our prosperity are largely self-evident to conservatives and represent perhaps our greatest ideological difference from the Left.

Daniel J. Mitchell is a fiscal policy expert at the Cato Institute focusing on the economics of government spending and tax reform. Prior to joining Cato, Mitchell was a senior fellow with the Heritage Foundation, and an economist for Senator Bob Packwood and the Senate Finance Committee. Mitchell earned a Ph.D. in economics from George Mason University and his undergraduate and master's degrees from the University of Georgia.

EVERYTHING YOU WANTED TO KNOW ABOUT ECONOMIC POLICY

Daniel J. Mitchell

◆ ◆ ◆

This chapter covers something that should normally fill an entire textbook. We are going to explore the entire history of economics as it relates to public policy. Out of necessity, then, we are going to touch on lots of issues and focus on only the most important implications.

Let me start by explaining a little bit about economic growth, because that is really what this discussion is all about. If you want to know what causes economic growth, there is a consensus among economists. Everyone agrees that the way to get economic growth is through the two factors of production: capital and labor. If you want more economic output in your economy and you want people to have higher living standards, you really have only a handful of options: you can provide more labor to the economy or more capital to the economy, or you can utilize the existing labor or capital more efficiently. But that's it. There are no other factors of production. Everything that you think might lead to economic growth is in some way tied to those two factors of production.

But what's important is how you mix those factors of production, and this is where government policy enters into the
discussion. Capital and labor are like two ingredients; think
about it as if you are making a cake. Who is the chef? How do
those two ingredients—capital and labor—get mixed together?
Is your chef the private sector, broadly speaking? Are you relying on people like Steve Jobs to be the chef who's mixing the
capital and labor together? Or are you relying on the political
class to do it? Are you relying on central planners in Washington? Are you relying on politicians in a national capital?
Who is the person who is actually mixing the capital and labor
together? Finally, what are the implications of those decisions
for economic prosperity? This is the theme of this chapter.
We will be figuring out the best way—from a fiscal policy
perspective—to ensure the maximum economic output for the
given amounts and efficiency levels of capital and labor that are
in the economy.

This discussion matters, because economic growth over
time makes a big difference in the prosperity of your people.
If your economy grows at 7 percent per year, you will double
your GDP in ten years. If your economy grows at 1 percent per
year, you will double your GDP in seventy years. If you look at
the high-growth, "tiger" economies that grow between 5 and
7 percent per year (i.e., some of the Baltic nations like Estonia,
Ireland in the 1990s, or Hong Kong over the past fifty to sixty
years), you can see by looking at their long-run data that these
countries were, within at least our parents' lifetimes, very poor
jurisdictions. However, they became much more prosperous
because they managed to have sustained, rapid rates of eco-

nomic growth for multiyear periods. On the other hand, if you look at some of the stagnating European economies that are in trouble, you will see that they have had between 0 and 2 percent growth for a period of several decades. Perhaps they are still growing, but they are falling behind compared with the rest of the world.

If I were to choose one thing for you to take from this chapter and to remember when evaluating public policy, it would be that long-term trend lines are critical. If an economy is growing at only 1 percent per year over the long run, then regardless of where that economy starts, it will eventually fall behind a country that is growing at between 4 and 6 percent per year. Conversely, if one country starts out richer than the other *and* has between 4 and 6 percent growth, while the other country has only 1 percent growth, then that country with 1 percent growth is going to fall further and further behind. Another way to think about this is in terms of your own household. Imagine how much better off you are (at least if you're the typical case) than your grandparents, and how much better off your grandparents were than their grandparents before them. That is all simply a function of how much economic growth there is in a society.

Just by way of background, the United States (for the last one hundred–plus years) has been averaging about 3 percent real growth. (What do I mean by "real growth"? It's "real" growth in the sense that it is adjusted for inflation. We might have five or ten times as much income as our grandparents, but that number is in nominal dollars. We really want to measure in "real" dollars, because that actually captures things we want to know: how much more purchasing power we have compared with our ancestors, what the living standards are for the average American today versus thirty years ago, etc.) We have had this adjusted-for-inflation 3 percent economic growth going back to about 1870. If you chart the trend line with actual economic growth, the actual economic growth always oscillates around that 3 percent line.

Therefore, the key question is whether or not we could be doing something to get more of the 5 percent–type growth that you see in Hong Kong or Singapore. Also, are there things that we should be doing to avoid the 1 percent growth that you get in a country like Italy? Much of my analysis is centered on these questions. What is the role of public policy in determining why some countries have faster economic growth and better economic performance than other countries?

THE FIVE FACTORS
THAT DETERMINE PROSPERITY

The best way to start answering these questions is to look at the different indexes of economic freedom. The Fraser Institute in Canada publishes something called the *Economic Freedom of the World Index*, my old employers at the Heritage Foundation publish something called the *Index of Economic Freedom*, and you also have the *Global Competitiveness Report* from the World Economic Forum. If you look at all of these different measures, you will find that they are very similar. In fact, you can actually break down the building blocks of economic prosperity into five basic categories, and they are: rule of law, trade, regulation, monetary policy, and fiscal policy. I am a fiscal policy economist, so my analysis will mostly focus on the role of taxes and spending. But if you look at these indexes, fiscal policy is only 20 percent of a nation's "grade." All of these five categories, roughly speaking, are responsible for 20 percent of how a nation performs economically.

The rule of law doesn't just refer to "the rule of law" normally understood. It also refers to property rights, the legal system, the presence of corruption versus honest government, etc. There are a whole series of institutional structures that, in some sense, serve as the foundation for an economy. If, for example, you have basically honest rule of law, legal systems, court structure, honest policing, and non-corrupt government, and the citizenry doesn't have to pay bribes to get things done, etc., then you can build a house of economic policy upon this foundation. But if you don't get that foundation right, it doesn't matter what sort of house you build, because the foundation isn't going to be very strong. When you think about, for instance, why so many countries in the developing world are staying poor, it is not because they have big, bloated governments. It is not because they have heavy regulation. The real problem in the developing world is that they don't have the right institutions.

To think about this in more detail, remember the two major ingredients that give us economic growth: capital and labor. People put capital to work in the economy because they expect deferred benefits. When you invest, generally speaking, you are not making money in the first year. You are hoping to make money down the road. But how likely are you to invest in an economy where you can't trust the institutions of government to treat you fairly? The main problem in the developing world is that the rule of law, property rights, and honest government are usually what is missing. We are lucky in the Western world that even the big, high-tax European welfare states, for the most part, all still satisfy these basic conditions.

Let's now look at monetary policy, trade policy, regulation, and fiscal policy. Let's take monetary policy first, because it is the area in which governments are most likely to throw an economy off the tracks. In fact, you will almost always find monetary policy somehow involved when a major dislocation occurs. If you look at some of the big downturns in our economy's history—the Great Depression, the 1970s, the recent financial crisis—you will almost always find a situation where the Federal Reserve engaged in a boom-bust policy; it initially had a period of too much monetary creation (in other words, creating too much liquidity in the economy), and then, when it realized that it had made a mistake, it pulled back. Unfortunately, the very act of creating too much money inevitably means that it has to pull back and, in effect, bake into the cake some sort of economic dislocation. This dislocation can take the form of a financial crisis, 1970s-style stagflation, something like the Great Depression, etc.

Note that I am not implying there exists one single explanation for these issues at any time. In the Great Depression, for instance, monetary policy may very well have been a triggering factor, but protectionism with the Smoot-Hawley Tariff, Hoover's raising of the income tax rates from 25 percent to

63 percent, a doubling of the burden of federal spending, and all sorts of other government interventions were also important. Anytime that you are looking at a period in our economic history, it is important to keep in mind that you always have those five big factors, and each of those big factors is responsible for 20 percent of a nation's economic performance.

It is also important to note that monetary policy isn't noticed when it is going well, and neither is the rule of law. Monetary policy is simply something in the background of an economy, allowing it to function smoothly. If money and purchasing power are stable, and there are no efforts by the politicians to tinker with and use monetary policy for short-term "goosing" of the economy, you don't notice it. In the same way, you don't notice honest, sound government and rule of law; it just gives you an environment in which you can function. You notice if you're in Argentina and inflation is 30 percent, or if you were in Zimbabwe during the hyperinflation. It is under these circumstances that you actually notice monetary policy. Similarly, if you are in a developing country where you can't open a business without paying bribes to ten different people or ten different departments of government, then you will also notice that the rule of law is missing. If you are an investor and the government expropriates your property, and you have no access to an honest court system, then you notice that the rule of law isn't there. But the rule of law is the foundation; you ideally never notice it when it's being done right. Monetary policy is similar. It is like the "oil in the engine" of the economy; you notice monetary policy only if all of a sudden your engine freezes up and you realize that you have a big problem.

Let's now talk a little about trade. This is another area where there is definitely a consensus. Almost everybody today (with only a few exceptions) understands that free trade is a good idea. All the way back to Adam Smith's *Wealth of Nations* (and even before then), there existed the notion that the bigger a market is, the more people are able to specialize, allowing us to trade with one another and become richer as a result. Let's be very simplistic about it. Imagine if every one of us were responsible for growing our own food, producing our own clothing, and building our own house. We would obviously be a lot poorer, because none of us could be good at all of those things. We would not able to specialize and utilize the efficient allocation of labor and capital on our own. This is why trade is a very good thing.

It used to be that governments were very protectionist, especially in the pre–World War II era; one of the big factors in the Great Depression was protectionism with the Smoot-Hawley Tariff. But the notion that free trade as an economic policy is a very good idea also has been around for a long time. Adam Smith wrote his *Wealth of Nations* back in 1776, but it took a while for that to seep into the political system and the consciousness of policy makers. They began to understand that protectionism necessarily made an economy poorer, and free trade began to take off, first with England as an island trading nation. Then, almost everyone backslid with the Smoot-Hawley Tariff and other protectionist initiatives around the world. After World War II, though, there was a very conscious decision on the part of policy makers. They saw how world trade collapsed by about two-thirds with the protectionism of the 1930s. Of course, there was a depression, so that would have necessarily reduced world trade as well, but the policy makers still learned a very big lesson: when you put protectionism in place, you are going to make your economy poorer.

So this is yet another area where there has definitely been a consensus. For the most part, I think there is a consensus that inflation is a bad idea and that the rule of law is a good idea, so these are some areas where the consensus is that we should move government out of the way, allowing people to trade freely with one another and allowing economies to focus on the areas where they are most efficient. The logic of trade, and the logic of free trade between nations, to be more specific, is the same as the logic for free trade between South Carolina and North Carolina. The argument for this type of free trade is the exact same argument for free trade between the United States and Canada. Or it's the exact same argument for free trade between you and the local supermarket. In the end, you do not want government hindering people in the economy— whether it's labor, consumers, or capitalists. You do not want the government hindering people from making the most efficient and effective decision possible for improving their living standards. Trade, in the end, is a big success story.

Let's look now at the last two issues, where the consensus isn't quite as strong. Consider the issue of regulation. The simple way of thinking about regulation is as the area where the government steps in to allegedly correct a market failure, or to protect some sort of health and safety goal. A market failure would be something like pollution. If there is no regulation, and I set up some sort of chemical factory to produce something, I might, if I was not a very ethical person, decide to dump some toxic chemicals into the river that runs behind my factory. In theory, and in the era before regulation, the tort system protects against this, because people who live downstream and are damaged by the pollution will go to court. But the tort system was viewed as an inefficient way of doing those things, and so we began to address such things through regulation. In addition, you also have regulation for things like basic safety. You create "school zones," and ask important questions: Are you going to have a speed limit in front of the school zone? If you're going to have a speed limit, what is it going to be? Is it going to be five miles per hour, fifty miles per hour, or one hundred miles per hour? These are the decisions that have to be made when looking at the regulatory apparatus.

One of the most common things that you should have is cost-benefit analysis. This *sounds* very simple. And it is, of course, actually a simple concept. But how does it actually work? That's where things get more challenging.

Everyone (presumably) agrees that there should be speed limits. I gave the example of a school zone, but let's talk about an interstate highway. There are about 30,000 deaths on the road every year, and let's assume that thousands of those deaths are caused by accidents on interstate highways. We could eliminate all of those auto fatalities by having national speed limits of five miles per hour. But would that make sense? Even though there's a clear benefit (we would save thousands of lives every year by having five-mile-per-hour national speed limits), we don't do that because we recognize that the regulation has a very high cost. Transportation between places would take forever, and there are all sorts of additional costs that the regulation would impose upon the economy.

So instead each state looks at its traffic density, driving patterns, enforcement capabilities, etc., and makes a cost-benefit trade-off. The same procedure exists in other areas as well. For example, there is a division of the Office of Management and Budget in Washington called the Office of Information and Regulatory Affairs (OIRA), and one of its responsibilities is to be the regulatory overseer of all the different regulations proposed by different government agencies. One of the things that OIRA looks for is the cost-benefit analysis. Agencies say: "We want to do X. We want a national speed limit of five miles per hour because our job is to reduce highway fatalities." But an agency like OIRA acts as the adult with oversight in the conversation, saying: "Well, wait. You guys are looking at only one side of the equation. You're looking at the reduction in highway fatalities, and we have to consider the overall economy." That's how, at least in theory, regulatory decisions get made in Washington.

But these decisions still become very controversial, because not everyone makes the same assessments of the costs and benefits. For example, another thing that you may have to add to the equation is the implications of slower economic growth for the health and longevity of your population. There are very clear relationships in economic literature between the income of a country and the life span of its people. If you are in a very poor nation, your life span could be under fifty years. But if you are in a very wealthy nation, life spans are approaching eighty years. Therefore, if you pass a very expensive regulation

that harms the economy, even though the intended goal of the
regulation is to save a certain number of lives, a potentially
resulting drop in GDP can have counterbalancing negative effects. In some of the academic literature, there are data showing
that a $13 million drop in economic output causes one prema-
ture death, as a relationship over time, through an economy.
Most government regulations are intended to prevent premature deaths. We want to limit the sulfur dioxide that comes out
of certain coal plants, for instance, because we think that this
regulation will prevent premature deaths caused by poor health
or other harmful consequences. But if you are reducing deaths
at a high cost, and $13 million less of economic output leads to
a premature death according to economic research, you have to
somehow balance these two factors and decide what your sacri-
fices will be in terms of economic output and the implications
of that same sacrifice.

In summation, the way to think about regulation is that
there are always trade-offs. You are never going to completely
reduce risk in a society. Every time that you wake up and cross
the street, drive a car, or fly in a plane, you always face risk. For
example, how many people know that peanut butter is a car-
cinogen that the federal government measures? Every peanut
butter sandwich you eat increases, in some infinitesimal way,
your risk of cancer. Obviously, it increases your risk a lot less
than every cigarette would, but that's what regulatory analysis
is all about; it's very complex. In theory, though, it should be
very science-oriented, and you should be trying to figure out
the costs and benefits.

That's the way it should work. Oftentimes, however, we

get regulations that arguably have no economic benefit. State governments, for example, have passed laws that say you can't be a florist unless you pass a government exam, or you can't be an interior decorator without a government license. There are even regulations in different states for funeral homes that require you to purchase caskets to get cremated in. Of course, that's mostly because the casket-building industry will lobby the state legislators to put in this requirement, even though cremations clearly do not require the purchasing of a casket. In situations like this, you might have regulatory burdens imposed even though there is no measurable benefit. Therefore, when I mention how government regulation should work, keep in mind that this is in a theoretical world. It is also important to consider how regulations actually work in the real world. You will see, in terms of the real world of regulation, that different industries will often use the process to try to obtain unearned wealth. This is the theory that the late George Stigler, a Nobel Prize winner at the University of Chicago, entitled "regulatory capture." Regulatory capture exists when the government creates a regulatory agency that is supposed to do certain good things for the economy, but over time the regulated industry figures out how to use lobbying resources and take effective control of the regulatory body. Once this happens, the regulatory body will actually pass rules that help the big, powerful companies in the industry.

That is, in reality, what you often see. Regulations wind up benefiting big companies at the expense of small companies. Why is that? If you are a big company, you already have a very big legal staff, accounting staff, compliance staff, etc. If there's some new regulation that will cost every firm $10 million, it might be an asterisk in the budget of a large corporation. For small competitors, on the other hand, $10 million might put them out of business. In summation, how regulation works in the real world is often different than in theory.

I should also say that regulation is not just about economics. Hang gliding, for example, is a very hazardous hobby to undertake. I suppose if you want to be an actuary or accountant, you could point to how little of an effect hang gliding has on our economy versus how many deaths it causes per year. A regulator might decide, therefore, to ban hang gliding on the premise of saving lives without sacrificing a noticeable amount of economic output. But under this scenario, you have to decide whether other things should be a part of your calculation, namely human liberty, freedom, and the ability to decide for yourself. If you want to go out and surf twenty-foot waves in California, or become a skin diver and take the risk of a shark attack, should you have that choice? There are inherently dangerous activities, and the question is whether or not people should have the freedom and liberty to engage in those activities. In theory, if you just did a completely dispassionate cost-benefit analysis, you might decide that people shouldn't be allowed to take any risks. For example, in New York City, Mayor Bloomberg wants to ban restaurants from having salt. He also recently made a new decision that stops companies or restaurants from contributing food to homeless shelters if the fat and salt are above a certain level. Isn't that wonderful? He would rather have homeless people go hungry than, heaven forbid, there be a little bit too much salt in their food. These are some of the different issues that you raise when you look at regulation and how it works on the economy.

THE ECONOMICS OF FISCAL POLICY

Let's now shift to fiscal issues. When I say "fiscal issues," I am really talking about three different things, and I'll break them down as we continue with this part of the discussion. We are talking about deficits and debt, government spending, and the tax code.

But before I break down those three things, let's walk through a very abbreviated fiscal history of the United States. Basically, from the founding of our country through the first 130 to 170 years (depending on how you want to calculate it), we had limited government. This is what our Founders envisioned. If you look at the Constitution, and specifically at Article I, Section VIII, you will read the enumerated powers of the federal government. Article I, Section VIII gives the federal government, and more specifically Congress, the power to levy and collect taxes, to do patent and copyright laws, to build post roads, to maintain a national defense, etc. There are about twenty specific clauses outlining the powers of Congress and the federal government.

Powers that you will not find in Article I, Section VIII, include a Department of Agriculture, a Department of Energy, a Department of Education, Social Security, Medicare, Medicaid, etc. In fact, most of what the federal government does today would probably cause the Founding Fathers to roll over in their graves, because Article I, Section VIII is very clear in defining exactly what the federal government is authorized to do. The rest of the Constitution is also pretty clear; if the federal government is not specifically given the authority or permission to do something, it is not the business of the federal government.

That system pretty much operated through the 1700s and 1800s and into the 1900s. Probably the first hiccup was the Progressive Era. The Progressive Era (late 1800s to early 1900s) was characterized primarily by a change in the view of the role of government. If you read the Federalist Papers, or any of the early writings, the Founders very clearly believed that government was a dangerous thing. The purpose, originally, of the Articles of Confederation, and later of the Constitution, was to figure out how to balance the necessity of a government with distrust of government. The purpose of the Constitution was to figure out how to fence in government and guarantee individual rights so that people wouldn't have to worry about this dangerous entity that throughout the history of the world was associated with oppression, tyranny, and abuse. The Founding Fathers took this idea that government is a dangerous and risky, though necessary, thing, and put in place this system that was designed to limit government.

What characterized the Progressive Era was the notion that government is not a dangerous thing that we should curtail, but a wonderful force for good. If we unchain government from the Constitution, we can therefore have government go out and start doing things to make the world a more wonderful place. Something that coincided with the Progressive Era that basically enabled the process to begin was the adoption of the Sixteenth Amendment, which made income tax permissible.

We actually did have an income tax between 1863 and 1872 (it came into place as part of financing the North in the Civil War). We then had an income tax adopted in 1894, but an 1895 Supreme Court decision said that the power to tax income was not authorized by the Constitution. Article I, Section VIII does give government the ability to levy and collect taxes, but they had to be apportioned among the states, and obviously it's very difficult to design an income tax that collects an equal per capita amount from each state. At the time, that decision pretty much killed the income tax.

I should note that I am an economist, not a lawyer, so the situation is probably much more complicated than my analysis. But what essentially happened is that the politicians then put forth a proposed constitutional amendment, which took two-thirds of both the House and the Senate to get out of Congress, and in 1913 was ratified by three-fourths of the states. The result is that what started out as a fourteen-page law with one two-page tax form with a top tax rate of 7 percent has morphed into the lovely Internal Revenue Code that we all know and love today. That was a very important point in time for the fiscal and economic history of the United States.

The next significant thing was the New Deal. The New Deal was when we began to put in place some of the welfare state, and particularly welfare and Social Security. After that was the Great Society, and the Great Society was when we got Medicare and Medicaid. This was during the 1960s, when we also began the so-called War on Poverty.

To briefly digress, it's important to understand that these programs have not been very successful. The poverty rate was falling prior to the enactment of Great Society programs in the 1960s. Once the new welfare programs were implemented, however, that progress came to a halt and the poverty rate since then has hovered between 11 percent and 15 percent of the population.

Returning to fiscal history, the next thing that happened was that we had a twenty-year period between 1980 and the end of the century when under both Reagan and Clinton there was a consensus that government was too big and that the burden of government spending should shrink. By and large, policy did move in that direction during the Reagan and Clinton years.

But then we have this century, the Bush–Obama years, which are basically the opposite of the Reagan–Clinton years, because we have seen a fairly constant expansion in the burden of government spending. Indeed, all of the progress that was made during the Reagan–Clinton years has been reversed.

Keep in mind that this is the one area where there is certainly not a consensus. Perhaps there was a consensus during the Reagan–Clinton years about shrinking the burden of government, and then maybe there was a consensus (at least in Washington among politicians) to increase the burden of government during the Bush–Obama years, but a lot of the fiscal fights that we are now seeing in Washington reflect a lack of contemporary consensus. People are fighting over what the proper role, size, and scope of the federal government should be. And not only are we looking at history, we are also considering the future. Everyone is aware of the fact that, because of the demographics of the population (the baby boom generation is beginning to retire) and the structure of the entitlement programs, the very same problems that we are looking at in Greece today are going to happen to the United States unless something changes.

Let's now look at these three big fiscal policy issues: deficits, spending, and taxes. (Just by definition, deficits are the annual borrowing we do to finance government. We are spending more than we collect in revenue, and the annual borrowing is our "deficit." "Debt" is simply the collection of all the past deficits, added up.)

We now have a deficit that is roughly 6 percent of GDP. Calculating our debt is a little more complicated, because there are actually several ways of measuring the national debt. There is the gross national debt, publicly held debt, and unfunded liabilities (which is more of an actuarial measure). Simply stated, we have an annual deficit of 6 percent of GDP and a gross national debt of more than 100 percent of GDP. Our publicly held debt is around 75 percent of GDP. The unfunded liabilities of the entitlement programs amounts to nearly 400 or 500 percent of GDP. (This is actually very hard to measure because you have to do calculations of present value, and make an assumption on the interest rate in that calculation. As a result, it is a very amorphous and fuzzy way of trying to define the national debt. In the end, it is simply a measure of how much we have promised to spend in the future versus how much we plan to collect in revenue.)

When discussing deficits and debt, the number one thing

that I want to get across to people is that deficits and debt are not actually the problem; they are merely the symptom of the real problem. The *problem* that we have is the burden of government spending. Government spending, regardless of how revenue is collected, is what diverts resources from the productive sector of the economy. As the level of government spending rises, the politicians increasingly become the chefs who mix the capital and the labor in the economy. Consequently, there are fewer resources in the private sector for the entrepreneurs to mix the capital and the labor.

Sometimes, people will disagree with this assessment because they believe deficits lead to high interest rates. This is because interest rates are the price of borrowing. As the government borrows more and more, traditional supply-demand analysis dictates that there will be more upward pressure on the price of borrowing. Because the price of borrowing is the interest rate, this analysis would indicate that deficits lead to high interest rates.

I'm an economist, so I believe in supply and demand curves, and I agree with that analysis. But here is the key thing: just as it is very interesting and challenging to measure costs and benefits when talking about regulation, it is very interesting and challenging to measure the impact of government borrowing on the price of borrowing. Here is the example that I often use: I sometimes go to McDonald's and buy McChicken sandwiches, each for a dollar. Sometimes, I may even purchase up to three McChicken sandwiches at a time. In theory, then, my purchase of McChicken sandwiches at McDonald's has increased the demand for McChicken sandwiches, which should put upward pressure on the price. But if my purchases of McChicken sandwiches are just a tiny drop of water in the "lake of demand" for McChicken sandwiches, then it is going to be very difficult to measure whether my personal purchases are having any effect on the price of McChicken sandwiches. Likewise, in a world capital market of tens of trillions of dollars, even very large amounts of borrowing by the U.S. government might not be enough to have a significant effect on interest rates.

At this point, the smart people reading this chapter will point to Greece. Interest rates in Greece have increased dramatically since its economy's crisis. But the reason that interest rates in Greece have shot up is not the supply and demand of credit in the global economy. In reality, it is an assessment on the part of international investors that the Greek government is not trustworthy; it may not be able to pay back its loans. That is what is driving the interest rate increases in places like Greece. That is why we are seeing interest rates on government debt for some European nations begin to climb. That is why, historically, there are relatively high interest rates on government debt for developing countries, because these are the countries that have a greater history or likelihood of default. So it is the probability of default that is driving the higher interest rates, not the demand of government to borrow money. In fact, we have more government debt in the world today than ever before, and yet global interest rates are very low.

Of course, as with anything in economics, you always want to look at more than one factor. Interest rates are very low not in spite of government borrowing, but because the overall world economy is not that strong. There is a lot of capital in the world economy, but there is not that much demand for private investment, because governments are making policy mistakes that make it less likely that you can earn a profit by investing. If there are lots of savings and capital being *provided* (especially by the East Asian economies), but little being *demanded*, that is going to affect the world interest rate. That is why the cost of capital right now is very low even though the demand by governments to borrow is at record levels. To summarize, I do think that government borrowing puts upward pressure on interest rates, but I think that the reason some countries have very high interest costs is all about their risk of default, not the supply and demand of capital available for government borrowing.

I should probably note that if you had someone from the Congressional Budget Office writing this chapter, he would make a slightly different argument. The CBO would argue that even if interest rates aren't high, government borrowing has a very negative effect on the economy because it diverts capital from private to public uses. I wouldn't disagree with that, but the CBO analysis also acts as if this is only thing that matters. If you look at some of the Congressional Budget Office research, it will actually argue that higher tax rates are good for the economy. Why does the CBO argue that higher tax rates are good for the economy? Its argument supposes that if you have higher tax rates, they will lead to less government borrowing (or maybe even a government surplus), and that this means there is going to be more capital for the private sector, leading to more economic growth.

The CBO makes some sound arguments, but to assume that tax rates won't discourage economic growth is a mistake. I also think that the CBO is a little naive if it thinks that after raising tax rates, politicians will actually use the money to reduce deficits instead of just spending it (we will get to this a little later in the discussion).

There are many problems with the CBO's argument, but there is also some truth to it. Obviously, at some level, too much government borrowing will get an economy into trouble. Again, however, I want to stress what I said before: it is the *diversion of money from the productive sector of the economy* by government spending that—whether financed by borrowing or taxes—is what we should worry about.

One last thing about deficits and debt. There is some very influential research, and there are many follow-up studies associated with it, arguing that 90 percent of GDP is a critical level. Government debt, beyond that level, begins to have very negative consequences for economic growth. That analysis is based on cross-country data, aggregated together. I personally do not think that this is a magic number. Japan has government debt of 200 percent of GDP, and it hasn't hit the brick wall yet. I think that the Japanese will at some point, because of their demographics, but they have 200 percent of GDP as debt and they are still surviving. After World War II, we had 125 percent GDP government debt and it did not stop us from growing. England was over 200 percent GDP in debt after World War II and it did not stop the country from growing. On the other hand, Spain and Portugal have already gotten into trouble and required bailouts when they had government debt of only about 65 or 70 percent of GDP. So 90 percent of GDP might be an average, but you must also consider the characteristics of the country. Some countries will get into trouble at much lower levels; I can guarantee that Argentina would default well before it got to 90 percent GDP, whereas a country like Japan might survive just fine until it got to 300 percent GDP. It's hard to know.

Let's now shift to spending. I've already mentioned that government spending is the most important variable to consider, since it is government spending that diverts resources from the private sector. As with deficits and debt, there are multiple ways to measure the cost of government spending. There is the "diversion cost" (which, as I mentioned, is the fact that labor and capital are being allocated by politicians in Washington instead of entrepreneurs in the private sector), and there is the "extraction cost" (which is simply the measure of how government spending is financed, via taxes and borrowing). They both have specific negative costs on your economy, but there are other "micro-effects" of government spending as well.

The extraction and diversion costs apply to every single penny of government spending, but it is important to realize that not all government spending is created equal. Public finance economists break down government spending into categories. First, there is basic rule of law and institutional spending (providing the rule of law, the court system, etc.). Those types of spending are actually associated with better economic performance, because government is creating the environment that allows "chefs" in the private sector to mix labor and capital without having to worry about theft, expropriation, invasion, and the like. These core public goods (sound institutions, rule of law) are associated with better economic performance.

Another category is physical and human capital. What are physical and human capital? Roads are an example of physical capital; education is an example of human capital. We need to have a good infrastructure network and an educated workforce in order to achieve a healthy and growing economy.

The problem, though, is that governments usually do these things very inefficiently. Sure, the interstate highway system gave us a good return on our money, but building "bridges to nowhere" gives us a very bad return on our dollars. What do governments tend to do more of today? They tend to do more bridges to nowhere, earmarks, and pork-barrel spending. Thus, even though capital spending can be associated with better economic performance, physical capital spending can also be associated with *worse* economic performance if politicians misuse their appropriations authority.

Human capital is another example. We spend more per capita than any other country in the world on education. Yet if you measure all the industrialized economies in the world, we have one of the worst performances. It turns out that our monopoly-structured government school system is extraordinarily expensive and gets us a very low rate of return in exchange. If you look at countries like the Netherlands, Germany, and Sweden that have school choice systems, they spend a lot less and get much better results for the amount of money spent.

This is true for anything you do. Depending on how good a negotiator you are, you might go out and buy a car for a great price, or you might get ripped off. The problem with the way that the government is providing physical and human capital is that we, the taxpayers, are getting ripped off. We are paying a lot and getting very poor results. Even though we know that physical and human capital spending are very important for an economy, we should always ask whether it is important that they be provided by the inefficient system of our government.

There are two other types of government outlays: transfer spending and consumption spending.

Most of the academic research indicates that such spending is negatively associated with economic performance, because this is the kind of spending that tells people not to work as much (since the government will replace that income), and not to save or invest as much (since the government will take care of you). This is the type of spending that has terrible inefficiency and systematically encourages dependency. Unfortunately, this is actually the vast majority of what the federal government does.

The government also spends on things like regulatory agencies, which can be deceptively expensive for our economy. Our budget for the Securities and Exchange Commission (SEC), for instance, is about $1.5 billion dollars. But the cost imposed on the private sector by just one law alone, Sarbanes–Oxley, was approximately the same amount, and it applied to only one segment of the business community. Therefore, the amount of money that we actually spend on a regulatory agency is trivial when compared with the cost that the regulatory agency might be imposing on the overall economy. But, of course, remember our discussion on regulation; you have to figure out if the regulation is efficient or inefficient by looking at the cost-benefit structure.

Considering these issues of government spending in aggregate, it is important to consider the Rahn Curve (see below). The Rahn Curve is the spending version of the Laffer Curve; it argues that if government is not spending anything (isn't providing rule of law, infrastructure, or human and physical capital), then the economy will be very weak. In essence, you need some government spending in order to enable your economy to grow. But when government gets too big, the curve bends downward and government growth is associated with weaker economic performance. The research shows that once total government spending in an economy exceeds approximately 20 percent of GDP, it begins to be negatively related to prosperity. And today, federal, state, and local spending consumes

The Rahn Curve

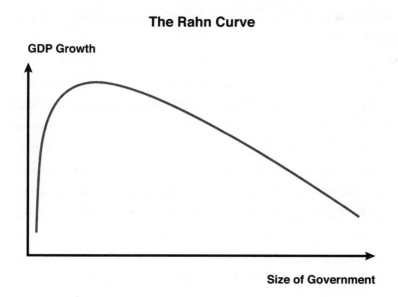

nearly 40 percent of GDP. (I actually think that the cutoff for government spending is empirically closer to 10 percent of GDP, but we don't have space to get into that.)

Let's now discuss Keynesianism and stimulus. Basically, the theory of Keynesianism is that you borrow money from some people and give it to other people. Here is a question to determine whether or not any of you are qualified to be a member of Congress: Who thinks that there is more money in the economy when that happens?

Keynesianism is the theory that taking money from the right pocket of your economy and putting it into the left pocket of your economy makes you richer as a result. It doesn't work. It didn't work for Hoover or Roosevelt in the 1930s, it didn't work for Japan in the 1990s, it didn't work for Bush in 2008, and it didn't work for Obama in 2009. Keynesianism is simply an excuse that the politicians have come up with, I think, to enable them to do what they truly like doing, which is spending money.

Let's now talk abut taxes. Remember the earlier discussion that not all government spending is created equal? This also applies for taxes; not all taxes are created equal. The Hong Kong flat tax, for instance, collects almost the same amount of money, as a share of GDP, as the U.S. income tax. Yet the Hong Kong flat tax is much less destructive to growth than the U.S. Internal Revenue Code. Hong Kong has a nice and simple 16 percent flat tax. The entire tax code is less than two hundred pages. The United States, by contrast, has this monstrosity of an Internal Revenue Code—74,000 pages of law and regulation, pervasive double taxation between the capital gains tax, corporate income tax, double tax on dividends, and the death tax. A single dollar of income can be taxed four different times.

Good public finance theory says that at any given amount of revenue a government wants to collect, it should collect at the lowest possible rate to achieve that amount. A government should not be double-taxing savings and investment. Every single economic theory (even socialism and Marxism) agrees on the importance of capital formation. If you don't have capital, labor isn't going to be productive, and that is what determines the health, prosperity, and vitality of the economy. Yet our tax system goes out of its way to penalize the provision of capital to the economy almost as if we deliberately designed a tax code to reduce our long-term growth rate.

We also have a monstrosity—a Rube Goldberg system of loopholes and exemptions, exclusions, deductions, credits, and shelters that winds up putting industrial policy into our system. In other words, the government, through the tax code, is being the chef, trying to determine how labor and capital get allocated. That necessarily means a less dynamic and less vital economy.

If you fix all of the problems in the tax code—if you have the lowest possible rate and you get rid of the double taxation and loopholes—what do you have? You have a flat tax. Or, to be more accurate, you have a single-rate consumption-based tax system. (When public finance economists refer to consumption-based tax systems, they are really just referring to a tax system in which income is taxed only one time. This is called the "consumption-based tax system.") The other model of taxation (which unfortunately is followed for the most part in Washington) is called the "Haig-Simons tax system," and that is the principle that not only should you tax income, but you should also tax net worth, changes in net worth, transfers of net worth, etc. This is where much of the double taxation in the tax code exists. If you want the right type of tax system, where you collect revenue while doing the least amount of damage to the economy, a consumption-based tax system with a low rate is much better than a Haig-Simons–based system of double taxation with high rates.

This, of course, gets into issues like "fairness." But fairness, like beauty, is in the eye of the beholder. Does fairness mean that you treat everyone equally? Or does fairness mean that you impose higher tax rates on individuals who are providing more output for the economy? There is a cost to the second definition of fairness; if you decide to go with the latter definition of fairness, it means that you are going to penalize the entrepreneurs, the people who produce the most per hour of labor they provide to the economy. They generate a much bigger amount of output. (In economics classes, that is known as the value of marginal product of labor. How productive you are per hour of work and how much wealth you can generate for an economy are what determine how much your wages are going to be in the long run.)

Let's look at some specific tax issues. Earlier, I mentioned the Laffer Curve. This is simply the notion that tax rates, at some point, can become so high that they are self-defeating. Here's the theory: at a 0 percent tax rate, the government collects nothing. At a 100 percent tax rate, the government also collects nothing. (Perhaps there are a few genetic socialists in the world who would still work and earn income even if the government took 100 percent of it, but for the most part a 100 percent tax rate would mean no revenue for government, and a 0 percent tax rate would also mean no revenue for government.) (See the Laffer Curve below.)

The real debate is over deciding which tax rate on the Laffer Curve corresponds to the revenue-maximizing point, and, more important, the growth-maximizing point. I personally do not want to maximize revenue for government, so I have never looked at the Laffer Curve and tried to find the point that gives politicians in Washington the most amount of money possible to spend. I care about the growth-maximizing tax rate. The growth-maximizing tax rate, in effect, automatically

The Laffer Curve

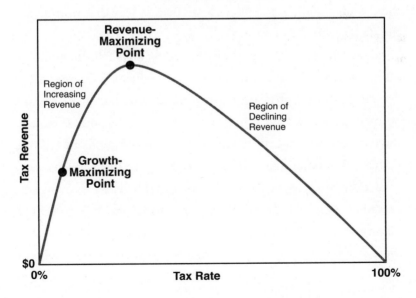

comes from the Rahn Curve and its growth-maximizing size of government. If the growth-maximizing size of government is 10 percent of GDP, for example, then you simply examine the Laffer Curve and find the least destructive way of collecting 10 percent of GDP. Or perhaps you think that the right level is 20 percent of GDP or 5 percent of GDP. Either way, your decision about what government should do and at what level government should do it should always come from the growth-maximizing point on the Rahn Curve.

If you want to honor what the Founding Fathers had in mind, then you will have a very limited central government. For much of our nation's history, the federal government spent only about 3 percent of GDP. Most government was at the state and local levels. So you have separate decisions: How does the federal government collect revenue, and how do state and local government collect revenue? In both cases, however, you want them to decide how to collect revenue in a way that minimizes the damage to the economy.

There are still a couple of other issues that I want to touch on quickly. One is the issue of "starve the beast." There is a big debate in Washington right now about whether taxes should be increased. We have a huge pile of red ink. You can look at the data and see that the reason we have this big pile of red ink is that government spending under Bush and Obama has exploded. If you look at taxes as a share of GDP, even without any extra tax increases, we are soon going to be above our average historical level of 18 percent of GDP. Therefore, I think that there is a very strong argument that 100 percent of the problem is on the spending side. Why on earth, then, would you want to have higher taxes?

But separate from that is the question of whether or not increasing tax rates is even capable of reducing the deficit. It turns out that when you raise taxes, you may simply encourage politicians to spend more money, making the fiscal situation worse. This is in part because the politicians spend more money, but also in part because of the Laffer Curve effects.

This is the situation in Europe. Forty or fifty years ago, the burden of government spending in Europe was similar to that in the United States. Over time, European countries kept raising taxes, and they also kept raising spending. This is why we have the "starve the beast–feed the beast" debate: Does cutting taxes reduce the size of government? During the Bush years, the answer was definitely no, so I wouldn't want to argue strongly that "starve the beast" always works, but the other side of the argument is "feed the beast." The evidence from Europe is clear. When European countries put in place the value-added taxes (which are their European form of a national sales tax), what happened? Before the VAT, and before the tax burden increased, there were southern European economies with medium-size government and big deficits and northern European economies with medium-size governments and small deficits. Now, they all have much higher tax burdens, they all have value-added taxes, and what do you find? You now have southern European economies with big governments and big deficits and northern European economies with big governments and small deficits. The only thing that has changed is that they have higher taxes, which only enabled, for all intents and purposes, a one-for-one trade-off of higher spending. What position you take in the "starve the beast–feed the beast" debate will say a lot about whether or not you think it is appropriate to give the politicians in Washington more revenue.

I just mentioned the value-added tax. I predict that the VAT is soon going to be a giant fight in Washington. Maybe not one year or two years from now, but somewhere in the next five to ten years, there is going to be a major fight over whether we should have this new levy. And the outcome of this battle will determine whether or not the politicians have a giant new source of revenue, as they did when they put the income tax into place in 1913. I fear another giant broad-based source of revenue would facilitate a leap to European-sized government. Whether that is a good leap or a bad leap depends on your underlying philosophy, but I personally think that it would be very unfortunate. We can certainly see what's happening in Europe now. Why would we want to copy their fiscal policy?

But the argument for a VAT is that, on a per-dollar-raised basis, it does less damage to your economy than higher income tax rates. This is true. If you have a pessimistic view that government will inevitably get bigger and that taxes will climb, a VAT would be the least damaging way for this to happen. But you should ask whether or not giving politicians a VAT will enable them to dramatically increase the size of government and the burden of government spending. In Europe, they enacted the VATs and used them as an excuse not only to raise spending, but also to raise standard income tax rates anyway, because they had to "maintain the distribution of the tax burden," in order to satisfy the left-wing definition of "fairness."

In the interest of space, I will discuss one last thing. Let's bring everything we've talked about—the history, the theory—all together and discuss where the political process is right now in Washington. There is basically a fight between the kind of vision proposed by Congressman Paul Ryan (the chairman of the House Budget Committee), which deals with fundamental reform of the entitlement programs, and the vision of those who oppose meaningful spending cuts and entitlement reform. If you look at the long-run forecast for the U.S. government, we are going to be Greece, plus some. Because of the demographics of an aging population, as well as the way our entitlement systems are structured, all the long-run fiscal forecasts show that government will become a far more expensive burden.

When Bill Clinton left office, the burden of federal government spending was 18.2 percent of GDP. Now, we are at 22 percent of GDP, a significant increase in the aggregate burden of government in just eleven or twelve years. Within the next several decades, as the baby boom generation fully retires, the federal government will consume approximately 40 percent of GDP (and perhaps even more, depending on which forecast you believe). Obviously, if you have a doubling in the size of government, it means that we are going to be more like Italy, France, Spain, and Greece, and that almost certainly is going to have very negative consequences on our GDP, employment levels, the amount of red ink that we have, and the type of tax system that we have.

I suppose this is a very pessimistic way to close this chapter. People who will be entering the workforce in the next couple of years face a dismal outlook. Assuming there is no reform, America will endure a period of Greek-style fiscal crisis during their prime earning years. This is why I am discussing the fight between visions. On the one hand, we have the budget prepared by House Budget Committee chairman Paul Ryan that restructures the entitlement programs. On the other hand, we have the vision of Bush and Obama of making government bigger and adding new entitlements. That vision, I think, basically puts us on a path to becoming Greece. But I want to be fair; it could also put us on the path to becoming Sweden. The northern European economies do the welfare state in a much more responsible way. So if you want a welfare state, you had better make sure that we wind up like Sweden, not like Greece. My personal fear is that our political system is much more likely to give us Greek-style results, not Swedish-style results.

But if we happen to do entitlement program reforms—block granting Medicaid to the states, restructuring Medicare so that it resembles a voucher system like what members of Congress have for their own health care, doing personal retirement accounts for Social Security as thirty-plus countries around the world have done—then this projection of ever rising costs of government spending could actually curve downward.

I will leave you with this: the most appropriate way to evaluate fiscal policy is something that I have very humbly named after myself. I call it "Mitchell's Golden Rule." Mitchell's Golden Rule is very simple: government spending should grow more slowly than the private economy. Notice that I am not focusing on balancing the budget. I am not talking about deficits and debt. I am focusing on the underlying disease, not the symptom. If I go to a doctor and I have a headache, and it turns out that I have a brain tumor, I do not want the doctor to give me aspirin for my headache. I want him to deal with the tumor, because I want to actually solve the problem. Likewise, if you have an economy where the private sector is growing faster than the government, sooner or later it is a mathematical certainty that you will balance your budget, even though that should not be your first priority. Your first priority should be making sure that you have government as a small share of the economy. If those two lines are reversed, however, and government is growing faster than the private economy, sooner or later it is a mathematical certainty that you become the next Greece.

And that is really what our future is all about, because there is no way taxes can ever keep up with spending if the public sector is growing faster than the private economy. This is because the private economy is your tax base. Greece got into trouble, the rest of Europe has gotten into trouble, and the United States is on the path to trouble because we all suffer from the same problem: government has been growing faster than the private sector.

In closing, our country needs to go back to the policies under Reagan and Clinton, where those lines of private- and public-sector growth were reversed. At that time, the private economy was growing faster than the government. In my mind, that is the path to virtue.

CHAPTER 12

◆ ◆ ◆

The modern conservative movement is divided on foreign policy. On one side are the conservatives who argue that America must stop acting as the world's policeman and minimize its foreign commitments. Conservatives holding this position are opposed to nation building and possibly also foreign aid, sometimes for ideological reasons and more often for fiscal ones. This non-interventionist viewpoint is often held by libertarians and may be called "isolationist" by its opponents.

On the other side are the national security conservatives, sometimes called "national security hawks," who have our nation's foreign policy and domestic security as their core issues. National security conservatives argue that where a material American interest is at stake, America must act swiftly and boldly. And they look at American interests more broadly, when compared with non-interventionists.

National security conservatives tend to be strong supporters of the state of Israel, which is a majority American position that is held by many on the left as well. While the national security conservative viewpoint is largely consistent with neoconservative foreign policy, not all national security conservatives consider themselves neoconservatives. And many do not share the history of the original neoconservatives who defected from the Left to become conservatives.

Former secretary of defense Donald Rumsfeld is considered by many within and outside the conservative movement to personify the national security conservative viewpoint. In this essay, Secretary Rumsfeld shares his profound personal insights into the Bush administration's foreign policy including the Iraq War and the War on Terror.

Donald Rumsfeld has served as both the youngest and the oldest secretary of defense, first under President Gerald Ford, and then under George W. Bush a quarter century after. A former naval aviator, Secretary Rumsfeld previously served as U.S. congressman, U.S. ambassador to NATO, White House chief of staff, special presidential envoy to the Middle East, and chief executive of two Fortune 500 companies. Secretary Rumsfeld chairs the nonprofit Rumsfeld Foundation with his wife, Joyce.

THE BUSH DOCTRINE, COMPASSIONATE CONSERVATISM, AND THE WAR ON TERROR

Donald Rumsfeld

◆ ◆ ◆

The twenty-first century brought with it not only the promise of the Information Age and the power of instantaneous communication and 24/7 media, but also the peril that civilization's enemies could harness these tools to subvert and attack the free societies that gave rise to information technology. Where some could create and use Wikipedia to share knowledge on just about every conceivable topic, others could create and use Wikileaks to post sensitive and classified documents endangering U.S. diplomatic, intelligence, and military operations. Where some could use Twitter and Facebook to gather by the thousands to protest authoritarianism as we saw across the Middle East during the so-called Arab Spring, others could use social media to spread propaganda of hate and radicalism. While the Information Age has opened avenues of expression to parts of the world that have not known free speech before, it has also made free societies more vulnerable to intimidation and terrorism than ever before.

That was the central challenge those of us in the Bush administration faced in the days after 9/11. The goal of the nineteen hijackers who boarded commercial aircraft the morning of September 11 was to inflict mass casualties but also to usher in an era of terrorism that would cause America to cease being the free, civil-liberty-minded society it has been since its founding. Maintaining the liberal, pluralistic, open society enshrined in our Constitution has long been the paradox in American conservatism. From my vantage point, that remained our task in an era when terrorists could use weapons of mass destruction to kill, terrorize, and force Americans to give up their freedoms. As Lenin wrote with characteristic terseness, "The purpose of terrorism is to terrorize." It's not to kill people. It's to terrorize. It is to alter behavior. With 9/11, al-Qaida sought to alter the behavior of our entire society by instilling fear that no one was safe. The intelligence we were receiving was clear that the group wanted to inflict yet more deadly attacks on the American people.

My earliest experience with terrorism came when President Reagan asked me to serve as his Middle East envoy after 241 marines and navy corpsmen were killed in 1983. A truck loaded with explosives drove into the barracks in Beirut. I received a call from the secretary of state, George Shultz, asking me to take a leave of absence from the pharmaceutical company I was running. Dealing with terrorism was a new experience for me. I'd served in the Pentagon during the Cold War, but this was something that was notably different from the Cold War.

After the attack on the marine barracks, the next day our forces put revetments around all the buildings. What did that do? Nothing: terrorists started lobbing rocket grenades over the revetments. The next place they attacked was the U.S. embassy in Beirut, which had a wire mesh hung over it to bounce the rocket-propelled grenades off. Sounds logical. But for every offense, there's a defense; for every defense, there's an offense. So what did the terrorists do? The next thing they did was to start hitting soft targets, people going to and from work.

The point is that there isn't any way to simply defend. That reality leads anyone with an ounce of sense to understand that you have to go on offense. The only way you can deal with that problem is *not* to treat it like a criminal act, where once it happens, you're going to try to capture the person, put him in jail, and punish him—or more likely, indict him in absentia because you can't find him. Those are the lessons I came away with way back in the early 1980s.

THE BUSH ADMINISTRATION

Shortly before the 2000 election, Governor Bush spoke here at The Citadel and talked about the future. He argued for the need to bring the military, the armed forces of the United States, into the twenty-first century, out of the Industrial Age and into the Information Age. Then came 9/11: the attack on the seat of economic power in New York, the attack on the seat of military power in the Pentagon—and except for the courage of the passengers on the flight that crashed in Shanksville, Pennsylvania, undoubtedly, the terrorists intended an attack on the seat of political power, either the White House or the U.S. Capitol.

It was a day none of us will ever forget. The president of the United States properly recognized that the purpose of terrorism was to terrorize, to try to alter our behavior and cause us to change the way we live. He made a decision that was notably different from those made by earlier administrations of both political parties: he decided that we had to go on offense, declaring that terrorism could no longer be considered something to be solved through law enforcement. It was something that required a new approach. President Bush understood this immediately. Given the lethality of weapons in this new century and the risk that a terrorist attack could result in not 3,000 people killed but 300,000, 9/11 caused him to conclude that he had to declare a war on terrorism.

I remember a week or two after 9/11 I went to the Middle East and Central Asia to secure overflight and basing rights for our coming campaign in Afghanistan. One of the nations I visited was Oman, where I met with Sultan Qaboos. He had decamped to the desert, where he apparently regularly met with his constituents. It must have been 140 degrees in the tent. He sat there without any visible reaction to the heat, while we perspired through three layers of our clothes. British-trained, he spoke English perfectly. He said something to the effect that the attacks of 9/11 may have been a "blessing in disguise, as terrible as they were." Not sure what he meant, I asked, "In what sense?" He said, "It may be the wake-up call for your country and the world so we will take actions and work together in ways that will be able to prevent not three thousand, but three hundred thousand, or three million people from being killed, as a result of the use of more powerful and more lethal weapons."

President Bush had to do everything conceivable not just to defend, but also to make everything that terrorists do harder: make it harder for them to move around between countries, harder to talk on the phone, harder to raise funds through their financial networks, harder to find a country willing to house them and be hospitable to their planning and training and launching of attacks on free people. Around that time, Johns Hopkins University organized an exercise called Dark Winter, which would give a scientific basis to Sultan Qaboos's point. The participants theorized about a biological attack with a smallpox outbreak in three locations in the United States. Within a year, that independent study concluded that there would be up to one million Americans dead as a result. There was likely to be martial law, states guarding their boundaries. When I grew up, if you had smallpox, chicken pox, or measles, the authorities would put a "quarantine" sign on your house; you weren't allowed to go out, and no one was allowed to go in. Well, you can imagine our entire country doing that because of a fear of smallpox.

This was very much on President Bush's mind. So we went to work to put in place a set of structures so that we could preserve our free way of life, so that we could avoid the hard choices that might accompany a major chemical, biological, or nuclear terrorist attack. One was the Patriot Act and an update to surveillance programs, some of whose existence has been leaked on the front pages of our newspapers. Another was Guantánamo Bay and military commissions, which had been a practice of our country since George Washington. Our armed forces had experience managing detentions of prisoners of war—POWs—people who wore uniforms, carried their weapons openly, and had a command structure. The terrorists being captured were not POWs because they violated these basic laws of warfare, so therefore they were not entitled to the rights and privileges that went with POW status. They were enemy combatants who were entitled to humane treatment, but the Justice Department argued that we also had a right to ask them questions and interrogate them. It is worth noting that despite campaign rhetoric to the contrary, President Barack Obama has kept in place these structures.

Another concept that President Bush and his administration embraced as part of the War on Terror was anticipatory self-defense, or preemption. It is a fundamental tenet of international law to respect national borders; every country has the right to do what is needed within its own country—unless it is threatened by another country. The right of self-defense is an equally fundamental tenet of international law. The question becomes not *if* but *when* a nation has a right to take action to stop an attack originating from outside it. The idea of waiting until you're attacked to defend yourself is one thing if someone's going to come across your border with conventional forces. It is quite another thing if you're going to be attacked with weapons of mass destruction. In that case, no responsible leader would wait until attacked. That caused President Bush to consider anticipatory self-defense and the realization that if you wait, it's too late. That is a difficult calculation, particularly given the unevenness of intelligence and the difficulty of the intelligence gatherers' tasks.

Another challenge that came up was the issue of language.

Take, for instance, the phrase *War on Terror*. First, if you say "war," it sounds as if you are going to win with bullets, that the task is conventional, and, as such, it's a problem for the Department of Defense. In fact, it is something quite different. It's not going to be won with bullets. It's much more like the Cold War, a battle of ideology and a competition of ideas, and it will take all elements of national power to prevail. I argued that the phrase *War on Terror* might mislead people and cause them to expect things that aren't realistic. I struggled with trying to come up with a better phrase, and I failed. I thought about *A Struggle Against Violent Extremists*, but the president stuck with *War on Terror*.

Even more problematic was the unwillingness of many in and out of government to identify the enemy, a problem that is even worse today. If you think about it, in the Cold War, communism was identified as the enemy. We pinned the tail on the donkey. We talked about it; we said what communism did, how it didn't work, how command economies were inefficient, how unfree political systems were not the kind of systems that unleashed human energy and creativity. In this new war, I worried that we weren't calling our enemies what they really are: radical Islamists.

Too many in the Bush and Obama administrations have been unwilling to say so. Somebody asked me one day, "What kind of grade do you give the Bush administration on the subject of competing in the competition of ideas?" I said, "Well, I'm an easy grader and I'd give us a D." Too many were nervous about being seen as being against a religion. Maybe that's understandable, because we are not against any religion. A large fraction of people on the face of the earth are Muslim. But the fact remains that it is a relatively small group of Islamists in that religion who are the extremists and who are training people to kill innocent men, women, and children, and we make a serious mistake by not saying it, by not calling it what it is. The idea of imposing a caliphate and imposing that particular set of views and behavior patterns on the world is something that has to be resisted and argued against. I don't believe we can achieve success unless we are willing to say what it is, identify it, and find ways to help other Muslims to resist the extremists.

We have to be patient. This struggle is not going to end like World War II with a signing ceremony on the USS *Missouri*. It isn't going to end in two or three years. It will take time. The Cold War took decades. We have to expect that this struggle is going to take decades.

THE "FREEDOM AGENDA"

There were discussions inside the administration about the importance of promoting democracy as an element of national security strategy. President Bush made democracy promotion a centerpiece of his foreign policy, especially in his second term. "It is the policy of the United States to seek and support the growth of democratic movements and institutions in every nation and culture, with the ultimate goal of ending tyranny in our world," he declared on the steps of the Capitol in his second Inaugural Address.

That's a tall order. And some individuals frequently interchange the word *freedom* with the word *democracy*. When the word *democracy* is used outside our country, I've long been concerned that the risk is that people think we are trying to impose our particular model of democracy on the rest of the world, and most people don't want to have our template or any foreign template imposed on them. They know they have different cultures, different histories, different neighbors, and different circumstances. I kept trying to push, within the administration, the use of the phrases *freer political systems* and *freer economic systems* instead of the word *democracy*.

There was and remains a divide among conservatives about whether to promote democracy as a matter of national security. The divide dates back to the Cold War when a group who self-identified as "neoconservatives" opposed the Nixon and Kissinger policies of détente with the Soviet Union. They argued for policies that made human rights and governance central to U.S. policy toward the Soviet Union. I was sympathetic to this view, especially during the Cold War, although I wondered whether culture and history might be more determinative of the makeup of foreign governments than the Western tradition of liberty, which has evolved considerably in the past three hundred years.

For example, in Uzbekistan, the United States faced an important question: what to do after violence broke out in the country and the Uzbek government put it down. I had been in Uzbekistan and met with President Karimov. He had agreed to let us use his base to put Special Forces in Afghanistan. He was cooperative even against Russian pressures. It was an enormous advantage for us. We couldn't get to Afghanistan from the sea.

We needed Karimov's cooperation; that said, I had no illusions about his democratic aspirations. What was important was that he was moving in a positive direction. He had been a politburo member in the old Soviet Union.

In 2005, a group of Islamists stormed a prison in the country. The government stepped in and put the revolt down. Nongovernmental organizations and human rights groups began issuing condemnations of the Uzbek government. They became judgmental, I believe, before all of the facts were assembled. Then the State Department and members of Congress criticized Karimov. I knew I didn't know the facts. We do know what the result of the U.S. government action was. The result was that the president of Uzbekistan threw U.S. forces out of the base we were using. He said, "We now know who our friends are," and then moved back into the Russian sphere of influence. That action did not advance U.S. interests or, for that matter, human rights in the country. Rather, it was a setback to human rights as well as for our national security.

Now, what does this example suggest? My view is that if someone is on what we consider the wrong side, but is moving in the right direction, improving on human rights, moving toward freer political and freer economic systems, that's a good thing and we ought to encourage it. That was the case with Uzbekistan. But, instead, the United States stuck a stick in President Karimov's eye. We disadvantaged our country from a security standpoint, and we disadvantaged the people of Uzbekistan by causing them to move back toward Russia and not maintaining the progress with respect to human rights and toward freer political and economic systems.

Uzbekistan isn't the only country to move through a transition. Consider what America went through. The United States had slaves into the 1800s. Women didn't vote until the 1900s. We had a Civil War that killed six hundred thousand human beings. We didn't arrive the way we are today. We are still evolving. Those countries are still evolving. They don't go from a dictatorial system to a free system in five minutes; it's a tough journey, a very tough journey. It has been a tough journey for our country, but we've made enormous progress.

However, we seem not to have the same patience with other countries. In Pakistan, President Musharraf stepped up, supporting us and the War on Terror. But our State Department decided that it was important for Musharraf to go to work in civilian clothes instead of in his army uniform. Our president goes to work in civilian clothes; why shouldn't every country's president be a civilian? So the department pointed a finger and told him he should get out of the army. He did, and he was thrown out of the country. The result was that the civilian government that replaced him is weaker and less helpful, and today in Pakistan we run the risk of a failed state with nuclear weapons.

It seems to me that we should use judgment and balance. We should not expect perfection and we should not expect other countries to be exactly as we are today, because we weren't as we are today over much of our history. What is important is to look to see in which direction countries are moving, and hope that they're moving in a positive direction and encourage that, rather than judging that they are not perfect, criticizing them, and causing them to reverse course and move backward, rather than continuing forward, even if in a pace we consider slow.

WAR IN THE INFORMATION AGE

Afghanistan and Iraq were the first wars waged in the Information Age. These wars have been fought in a circumstance notably different from World War II, Korea, or even Vietnam. BlackBerries, iPhones, YouTube, and Sony video cameras mean that information moves instantaneously around the world. These advances have changed everything. We still haven't fully adjusted to the Information Age when it comes to warfare and national security.

At any given moment of the day or night, something's going on in the world that makes a difference to the United States of America. I'll offer one example. There was a report in *Newsweek* that a Koran had been flushed down a toilet at Guantánamo Bay, and there were riots in three countries where people were killed as a result of that report. As was said more than a hundred years ago by Mark Twain, "A lie travels halfway around the world while the truth is still putting on its shoes."

We can't lie. Terrorists can lie. So what happened after the Koran incident? *Newsweek* investigated and concluded that in truth it had never happened. The editors ran a retraction. They said they were sorry. Sorry? People were dead.

On a related media story, when people in the United States are asked, "How many people were waterboarded at Guantánamo?" answers vary widely. Some say, "A hundred or two hundred." Some answer, "Ten or fifteen." Others say, "I think I read three might have been." But the answer is: none. Zero. Not a single human being was waterboarded by the U.S. Armed Forces in Guantánamo, for the purposes of interrogation. The CIA, not the Department of Defense, *did* waterboard three people. But think of how it all has been inaccurately conflated because of irresponsible and sloppy reporting.

Today's news correspondents are under constant pressure to produce exclusives and breaking stories. Daily or weekly deadlines have turned into updates by the hour, even by the minute, to feed the insatiable demand of 24/7 cable news and Internet audiences. Terrorists have skillfully adapted to fighting wars in today's media age. Our country has not. Our enemies routinely twist the truth and launch attacks designed to attract headlines. Terrorist groups have media committees. The Taliban in Afghanistan have a Twitter account. Ayman al-Zawahiri once said, "More than half of this battle is taking place in the battlefield of the media. We are in the media battle in a race for the hearts and minds of Muslims."

The challenge of this glut of information is sifting through it and making the right judgment calls about what is true and what is not. Fortunately, the proliferation of technology and media means new alternatives and ways of getting information. Americans are no longer dependent on the three major networks and the *New York Times* to get the news. We have talk radio and blogs and cable news. The American people have sound inner gyroscopes. Over time, they come to the right decisions.

Another element of warfare in the Information Age is the prevalence of lawyers and the growth of a new phenomenon called "lawfare." Increasingly, our enemies are aided by headline-seeking lawyers and rogue prosecutors who are using the concept of "universal jurisdiction" to file lawsuits against U.S. government officials and military personnel. They file lawsuits in foreign courts hoping that a lone judge or prosecutor might take up the case and create an international incident. It's another way of creating an asymmetric advantage so that even if terrorists can't win on the battlefield they have a chance to win or at least to harass in courts. They're putting American officials and intelligence officials at risk of legal action in an attempt to intimidate them and their families and to sway policy decisions in their own favor. It is, in effect, an attempt to criminalize policy differences. It's a trend that tends to subordinate the American people and their elected leaders' actions, as well as the U.S. military, to foreign courts and rogue prosecutors. This is a growing threat to American sovereignty.

I was at a NATO meeting in Brussels and read in the paper that the Belgian Parliament had passed a law that allowed anyone in a foreign military to be prosecuted in Belgian courts. I thought, "We can't have military people go to Belgium, where NATO is located, if any rogue prosecutor can decide he wants to enhance his image by filing a lawsuit." In fact, one did file a suit against General Tom Franks, the U.S. CENTCOM commander. So I called the Belgian defense minister, and, not being a diplomat, I was not very diplomatic. I explained that the NATO headquarters did not have to be in Belgium and that if the Belgian government persisted, American personnel—military and civilian—would not come to Belgium. Within a matter of weeks, the legislation was repealed, nullified, and withdrawn.

But Belgium was just the beginning. Lawfare is a danger, not just for the United States but for the world. Consider the contribution our military made in the 2004 tsunami in Indonesia. Consider what we did during the earthquakes in Pakistan. Anytime the UN, the Organization of American States, or other international organizations are faced with a humanitarian crisis, they come to the U.S. Department of Defense and ask for help, and we provide it—generously and repeatedly. We wouldn't be able help others if this "universal jurisdiction" practice continues to grow. We wouldn't send U.S. military personnel on humanitarian missions if they could be prosecuted in foreign courts around the world. Even President Barack Obama, who had been personally authorizing drone strikes that kill people, would be vulnerable to such suits. I am convinced that if lawfare continues, it will inevitably lead to isolationism on the part of our country.

REFRESHING AMERICAN INSTITUTIONS

It may seem unusual to hear this from a conservative, but the fact is that the institutions created at the inflection point of the end of World War II and the beginning of the Cold War, during the Truman administration, are in need of repair and adjustment. They are in need of reform to be better able to contribute to stability in an era in which there is no longer the Soviet Union or a bipolar world. We are also in need of an update of our own national security institutions, which were created for a different age. Here at home, the Defense Department, the CIA, and the National Security Council were established after World War II. Internationally, the World Bank, the

International Monetary Fund, and the North Atlantic Treaty Organization all were established during that period.

In the 1990s, we reached another inflection point—the end of the Cold War and the beginning of the Information Age. But we have not moved forward to adjust those institutions— either here at home or within international agencies—to fit the twenty-first century. The changes and updates that have been made are, for the most part, only on the margins. NATO has seen some changes; it's been enlarged. The Defense Department has made some changes with the Goldwater-Nichols legislation. In the old days, Bolling Air Force Base was built right next to Anacostia Naval Air Station. Two air stations within fifteen seconds of each other. Separate runways, separate air controllers, separate security. This was a model of inefficiency rather than jointness. Thanks to Goldwater-Nichols, today we are fashioning a joint force and achieving leverage that is critically important. I believe we would benefit from a new Hoover Commission, as we had in the 1940s and '50s, to look at our national security and international institutions and make recommendations to bring them into the twenty-first century.

The problems we face in the world are not problems that are going to be solved by one nation—challenges such as the proliferation of weapons of mass destruction, piracy, terrorism, and drug trafficking. They will require us to work closely with other countries.

Necessity is the mother of invention. Fear does focus the mind. The events of 9/11, the number of terrorist activities at various places around the world, and the recognition of the growing lethality of weapons today have changed leaders' margins for error. The prospect that our country is facing growing and new challenges is registering on our people.

What's unique about American conservatism, at least in contrast to its European cousin, is that what it seeks to preserve isn't really conservative at all. American conservatives don't want to conserve monarchy or a church. They want to conserve our founding ideals enshrined in the Declaration of Independence and Constitution—ideals that by most standards are liberal, even radical some might say. The belief in the rights of the individual over the rights of the government is what unites American conservatism and what will propel it forward in this still new century, uniting libertarians, social conservatives, and the growing number of independents and Democrats who are witnessing the unparalleled growth and expansion of the federal government and increasingly questioning whether we are getting satisfactory results given the exorbitant costs.

There is a danger, however, that our country could reach a tipping point where behavior patterns alter the direction of our great country permanently away from the constitutional principles and toward big government. I had an Asian leader say to me, "I never thought I'd see the day when adults in the White House would be modeling America on Europe." That's a model, suffice it to say, that is not working.

I was in college in 1954 and Governor Adlai Stevenson gave a speech to my senior class. He said,

The power, for good or evil, of this American political organization is virtually beyond measurement. The decision it makes, the uses to which it devotes its immense resources, the leadership it provides on moral as well as material questions, all appear likely to determine the fate of the modern world. You dare not, if I may say so, withhold your attention. For if you do, if those young Americans who have the advantage of education, perspective, and self-discipline do not participate to the fullest extent of their ability, America will stumble, and if America stumbles the world falls.

Those words are as true today as they were then. That is our challenge. That is our responsibility.

CHAPTER 13

◆ ◆ ◆

As we have seen, centuries of Anglo-American history and faith inform the American conservative tradition and its core principles. A Judeo-Christian frame of reference was shared by all the American Founders. Even in our Declaration of Independence, the Founders specifically refer to "the Laws of Nature and of Nature's God" as giving men the right to separate from and dissolve their political bonds with England.

Social conservatism remains a prerequisite for mainstream Republican candidates, but it is also considered an uncomfortable legacy by some within the Republican Party. Many coastal Republicans, including some who provide a lot of support for the party, seem to prefer candidates who either are not socially conservative or sublimate their social conservatism in favor of economic conservatism or national security issues. At the same time, social conservatives form a larger and larger part of the Republican electoral base.

Grassroots political organizer Ralph Reed tells the

story of how evangelical Christians came to work with the Republican Party, ultimately becoming a very central part of the party's base. He shows us that the heart of the conservative movement still lies with traditional morality, and the role of religious conservatives in electing Republican candidates is larger than ever.

Ralph E. Reed Jr. is founder and chairman of the Faith and Freedom Coalition, a grassroots public policy organization with 700,000 members and activists in 400 local chapters nationwide. As executive director of the Christian Coalition from 1989 to 1997, he built one of the most effective public policy organizations in modern history. Reed was named one of the twenty most influential leaders of his generation by *Life* magazine and one of the fifty future leaders of America by *Time*. The *Wall Street Journal* called him "perhaps the finest political operative of his generation." Ralph Reed is chairman and CEO of Century Strategies, a public relations and public affairs firm. In 2000 and 2004 he served as a senior adviser to George W. Bush's presidential campaigns. Reed earned a bachelor's degree from the University of Georgia and a Ph.D. in history from Emory University.

HOW SOCIAL CONSERVATISM
CAN WIN

Ralph E. Reed

◆ ◆ ◆

I first became involved in the religious conservative movement in 1983 when I made a personal decision for Christ. At the time, I was the executive director of the College Republican National Committee working to organize students on the college campuses for Ronald Reagan's 1984 reelection campaign. After my faith experience, I felt a burden to organize as many Christian young people as I could to become involved in the pro-family movement and to work for Reagan's reelection. Those of us who were inspired by Reagan and felt the generational pull of the conservative agenda were, figuratively, the mirror image of the hippies, the Yippies, the Students for a Democratic Society, and other radical groups who protested the Vietnam War and drove Lyndon Johnson from office in 1968. One publication called us the "Red Dawn generation," after the movie that portrayed young patriots opposing a fictional Soviet invasion of the United States. The film developed a cult following among campus conservatives.

Reagan won his strongest level of support among any age

group in the electorate from eighteen- to twenty-four-year-olds, meaning the oldest man ever to occupy the Oval Office did best among the youngest voting cohort. This phenomenon befuddled many political analysts. But for those of us who came of political age in the late 1970s and '80s, it was an issue of whether America's best days would still be ahead or were behind us. Our commitment to Reagan and conservatism arose out of the searing experience of the failed presidency of Jimmy Carter, stagflation, the Soviet invasion of Afghanistan, the taking of U.S. hostages in Iran, and our country doubting its exceptional role in the world after Vietnam. This was particularly true among evangelical youth, who identified with Reagan because of his faith and his pro-life stance.

In September 1989, I was invited by Pat Robertson to attend a meeting of evangelical leaders held in Atlanta to chart the course of the movement after Reagan. I had met Pat at the inauguration of George H. W. Bush, and we were coincidentally seated next to each other at a dinner, where we had a spirited conversation about his recent presidential campaign, what he planned to do next, and the future of the pro-family cause. As a graduate student at Emory University working on my dissertation, I was a little surprised to be included in a meeting with such evangelical luminaries as D. James Kennedy and Tim and Beverly LaHaye. At the conclusion of the meeting, Robertson introduced me as the executive director of an organization that as yet had no name, which became the Christian Coalition. This meeting occurred two months after Jerry Falwell's closing of the Moral Majority, which he announced at the Southern Baptist Convention annual meeting in Las Vegas.

Many predicted that the religious right was dead. They could not have been more wrong. Within a few years the Christian Coalition had over two million members and activists in over three thousand local chapters. In 1994, the Christian Coalition distributed over forty million pieces of voter education literature and helped turn out a record number of evangelical voters, a net gain of nine million votes over the 1990 baseline. This contributed to the election of the first Republican majority in the House and the Senate at the same time in forty years.

Clearly, to paraphrase Mark Twain, the premature reports of our death were greatly exaggerated. This remains true today. Indeed, in the aftermath of the 2012 election results and the recent Supreme Court opinions on marriage, there are some who are repeating this error and suggesting that evangelicalism is a movement in decline. But as we shall see, the opinion elites always underestimate both the persistence and resilience of people of faith engaged in civic affairs.

It is difficult to overstate what a significant religious, cultural, and political development the rise of the religious conservative movement really was in American history. In 1976, when Jimmy Carter became the first candidate from the Deep South elected to the presidency since before the Civil War, he won two-thirds of the evangelical vote. Four years later, Ronald Reagan won 64 percent of the evangelical vote. This constituted an astonishing seismic shift in the party loyalty of a constituency that represented at least one out of every five voters. Carter went from carrying every state in the South except Virginia in 1976 to losing every state in the South except his home state of Georgia in 1980. This was due primarily to the dramatic change in the voting pattern of evangelicals. The Reagan coalition, which has proved to be among the most durable in American political history, is inconceivable and could not have succeeded without these voters.

Political engagement was not something evangelicals sought. From the time of the Scopes Trial in 1925, the so-called Monkey Trial, when a high school teacher, John T. Scopes, was convicted in Dayton, Tennessee, for violating Tennessee state law and teaching the theory of evolution in a science class, then saw his conviction overturned by an appellate court, until the mid-1970s, evangelicals lived in a kind of self-imposed political exile in their own country. As historian Edward Larson has documented, after the Scopes trial, *fundamentalism* became a term of aspersion in American culture, leading evangelicals to build a separate and distinct subculture of schools, colleges, seminaries, publications, and media outlets.[1] They largely withdrew from politics on a national level, a retreat that lasted for two generations and spanned two world wars, one hot, and the other cold. They reeled from their defeat in the debate over evolution. They smarted from the crude caricature drawn of them by harsh critics like H. L. Mencken, who denounced them as boobs and yokels and morons and accused them of polluting their society with what he called, and I quote, "theological bilge." They were buffeted by the twin forces of modernity and ascendant liberal theology. These evangelicals and fundamentalists, who from their rise during the Second Great Awakening in the 1830s and 1840s, throughout the nineteenth century and well into the twentieth century, played a central and pivotal role in American culture, education, and civic life, undertook a systematic and deliberate retreat from public life.

The failure and ultimate repeal of Prohibition, eight years after the Scopes Trial, seemed to signal their final humiliation. And for the next forty years, even though they were over forty million strong, they existed as a nation within a nation, a society within a society, and a people within a people, turning inward, building their own educational, cultural, and church-related institutions. Their isolation was so complete that it didn't come to an end even when the Supreme Court declared the New York Regents' prayer unconstitutional in the *Engel v. Vitale* case in 1963. It didn't end with the *Roe v. Wade* decision a decade later.

If one looks at the history of *Roe*, what is most striking, especially given what happened later, is the relative quiescence of the evangelical community at the time the Supreme Court rendered its decision. Certainly most evangelicals disagreed with the decision, but at the time abortion was not viewed as a political issue. In 1967, when then-governor Ronald Reagan signed California's Therapeutic Abortion Act, which became a model for other states seeking to liberalize their abortion laws prior to *Roe*, the issue had little resonance in evangelical churches. Most viewed abortion as a personal issue outside the realm of politics. Moreover, evangelicals had no grassroots organizations to oppose abortion on demand because they had been allowed to wither away in the previous forty years. Thus, the primary opposition to *Roe v. Wade* and the chief impetus for a human life constitutional amendment protecting unborn children came from the U.S. Conference of Catholic Bishops.

Ironically, what ended their political exile was their disappointment with one of their own, Jimmy Carter, the most
explicitly evangelical president since Woodrow Wilson and a
devout Southern Baptist. Carter taught Sunday school each
week at a Baptist church in Plains, Georgia. He was the first
president in modern times to say he was "born again," a phrase
that many Americans, and even more journalists, were unfa-
miliar with at the time. The virtually unknown Carter's victory in the 1976 Democratic primaries over more prominent
and established candidates like Hubert Humphrey and Henry
"Scoop" Jackson and in the general election over Gerald Ford
is the stuff of legend. In the post-Watergate period, Carter's
religious faith, his emphasis on piety and moral character, and
his promise to "never tell the American people a lie," a promise
made more compelling by his faith journey, were critical to his
appeal as a candidate. So striking was Carter's unabashed evangelicalism after decades of candidates treating their faith as a
private issue that after his election, *Newsweek* put Carter on the
cover and declared that 1976 was "the year of the evangelical."

Given Ford's defeat of Reagan at the Republican Convention in Kansas City in 1976 and his pro-choice views, evangelical leaders such as Lou Sheldon with the Traditional Values
Coalition and Pat Robertson either met with Carter, expressed
some sympathy for his candidacy, or openly supported him. It
didn't take long for them to be disappointed, and their disappointment reached a peak in 1978 when the Treasury Department proposed regulations requiring Christian schools across
the United States to demonstrate that they were not functioning as segregated academies seeking to sidestep court-ordered

desegregation—or lose their tax-exempt status. These regulations were a dagger aimed at the heart of Christian education in the country and evangelical ministries and churches expressed outrage. Over one hundred thousand letters descended on the White House and the Treasury Department, which quickly withdrew the regulations to try to contain the political damage. Evangelicals viewed the episode as an act of open hostility against their churches and schools by the administration of a coreligionist, a betrayal (added to a long list of others) they could not ignore. Though Carter undertook some feeble and belated attempts to mend fences, evangelical leaders began to search for a new political leader.

They found one in the unlikely person of Ronald Reagan, a former liberal Democrat, a former union president, a former B-grade actor who rarely attended church services, and the first divorced man ever to win a major party nomination. When asked if he was born again, Reagan said that they did not use the term in his church. But make no mistake: Ronald Reagan was a genuinely historic figure for evangelical Christians. First, he was a man of deep faith in God, a faith first inculcated in him by his mother, who took him to church and gave him devotional books to read, providing solace and comfort in the home of an alcoholic father who engaged in binge drinking, disappeared frequently, and lost jobs because of his drinking.

Reagan also believed that he had a mission and purpose in life: to defeat Soviet communism. And he held the strongly pro-life, pro-family, and traditionalist views that became the touchstone of the religious conservative movement. After formally accepting the Republican nomination for president in

1980, Reagan addressed the Religious Roundtable gathering in Dallas, telling thousands of evangelicals cheering him (and millions more watching on television), "I know that you can't endorse me, but I want you to know that I endorse you and the work that you're doing for a better America."

This event marked the formal marriage ceremony of the evangelical, pro-family, religious conservative movement and the modern Republican Party under Reagan. And there have really been only two significant demographic transformations in our politics in the last century that rival this movement of evangelicals from the Democratic Party to the Republican Party. The first was the movement of African Americans from the party of Lincoln to the party of FDR, which took place between 1932 and 1940. Even in 1932, Herbert Hoover carried a majority of the African American vote against FDR, and as late as 1960, Richard Nixon ran for president as a card-carrying member of the NAACP and battled John F. Kennedy for the black vote. Kennedy carried the state of Georgia by a larger margin than he carried his home state of Massachusetts. That is how well the Democratic coalition once performed among white voters in the South. The movement of African Americans from the Republican Party to the Democratic Party, from the party of Lincoln to the party of Franklin Roosevelt, is a legacy that lives with us to this day in the person and presidency of Barack Obama. Obama won 98 percent of the black vote in 2008 and slightly less in 2012.

The second major shift was the movement of ethnic Catholic union households into the Democratic Party. The political scientist V. O. Key has demonstrated that this movement really began in 1928, with the nomination of the first Catholic major party nominee in U.S. history, New York governor Alfred E. Smith, who ran against Prohibition and lost in a landslide. But just as Barry Goldwater's defeat in 1964 would later signal the emergence of a Republican South, so did Smith's defeat in 1928 presage the later victory of FDR and the rise of a huge Catholic union household vote. It was not uncommon for decades thereafter to go into the home of a middle-class Roman Catholic family and find two portraits hanging over the mantel: Jesus Christ and FDR. Later, FDR's portrait would be replaced by that of their fellow Catholic, Kennedy. These blue-collar Catholic voters would remain fiercely loyal to the Democratic Party until 1980, when in Catholic and union states like Ohio, Michigan, and Illinois they voted for Reagan and political scientists began to label them "Reagan Democrats." (As with their transition to the Democrats, which began with Smith but reached full fruition with FDR, their drift to the GOP began in 1972 in the Nixon landslide.)

Roughly half of the evangelicals in the U.S. reside south of the Mason-Dixon Line, so as they began to move into the Republican Party between 1976 and 1980, they helped move the South from being a solid-blue region to deep red. This represented a total change from the South's affinity for Democrats, which continued from the formative years of the party under Thomas Jefferson and Andrew Jackson until well into the 1960s. In 1946 when the Republicans gained control of the House of Representatives, there were 105 members of the House from the eleven states of the old Confederacy: 103 were Democrats, while only 2 were Republicans. After the 2010 off-year Republican landslide, there were 152 members of the House from the eleven states of the old South and only 47 of them were Democrats. In the Senate, there were 22 senators from those eleven states, and 20 were Republicans. This same pattern has now been repeated in state legislatures throughout the South. Following the 2010 elections, for the first time since Reconstruction, Republicans gained control of both chambers of the legislatures in North Carolina and Arkansas, two of the final holdouts of Democratic control.

For most of the 1980s evangelicals focused on a cluster of three primary issues. First, a constitutional amendment legalizing voluntary prayer in public school. Second, a human life amendment that would have declared unborn children persons under the Constitution and afforded them legal protection. Third, the nomination of conservatives and strict constructionists to the federal courts, and especially to the U.S. Supreme Court, since evangelicals, faithful Catholics, and other religious conservatives felt that the Supreme Court had been hostile to their beliefs and religious freedom. But the human life amendment never had sufficient votes to pass in the House or the Senate during the 1980s. The school prayer amendment passed in the House but narrowly failed in the Senate during Reagan's presidency, in spite of bipartisan support. Reagan's efforts to move the Supreme Court in a more conservative direction were frustrated by the confirmation of Sandra Day O'Connor (who turned out to be much more moderate than either Reagan or evangelicals anticipated) and the defeat of Robert Bork's nomination in 1987. David Souter's confirmation in 1990 added another justice to the high court who proved far less conservative than promised. As a result of these appointments, the court was two votes shy of a pro-life majority when it revisited the abortion issue in the *Casey v. Planned Parenthood* decision in 1992, upholding Pennsylvania's restrictions on abortion while also upholding *Roe*. This decision became a painful symbol of the frustration and disappointment evangelicals felt toward the Republicans, throwing a wet blanket on their intensity and enthusiasm in the three-way contest between Bush, Bill Clinton, and Ross Perot.

With the election of Bill Clinton and the shuttering of the Moral Majority, many pundits declared that the religious right was dead. But it wasn't dead; its members just had to retool and revise their playbook. Part of that playbook was to broaden their agenda and expand their basket of issues. In 1993 I wrote an essay for *Policy Review*, the flagship publication of the Heritage Foundation, entitled "Casting a Wider Net." That article argued that because the Bible contains principles and instruction on every area of life, evangelicals needed to work on a wider array of issues, not just school prayer and abortion. To gain credibility and become more relevant to the lives of not only secular voters but many voters of faith, they needed to work on spending, taxes, welfare reform, education reform, and foreign policy, bringing time-honored Judeo-Christian values to bear on all areas of public policy.

The second innovation was bold incrementalism. Evangelicals began to realize after fifteen years of civic engagement that they were not going to change the culture by throwing a single Hail Mary pass, electing a president and members of Congress, confirming a handful of new Supreme Court justices, overturning *Roe*, passing a school prayer amendment to the Constitution, and ushering in the millennium. This was a sobering but important lesson in the political education of evangelicals. Religious conservatives learned it just as others who preceded them into the civic arena did. Feminists found out the hard way with the Equal Rights Amendment that the framers made it extremely difficult to amend the Constitution. Certainly the Constitution is a living document, but it is not designed to change dramatically without broad, bipartisan support. The labor unions earlier found that the Constitution was not malleable to their purposes when they attempted to outlaw child labor by amendment. Child labor eventually became verboten by law and economic custom, but not by amending the founding document.

Social reform movements, it turns out, are highly adaptive organisms. So like hamsters trying to get a food pellet, the pro-life community simply tried a different path. Frustrated in their attempt to pass a human life amendment, pro-lifers sought another means to restrict abortion and protect life. The National Right to Life Committee, using model legislation that had passed in Ohio, proposed a federal ban on a procedure known as "partial-birth abortion," a rare and gruesome procedure in which a child is partially delivered and then dismembered. There was bipartisan support for the measure, with even liberals like the late Senator Daniel Patrick Moynihan calling partial-birth abortion "infanticide."

Republicans in Congress passed the partial-birth abortion ban three times before it became law when signed by George W. Bush (Bill Clinton had vetoed it twice and the Supreme

Court had earlier overturned an Arkansas law on the grounds that it violated *Roe*). This was the first federal ban on an abortion procedure since *Roe* became law in 1973. Meanwhile, working with Representatives Frank Wolf of Virginia and Tim Hutchinson of Arkansas, the Christian Coalition made its number one legislative priority the passage of a $500 per child tax credit, arguing that the tax burden on middle-class families with children had become excessive and deleterious to the family. We argued that the intact, two-parent family was the most successful Department of Health, Education, and Welfare ever conceived. Why, then, take 40 percent of such families' income and send it to Washington? Why not allow more of their money to stay in their pockets and in their homes so that they could use it as they saw fit, for the education and the nurture and the health care of their children? We also proposed eliminating the "marriage penalty," which forced married couples to pay higher taxes when filing a joint return than a couple living together and filing separately.

This $500-per-child tax credit and reducing or eliminating the marriage tax became mainstays of Republican fiscal policy. They became key provisions in the Republican budget alternative in 1993, under then-ranking Republican budget committee member John Kasich, and were included in the Contract with America. These tax provisions united social and economic conservatives, bringing them together in common cause to both cut taxes and strengthen the family, foreshadowing the Tea Party movement's ability to bring them together to reduce runaway spending and massive deficits. The child tax credit became law when Bill Clinton signed it into law in 1996 after previously vetoing the GOP-passed budget and shutting down the government. George W. Bush ran for president in 2000 proposing a tax plan that doubled the child tax credit to $1,000. And even as Barack Obama campaigned to repeal the Bush tax cuts, he always exempted the child tax credit and the amelioration of the marriage penalty as targets of his ire. In the so-called fiscal cliff negotiations between the Obama White House and Republicans in Congress, the child tax credit and marriage tax reduction were sacrosanct.

Similarly, the Christian Coalition and other pro-family groups lobbied for welfare reform, not based so much on fiscal grounds but making a moral argument that by subsidizing illegitimacy and penalizing marriage and work, welfare policy had cruelly consigned millions to poverty. Rick Santorum echoed this theme recently during his 2012 presidential campaign when he frequently cited a 2009 Brookings Institute study that found that if you didn't graduate from high school, didn't have a full-time job, and bore children out of wedlock, you had a 76 percent chance of being in poverty. But if you got a high school diploma, if you got a job and kept it—any job, no matter what it paid—and if you got married and stayed married, bearing children within the institution of marriage, you had just a 2 percent chance of being in poverty.[2]

During the 1990s, working with Republicans like Newt Gingrich, Dick Armey, and Santorum, pro-family conservatives adopted policy changes that helped move two million Americans from welfare to work, from government dependency to dignity and self-reliance. This policy agenda, focused on a better society built on stronger marriages and families, is the future of the religious conservative movement. The pro-family movement is more effective and sophisticated than ever. If one looks at the Tea Party movement, which flowered seemingly out of nowhere in 2009 in response to government overreach under Obama, it has steadfastly focused on fiscal and spending issues. But according to studies conducted by both the Pew Research Organization and the Public Religion Research Institute, 60 percent of Tea Party members are self-identified evangelicals, half of U.S. evangelicals consider themselves part of the Tea Party, and three-quarters of Tea Party members and supporters are social conservatives. They're pro-life, they're pro-marriage, and they're for religious freedom and liberty, and there's a remarkable overlap between social conservative voters and Tea Party voters. In the 2010 elections, according to a postelection survey conducted by Public Opinion Strategies, 41 percent of all voters who went to the polls in 2010 self-identified as Tea Party members and 31 percent of all voters identified themselves as born-again evangelicals or conservative Christians. Again, one can see a major overlap between the two constituencies.

Anyone who has attended a Tea Party rally or been at a Tea Party event knows the decided religious and spiritual flavor of their rallies and events. A popular Tea Party anthem is a song called "I Am America" in which Krista Branch sings, "I've got some good news. We're taking names and we're waiting now for judgment day." Some might quarrel with the theology behind the lyrics, but the music video features a girl holding up a sign that says, II CHRONICLES 7:14. This is a verse from the Old Testament that has tremendous significance and meaning in the evangelical community because it speaks to the need for personal as well as national repentance and humility. When Reagan took the oath of office as president on January 20, 1981, he put his hand on a Bible that had belonged to his mother and was open to this verse.

This is not to imply that the Tea Party and the religious conservative movement are one and the same, nor is it to suggest that they're synonymous, but it does demonstrate that evangelicals, often caricatured as caring only about school prayer, marriage, and abortion, are in fact engaged in a much wider array of issues. As a result, they have never been more effective or turned out to the polls in larger numbers. In 2012 they were 27 percent of the electorate and cast 81 percent of their ballots for Mitt Romney, who as a Mormon did not even share their theology.[3] They are a permanent fixture in American politics, and they are not likely to go away anytime soon. If past is prologue, they will stubbornly resist any attempt to stigmatize them or drive them from public life.

The final change in the religious conservative movement is the transition from a largely church-based movement led by pastors and religious leaders to a grassroots public policy movement led largely by political operatives, conservative community organizers, and elected officials. When Jerry Falwell founded the Moral Majority in 1979, he held "I Love America" rallies that took place mostly in evangelical churches. State and local Moral Majority leaders were usually independent Baptist or Southern Baptist pastors. This was natural and logical at the time because the evangelical church served as an incubator of the movement. In the intervening three decades, an entire generation of evangelical public policy advocates and political organizers have been credentialed. The president of the Family Research Council is Tony Perkins, who previously served as a highly effective and respected state legislator in Louisiana. His predecessor was Gary Bauer, who served as chief domestic policy adviser in the Reagan White House. The president of the Susan B. Anthony List is Marjorie Dannenfelser, a former Capitol Hill staffer and public policy activist. The executive director of the Faith and Freedom Coalition, which I founded in 2009 to mobilize evangelicals for effective civic action, is Gary Marx, who served as a senior operative in the Bush-Cheney campaigns. As a result of this, the pro-family and religious conservative movement has gone from being on the margins of our political system, with its nose pressed against the glass of the culture, to being in the mainstream, fully integrated with the most advanced and sophisticated voter registration and get-out-the-vote technology available. At Faith and Freedom Coalition, for example, we have built a faith-based voter database by marrying consumer databases with demographic information, micro-targeting data, and voter files of over thirty million evangelical and faithful Catholic voters. These citizens can be contacted by mail, phone, e-mail, text message, and social networking technology like Twitter and Facebook to work on public policy, to press for legislation, and to encourage them to vote. This represents roughly a tenfold increase in the voter universes that we had at our disposal at the peak of the Christian Coalition in the 1990s.

SOCIAL CONSERVATISM AND THE FOUNDING FATHERS

What binds faith-based conservatives with others in the conservative movement such as libertarians, despite differences on some important issues? Ultimately, it is the founding principles as enshrined in the Declaration of Independence, the Constitution, and the Bill of Rights. The genius of the Founders was that they predicated the entire organizing principle of our government around the concept that men are sinners and we live in a fallen world. This became the premise for the strict limits on the national government, the separation of powers, and the Tenth Amendment reserving all but enumerated powers to the states. Madison famously said in Federalist # 51:

> If men were angels, no government would be necessary. If angels were to govern men, neither external nor internal controls on government would be necessary. In framing a government which is to be administered by men over men, the great difficulty lies in this: you must first enable the government to control the governed; and in the next place oblige it to control itself. A dependence on the people is, no doubt, the primary control on the government; but experience has taught mankind the necessity of auxiliary precautions.

Men are not angels. Given unlimited power, they are certain to abuse it. This is a biblical principle that underlies our form of government. While economic conservatives and libertarians may favor limited government based on more secular beliefs, such as Austrian economics and the like, faith-based conservatives share their fears (albeit for different reasons) of a big government that taxes too much, spends too much, and regulates too much. Evangelicals and faithful Catholics understand that freedom is indivisible, and that restrictions on economic freedom will eventually restrict one's religious freedom.

The genius of the Founders was really twofold. First, to limit the federal government to specific, enumerated purposes. For example, in the minds of the framers, the federal government's power to regulate interstate commerce under the Commerce Clause was not unlimited. Under ObamaCare, the federal government argued it had the power to force citizens to engage in commerce by purchasing health insurance. Even the Supreme Court rejected that argument, concluding the only possible constitutional ground was the government's taxing power. The hostility toward the faith community found in ObamaCare's mandate on religious charities, colleges, and hospitals to provide health-care services that assault their conscience and violate their religious beliefs is further proof that both economic and religious conservatives oppose a government that is too big, too controlling, and restricts their freedom.

This truism was demonstrated yet again by the Supreme Court's recent decisions on marriage. In a single act of judicial fiat, the high court rejected ten thousand years of collective wisdom of Western civilization, the laws and customs of thirty-eight states, and a federal law (the Defense of Marriage Act) passed by a bipartisan margin large enough to pass a constitutional amendment, signed into law by a Democratic president, and declared the defense of traditional marriage a form of bigotry. Like the Massachusetts General Court decision a decade ago that found in the state constitution a right of same-sex couples to marry that had eluded legislators and governors of both parties in the two centuries since John Adams drafted it, the Supreme Court legislated from the bench and short-circuited the democratic process. While it did not order every state to adopt the most liberal marriage laws in the Western world—as it did with abortion law in *Roe*—the high court laid the predicate for such action in the future. This is why social conservatism is best understood as a largely defensive movement, seeking to defend the time-honored institutions of marriage, family, and the church from the infringements on their liberty by the government.

The Founders wanted to devolve that power back to states, to communities, and, most important, to mediating institutions like religious organizations, charities, voluntary associations, and the family. They also wanted to take whatever power there was at the federal level and disperse it among three branches that all constantly fought with one another. These were all ingenious ways to limit. But we can never lose sight of the fact that this limitation was based on the Founders' very clear notion that if one does not restrain the power of government, men will abuse all power that is centralized. This is why George Washington argued in his Farewell Address that freedom and prosperity are impossible without the twin pillars of religion and morality.

Social and economic conservatives also understand that a looming fiscal disaster awaits us. The ticking time bomb of entitlement obligations will explode within a decade. The government has been borrowing and spending, taxing and spending, printing money and spending, and slowly bankrupting the country. The music is about to stop. Kevin Williamson and Niall Ferguson have recently argued that unsustainable government spending is the next bubble. For the first time since Social Security began in 1935 we are paying out more in benefits than we collect in payroll taxes. According to the Congressional Budget Office, Social Security and Medicare will both be unable to pay their obligations by roughly 2030.

Some years ago an organization polled young people in their twenties and asked them whether they believed there was life on Mars and whether they expected ever to collect a Social Security check. A higher percentage of Americans under the age of thirty believed there was life on Mars than believed they would ever collect Social Security benefits. At the time that Social Security was passed in 1935, the average life expectancy for an American male was sixty-three, and beneficiaries did not begin receiving benefits until age sixty-five. Today, the average life expectancy of an American male is roughly seventy-nine, and the life expectancy for the average American female is eighty-three. Actuarially, the numbers do not add up. Fifty years ago there were sixteen workers for every retiree; today there are approximately three workers for every retiree, and by 2050 there will be approximately two workers for every retiree. To keep Social Security from going bankrupt, the government would have to double the payroll tax or cut benefits in half.

George W. Bush argued we should reform Social Security or it would not be there for future generations. There has not been a president since Social Security was created in 1935 who spent more political capital than George W. Bush did to try to save the system. He did eighty-two Social Security events all over this country but could not get the votes of the three Democrats he needed to move the bill in the U.S. Senate.

In the end, the Soviet system proved intellectually and morally bankrupt. In many ways it collapsed under its own weight. Margaret Thatcher famously said that Ronald Reagan gave it a push, and so he did. Entitlement spending is also unsustainable, but social conservatives and their economic conservative allies need to give it a push. They need to point out that it undermines the family by transferring from children and loved ones to the federal government the responsibility for caring for one's parents in their golden years. Government cannot replace with entitlement spending the individual's responsibility to prepare for retirement or the social responsibility of children to assist in the care of their parents, just as their parents cared for them.

We can assert these basic constitutional and Judeo-Christian principles and still make common cause with other conservatives. I support the separation of church and state to protect the church from the state, not protect the state from the church. The idea of a disestablishment of religion was not invented by liberals, and it certainly wasn't invented by the ACLU. The idea of the disestablishment of the church was an evangelical idea, and specifically a Baptist idea, especially in Virginia during the colonial period when Anabaptists were forced to pay taxes to support Anglican meetinghouses that they did not attend and whose theology they did not share.

The rule of law presupposes a moral code of conduct based

on societal consensus. The question is not whether there will be laws, for as long as there is civilization there will be laws that constrain and restrict human activity. The only real question is, "Based on what moral code?" Is marriage between a man and a woman, as we've believed throughout the history of Western civilization, or does it have a different definition? When it comes to bearing and raising children, who has the primary responsibility: is it the government and the school, or is it parents? These issues are resolved through the democratic process and ultimately a moral code prevails. This is why it is naive in the extreme to expect social issues to disappear from the political discourse; because they involve law and the common lexicon of right and wrong, they will always be part of the debate. Better for conservatives to understand this and develop a language for dealing with social issues than to stick their heads in the sand and try to wish them away.

In February 2009, after Obama's inauguration as president, *Newsweek* declared in a cover story, "We Are All Socialists Now." The punditry expected a conservative crack-up and the onset of a liberal renaissance more expansive and ambitious than either the New Deal or the Great Society. Within eighteen months after that cover story, *Newsweek* was bankrupt and Republicans gained sixty-three seats in the House of Representatives, the biggest landslide in an off-year election since 1922, largely because of a surge of evangelical and Tea Party voters.

This is not to suggest conservative triumphalism. The 2012 elections demonstrated there is still resilient support in the U.S. electorate for Obama and his agenda. But exit polls also made clear that Obama's reelection was not an unqualified endorsement of his agenda. By a healthy margin voters said the government was too big and doing too much, not too small and doing too little. And ObamaCare remains the most deeply unpopular entitlement program in history, with roughly half the electorate opposing it or calling for its partial or full repeal, while support for ObamaCare hovers between 35 and 40 percent of the electorate. Meanwhile, a majority of the American people now identify themselves as pro-life, according to recent polls by Gallup and other public opinion organizations.

Social conservatives have been declared dead on more than one occasion since they burst onto the political scene a little over three decades ago. Those critics who underestimated them failed to understand the persistence and passion of their citizenship. They love their country, they love God, and they believe they have just as much a right to make their voices heard in the political process as anyone else, not in order to establish heaven on earth, but to pass sound public policy and establish the common good. Those are both eminently desirable goals. They are here to stay, and they are likely to continue to shape our politics and the future of America as much in the future as in the recent past, or more, and the country will be better off for them.

CHAPTER 14

◆ ◆ ◆

National security conservatives view the rise of terrorism as the main threat facing the United States. They point out that America's enemies don't always use conventional weapons anymore. Instead, our enemies may use electronic hacking, targeting banks and secure information in order to use that information against the United States and its allies. Or they may manipulate the world markets on key commodities like oil.

While Secretary Rumsfeld discussed foreign threats to our national security, Ambassador R. James Woolsey, former director of Central Intelligence under President Clinton, focuses on domestic threats to America's defense, specifically relating to energy. These emerging threats represent something seemingly new in American history: an undefined enemy, working across borders, striking silently in ways both large and small.

Ambassador Woolsey is a Democrat, but his views are shared by most national security conservatives regardless of their party. He explains some of the major threats facing the United States, and the need to balance liberty concerns with preservation of our national security.

Ambassador R. James Woolsey is a former director of Central Intelligence under President Clinton. Ambassador Woolsey has held presidential appointments in two Republican and two Democratic administrations. He served as ambassador to and chief negotiator for the Conventional Armed Forces in Europe (CFE) Treaty, general counsel of the Senate Armed Services Committee, and undersecretary of the navy. He currently chairs the board of the Foundation for Defense of Democracies, the Advisory Board of the Opportunities Development Group, and the Strategic Advisory Group of Paladin Capital, and is a venture partner with Lux Capital Management. He has served as the Annenberg Distinguished Visiting Fellow at the Hoover Institution at Stanford University and as a Senior Fellow at Yale University's Jackson Institute for Global Affairs. Ambassador Woolsey was formerly a vice president of Booz Allen Hamilton in McLean, and a partner with Shea and Gardner in Washington, D.C.

WHY NATIONAL SECURITY
DRIVES OUR FUTURE

Ambassador R. James Woolsey

◆ ◆ ◆

Let me say a few words about three aspects of national security. First of all, you can color me "neocon," or close enough for government work. I was founder and president of Yale Citizens for Eugene McCarthy for president in 1967, 1968. I thus essentially headed up the antiwar campaign at Yale that year. And we were, by the way, the most conservative organized political group on the Yale campus. Everybody else was burning something—burning bras or burning draft cards or burning something. We organized a lot of the campaign in New Hampshire, and we had a bit of an impact on what happened in American politics as a result.

In the 1970s, I ended up working as general counsel of the Senate Armed Services Committee for a marvelous man, the late Senator John Stennis of Mississippi, who was chairman. The number two ranking Democrat was Scoop Jackson. Frank Gaffney, Richard Perle, and I all worked together for these marvelous men. Part of what was going on there, and went on for some years before and after, was holding the Democratic Party up to a high standard with respect to protecting the country. For example, Richard especially had a good deal to do with Scoop's Jackson-Vanik Amendment, which barred the extension of the most favored nation treatment to the Soviet Union until it liberalized the release of Jews to emigrate. We had something to do with countering some of the more accommodating aspects of détente, for example. That Scoop Jackson part of the Democratic Party is almost all gone.

That history, I would say, of working hard on making the United States sound militarily, having more defense capability than that which is barely enough, standing up to dictators when they need to be stood up to, and accepting America's leadership role among the democracies of the world is something that I think is extremely important for conservatives to espouse. They should not slip into the stance that some did, for example, in the 1930s in the America First movement, which was responsible for a more isolationist point of view, and which made it far more difficult for Roosevelt to stand up to Nazi Germany and imperial Japan before Pearl Harbor.

There are three basic threats to national security. First of all, this country needs well-trained, substantial military forces in order to be able to deter those who would exercise power against the weak. I'm thinking particularly about Iran in the Middle East, and I'm thinking about China with respect to East Asia. There is no doubt that the Chinese, without our being part of the picture, would be exerting control over major parts of coastal Asia, major countries in Asia, and would do so rather quickly and thoroughly. There is no doubt that without the United States taking some decisive stances and actions as well, Iran will survive its current difficulties and Iran will, before too long, have a nuclear weapon. And a nuclear weapon in Iran means that since Shiite Iran will have a weapon, Sunni Egypt, Sunni Saudi Arabia, and Sunni Turkey will have nuclear weapons before long. Because once you have a nuclear reactor for creating electricity, you can get into the fuel cycle, the enrichment of uranium and the reprocessing of plutonium, and thereby move toward having a nuclear weapon, the way the Pakistanis have, the way the North Koreans have, and the way the Iranians will. Unless we do something.

We simply have to keep Iran from getting a nuclear weapon. It's unlikely that this administration would use force. I don't think Israel can do the job; its air force is too small and it doesn't have the tankers. You'd need a bombing campaign to deal with this issue effectively, and there's only one air force and navy in the world that can do that: ours.

I therefore pray that the sanctions and the weakness of Syria will help stop Iran. Why did the United States crack down on Mubarak, who was our ally for many years, within the first two weeks of the Arab Spring, and leave Assad and Syria alone, not even bringing the kind of pressure to bear on them that it did on Libya? Syria's stability and the rule by the Assad family are at the heart of Iran's reach into the Sunni world. Nothing worse could happen to the Iranian rulers, except a revolution inside Iran, than for Assad to fall. We have not exercised a single iota of strategic sense in dealing with those three countries: Egypt, Syria, and Libya.

The problem here is that whereas we survived forty-five years of a Cold War, with us and the Soviets having nuclear

weapons, only one time did we come close to a nuclear exchange: during the Cuban Missile Crisis. We did have essentially an effective deterrent and containment and a nuclear
standoff with the Soviets. Since their lousy economy could not
keep them going, after some forty-five years it effectively collapsed. And we won World War III, in a sense, the Cold War,
without having fired a shot between the United States and the
Soviet Union. Certainly we had Vietnam and we had Korea,
but we won the Cold War without any kind of a U.S.–Soviet
military exchange, let alone a nuclear exchange.

It would be wonderful if we could deal with the rest of our
problems in the world as effectively as we did the Soviet threat.
But by the early/mid-1960s, I would say, the Soviet ideology
was dead. There were true, committed Marxist-Leninist revolutionaries back in the 1920s and '30s and '40s in the United
States, but I'd say that probably by the 1960s, there were more
true, committed revolutionaries in the bookstores of the Upper
West Side of Manhattan than there were in the Kremlin. I
negotiated with those guys four times, and they didn't want
to die for the principle of "from each according to his ability,
to each according to his need." They wanted to remodel their
dachas, their summer homes. We outlasted them because they
had an empty set of values and an empty economy. Would that
we could do the same as time rolls on. But we have a rather
different set of problems now, and a different type of enemy.

All of that took a substantial military establishment. The
world today must know that we can stand up to whoever would
come against us and deal with them effectively. We have to
have more than that which is barely enough. There is room for

reasonable disagreement over whether we need eleven aircraft carriers or ten or twelve, but there is, I think, not room for reasonable disagreement about the need to be able to protect the country, in very substantial measure, with military forces not much smaller than what we have now.

The second and third areas of security that I think it's particularly important for us to focus on both relate to energy. Unless we fritter it away, we will be able to deal effectively with most conventional military enemies, as we did with Iraq and as we did in the actions of the Clinton administration against the Serbs brutalizing Bosnia and Kosovo. Energy is different.

First of all, we have two basic large energy systems in the United States: electricity and transportation. Electricity is supplied for us by natural gas, coal, nuclear power, hydropower, and some renewables. Essentially, all of it is domestic. We don't have a foreign supply problem with respect to electricity.

One of the most deceptive things that are said in the current political campaign is that we have a problem because we have foreign supply of our oil; therefore, we need to build more solar and wind turbines, etc. Build more solar and wind turbines if you want; they're clean ways to generate electricity, and have advantages and disadvantages. But they don't have anything to do with our oil dependence. In the early 1970s we made over 20 percent of our electricity from burning oil. So then, back at the time of the Yom Kippur War, if you built a wind farm or a nuclear power plant, you were, in fact, reducing the country's demand for foreign oil. Today, less than 1 percent of our electricity comes from burning oil, most of it in Hawaii. Today, if you say, as the administration does perpetually, that you are

helping solve our foreign oil dependence problem by building solar or wind turbines or really anything else to produce
electricity, you are in fact dealing with less than 1 percent of
the problem. That is something of a record in modern political
rhetoric. Most political rhetoric is either 60/40 right or wrong,
or 70/30, or 80/20, or 90/10. Very few political statements
consistently made are 99-plus percent wrong, as this one is.

The problem with the electric grid is not that we have foreign supply issues. The problem with the electric grid is that it
is, although extraordinarily capable and a wonder of its time in a
way, extraordinarily fragile in some key ways. First of all, when
we went through the Y2K issue, the Internet was just coming
into heavy use. And the people who were fixing our grid and
all of our other operations of computers and everything else in
the country so they wouldn't crash when the calendar turned
to 2000 decided that as long as they were changing things,
maybe what they'd do would be to create a situation whereby
they would put the control systems for the electric grid on the
Internet. That way was cheap; it was also easy. The Internet
was getting upgraded, why not? What a good idea!

But there's a problem. The problem is hacking. The problem is cyber excellence on the part of the Chinese and the Russians. The problem is that if you are modernizing the Web and
the electric grid in such a way that you have a "smart grid," and
you can turn down your air-conditioning at your home from
your cell phone, you may be making it possible for a teenager
in Shanghai to turn down your air-conditioning from his cell
phone, or more, something worse than just turning down your
air-conditioning in a way you don't want.

The fact that the SCADA systems (the Supervisory Control and Data Acquisition systems) of the electric grid operate in many cases over the Web has created a remarkable set of vulnerabilities to terrorists, and not only to those who are merely seeking to cause mischief, or those who would steal money from the utilities. A great deal hangs on our ability to do something relatively quickly to make it possible for us to manage our electric grid, other than the way it's being managed now.

Now why is this important? The United States has eighteen critical infrastructure systems: water, sewage, food delivery, etc. All seventeen of the others depend on electricity. If the electric grid goes down for a few days, as it did in the Northeast and part of the United States and eastern Canada back in '03, we can pretty much deal with it. You've got usually a few gallons of fuel for a generator, or you go stay with somebody who was more farsighted than you were and has a few gallons of fuel for a generator. It usually works itself out. But intentional interference could take the grid down for much longer than that, many days to weeks to months.

So we have, in the first place, a very serious problem: if the grid goes down, pretty soon, these other systems go down, too. And we are not back in the 1970s, pre-Internet. We are back in the 1870s, pre-electricity, and I doubt if any of us has enough plow horses or water pump handles to deal with the situation. Chalk that up as one very serious problem connected with our electricity grid.

There's another. The transformers that we have—which step up voltage so you can have very long-distance sending of electricity, and then step down the voltage so it can be sent to your home and used—are very hard to find. They're absolutely vital to the system. They cost a great deal. They're extremely heavy, very difficult to move. There are two places where they're built, South Korea and northern Europe (northern Germany, last time I looked). And you need to go stand in line to have them built, because they are designed in such a way that they fit into a specific slot for a specific transformer. They're not generic; they're not modular. The utilities just put them behind cyclone fences, a hundred or two hundred feet away from the highway. If you want to know what the transformers are and what you would shoot with a .45 pistol to take them out, they are the things that the signs point to that say "Danger! Do not touch." In case a terrorist speaks only three or four words of English, like "Danger, do not touch," he's in business.

So the danger and the risk of not having a way in which we can protect our electric grid either from individuals or from terrorist groups subordinate to rogue countries, or from countries themselves, are a very serious problem.

The third problem is electromagnetic pulse. A nuclear detonation sends a series of pulses. Even a simple nuclear weapon, if detonated, say, a couple of hundred kilometers up, can send out an electromagnetic pulse that, based on a recent major congressional study, would seem to be able to take down huge sections of the electric grid. Now, don't we have ballistic missile defense? Couldn't we stop something like that? It doesn't have to be an intercontinental ballistic missile from someplace like China. It could be a small SCUD missile, which forty countries have, based on a fishing boat out of Iran. All you have to do is launch it—you detonate it as it's going up. We have no ballistic missile defense that deals with something in the ascent phase; it's only when it's in midcourse, or coming down, when it's terminal. So if Iran or somebody Iran is working with decides to disable a huge share of the American electric grid, that is, I'm afraid, open to them. And the changes that have recently been made in our ballistic missile defense, in order to accommodate the Russians, go the wrong way, rather than in a helpful way, in terms of dealing with a problem like this.

These three aspects of vulnerability of our infrastructure— there are others, but these are three rather salient ones— suggest to me that it is extremely important to focus on the future. Conservatives, in order to be able to deal with the worst that can happen to the United States, and have the confidence of the population that they'll be able to deal with that, need to learn about these issues, take them seriously, and not brush them off, because we are, unfortunately, far easier to reach by, say, someone using an Iranian fishing boat, than by most weapons systems anyone has had remotely in mind, even in recent decades.

There's a second aspect of energy that is also a huge problem, and I'll close with this. We borrow about a billion dollars a day in order to import oil. Even when we pump more, that just means the price still stays up, because the added supply doesn't take the price down. OPEC reduces what it's pumping in order to keep the price up around a hundred dollars a barrel. OPEC controls nearly 80 percent of the world's reserves of conventional petroleum. We control two. OPEC lifts oil for five to ten dollars a barrel throughout the organization. The eight OPEC states of the Middle East lift oil for about five dollars a barrel. When you lift oil for five dollars a barrel and sell it for a hundred and five, as they do, you're doing reasonably well. It doesn't matter that we buy most of our foreign oil from Canada. There's one worldwide market. If we buy more from Canada and less from Saudi Arabia, somebody else buys more from Saudi Arabia and less from Canada. It's a giant pool. There are temporary offsets such as needing the right kind of refinery for the right degree of sulfur in the oil, but they're not the heart of the matter. The heart of the matter is that we don't solve the problem by either buying oil from countries that are nearer to us, like Canada, or even buying it from ourselves. Buying it from ourselves is a good idea. Drilling for more oil in order to produce more helps with our balance of payments. Instead of borrowing a billion dollars a day, if we get really successful, we might borrow only nine hundred million dollars a day, or really, really successful, borrow eight hundred million dollars a day. But OPEC is still in the driver's seat. So "Drill, baby, drill!" is positive for our balance of payments, but it certainly doesn't solve the problem.

The same thing is true of getting more oil production from a country that's either nearer us or more friendly. As I said, it doesn't make that much difference. The same thing is true of improving the mileage of our cars. You improve it to a new standard, fifty miles per gallon instead of thirty miles per gallon. Good, that helps; that's a onetime drop in demand, and what happens is that OPEC simply pulls its supply down in order to keep the price up. OPEC pumps thirty million barrels of oil a day. On the eve of the Yom Kippur War in '73, when

this current situation began, OPEC pumped about thirty million barrels a day; it's about a third of what the world needs.
In between those years, '73 and today, it has pumped less in
order to try to keep the price up. Sometimes it's been successful,
sometimes not. But if you own nearly 80 percent of something
in the world, and you sell only a third of what the world consumes every year, and if you pumped thirty million barrels a
day back in the early 1970s, and now, forty years later, when the
world's economy has doubled and petroleum use has basically
doubled, you still are pumping only thirty million barrels a day,
there is only one term that fits you, a conspiracy in restraint of
trade, otherwise known as a cartel.

That situation means that it as long as we stay enslaved to
oil, we will stay, in a very real way, in a situation where we are
operating at the behest of OPEC. And I cannot think of a more
substantial challenge to our national security than that. OPEC
is twelve countries, two in Latin America, two in sub-Saharan
Africa, eight in the Middle East. And Iran, Saudi Arabia, and
many of the other members of OPEC do not have our best
interests at heart.

What can we do about some of this? With respect to the
electricity grid, someone needs to be in charge. It's not clear
who's in charge today of security for the grid. I know that
sounds strange, but there are fifty institutions that run the electricity grid in the United States in the fifty states: the public
utility commissions. The Department of Energy doesn't run
the grid; it has a small office of a few people who watch things.
The Federal Energy Regulatory Committee, FERC, doesn't
run the grid; it sets rates for transmission over long distances.

The institution that comes closest, I suppose, is something called NERC, for the North American Electrical Reliability Corporation—it's really the trade association of 3,500 utilities, and with respect to important security issues it does, if you'll pardon my bluntness and directness, zip.

So if you want something done with respect to security on the electric grid, we have to find a way to put someone in charge. We need to find a way to do it that is consistent with our history and the local focus of electricity, and the need for us to take account of consumers' needs and the rest.

The largest change that came about when our Constitution was drafted was that Madison and his colleagues were using as a model, in many ways, the Roman Republic. The Roman Republic had one tragic flaw, which was a lack of clarity about who was going to control the military, and that's what brought it, effectively, to its end. In our Constitution, we've got that straight: the president is the commander in chief; Congress has the power of the purse. But the problem is that under the current situation, we are coming close to being nearly at war with terrorists and Iranian hackers and the rest, and instead of a commander in chief the way our Constitution sets it up, we've got a trade association of 3,500 utilities sort of, kind of, a little bit responsible, sort of, for the security of the grid, and kind of, occasionally, maybe talking about doing something.

With respect to oil, if we want to get out from under the thumb of OPEC, we have to break oil's monopoly over transportation, and we have to break OPEC's cartel. I'm afraid there is no other way to do it, and we won't do it by any of the remedies that have been talked about much so far. We have to make it possible for American consumers to do something different from what they do now. Today, they drive with oil products in their cars. We're not addicted to oil, but our cars are. You can't put anything in there except oil products. And so if the price goes up because OPEC wants it to go up, it goes up. We need to come up with a way to do something as sound as what the Brazilians have done. They have made it possible to drive into a filling station and choose between fuels—for them it's gasoline and ethanol because ethanol is very cheap for them to produce on sugarcane— then, when gasoline goes very high, they just buy more ethanol and they're in control, the Brazilian consumers. We are not. We are way behind the Brazilians in our ability to control our own market for fuel. We could take advantage of the fact that natural gas now, as a result of hydrofracturing, is approximately one-fifth the cost per unit of energy of oil. We could use natural gas, including mainly domestic, American natural gas, in ways that it hasn't been used before, because when gas and oil cost about the same per unit of energy, it didn't make much sense to change from oil to natural gas. But natural gas can be used to produce fluids to drive on. Either you can compress or liquefy natural gas for large vehicles, trucks and buses, or you can turn the natural gas into methanol ("wood alcohol") to fuel the family car. Some companies are starting to experiment with turning natural gas into gasoline.

The point is to be able to move away from petroleum as a feedstock for the fuel that you drive on. If you can do that, and I think the technology is possible, then before too many years are up, we may be able to appear to the world as smart and clever as the Brazilians. That would be good.

Let me close with just one thought. A few years ago my sometime writing colleague, Anne Korin, came up with a wonderful illustration of what we need to do, and she and her colleague, Gal Luft, at their think tank wrote a book called *Turning Oil into Salt*. Salt, for thousands of years, was a strategic commodity. It was the only way to preserve food until the mid-nineteenth century, when canning came in, and even then, it was the only way for years to preserve meat. Salt was a very big deal. Roman soldiers were paid in salt. The word *salary* comes from salt. If your country had a salt mine and a neighboring country did not, you were in the driver's seat. Countries were going to war over salt mines in Latin America up until the 1890s. But in the 1890s something very important happened: a technological change. The electric grids started to come into operation in major cities in the world. And right away, people realized you could use electricity for little things called refrigerators and freezers, and they also realized that meat that had been frozen and thawed was cheaper than meat soaked in an expensive salt brine, priced by a monopoly; not only was it cheaper, but the meat tasted a lot better. So it was better and cheaper to freeze meat than to soak it in salt brine. Within a very few years, essentially salt was destroyed as a strategic commodity. It wasn't destroyed, period. We still use it on sidewalks in February, on corn on the cob. Salt has its uses. But when you went in to lunch today, I doubt that any of you looked at the saltshaker on the table and said, "I wonder where that comes from. I wonder if we're salt-independent." Nah, salt's boring, unless you're investing in Morton's. I would suggest what we need to do is just to make oil equally boring.

CHAPTER 15

◆ ◆ ◆

One of the core principles of conservatism is limiting the powers of government and preserving individual liberty. President Reagan was straightforward in his approach to government, stating flatly in his first inaugural address— "Government is not the solution to our problem; government is the problem." Many conservatives agree.

Senator Rand Paul, defender of liberty in the U.S. Senate, argues that for several generations the concept of preservation of liberty and limited government has been minimized within the Republican Party. Many people who identify themselves as conservatives today simply no longer observe the constitutional principle of limited government and have accepted the inevitability and permanence of big government.

Recently, however, a libertarian focus on limiting government and preserving liberty seems to be gaining ground within the conservative movement. Many young people in particular are responding to the simple libertarian message: "Get the government out of my life." A government that leaves its citizens alone has great appeal in this age of government regulation of health care, light-bulbs, gun ownership, and so many other areas of American life.

While some conservatives warn that libertarians are too ideological to win elections, Senator Rand Paul argues that the future of the conservative movement rests on libertarian principles. He urges conservatives to shift their focus toward reducing the size of government and respecting its constitutional limits. At the same time, he argues that America must preserve its traditional conservative values and principles.

Dr. Rand Paul is the junior United States senator for Kentucky. Elected in 2010, Senator Paul has focused on constitutional liberties, fiscal responsibility, and government overreach during his years in the Senate. Paul, the son of former presidential candidate Congressman Ron Paul (R-TX), was a practicing ophthalmologist in Kentucky prior to being elected to the Senate.

TOWARD A MORE LIBERTARIAN CONSERVATISM

Senator Rand Paul

◆ ◆ ◆

Reagan once said, "I believe libertarianism is the very heart and soul of conservatism." Too often they are portrayed as competing or even incompatible ideologies, but I agree with Reagan. Returning to a more libertarian conservatism would return us to a sharply more limited government and radically more pro-freedom agenda.

More and more Americans are becoming alarmed by the size and scope of government power and its daily intrusion into our lives. I often illustrate our distaste for this government power with the story of the little girl who wanted a hundred dollars. She says she'll do good things with the hundred dollars, so she writes a note. She writes, "Dear God, please send me a hundred dollars." The postmaster gets the letter and he doesn't know what to do with it, so he sends it to the White House. The president gets the letter and says, "Oh, that's cute. The little girl wants a hundred dollars. Send her five dollars; she'll be happy with that." So the little girl gets the five dollars. Her parents always told her to write a thank-you, and so she starts out her letter. She says, "Dear God, thanks for the five bucks. But next time, don't send it through Washington. They stole 95 percent of it."

If you're a conservative, you don't want to send it to Washington at all. If you're a moderate, you say, well, instead of five bucks, if they could only return ten bucks, everything would be okay, and if you're a liberal, you think the richest aren't paying enough; they've got to pay their fair share. You think they should send it all in.

But seriously, it is about a philosophy. A philosophy—to my mind and to the minds of a lot of conservatives—that started with Barry Goldwater. When I decided to run for the U.S. Senate, I reread Barry Goldwater's *The Conscience of a Conservative*, the first edition of which was published in my home state Kentucky in Shepherdsville, near Louisville. There's a quote toward the beginning of the book that I believe is a good summary of what undergirds American conservatism. Goldwater writes:

> I have little interest in streamlining government or making it more efficient, for I mean to reduce its size. I did not propose to promote welfare, but I proposed to extend freedom. My aim is not to pass new bills, but to cancel out old ones. I don't intent to inaugurate new programs, but to cancel out programs that do violence to the Constitution. I will not attempt to find out whether legislation is needed before I determine whether it is constitutional. And if my constituents complain and say that I am neglecting their interests, I will inform them that I

was told that their chief interest was liberty, and in that cause, I am doing the best that I can.

Goldwater's words encapsulate my own conservative philosophy. The conservative's task isn't simply to make government more efficient, but to reduce its scope to those functions given to government by the Constitution.

THE CONSTITUTION

Limiting government is one of the purposes of our Constitution. The Founders wanted our government's functions to be narrow and few. They wanted safeguards against government overreach and abuse. They wanted checks, balances, and explicit protections that were lacking in the government from which they had declared independence. The founding generation, as students of history and philosophy, understood that government anywhere will always try to expand infinitely and aggrandize itself at the expense of liberty.

Ronald Reagan said in his Farewell Address, "As government expands, liberty contracts." Our country was founded on this sentiment. The Founders feared government and loved liberty. The Constitution they created is essentially a conservative document.

It is also in many ways a libertarian document.

Some of the most prominent Founders would today be considered libertarians, as their strict limits on government also included outlining and protecting the rights of citizens. Their deep respect for the principles of individual liberty has always been an integral part of what has made America one of the greatest and most prosperous nations in human history.

What the Founders intended, and what many conservatives and libertarians want today, is a system that keeps decision making close to the people. Most conservatives and libertarians have always wanted government under which bureaucracy remains small and does not hamper the talents and aspirations of the individual. The federal government should not do what the states can do for themselves, the states should not do what local governments can do for themselves, and local governments should not do what families, faith groups, and individuals can do for themselves.

Today, we have a federal government that perverts aspects of the Constitution to supersede state, local, and individual rights.

EXPANDING THE POWER OF GOVERNMENT

Revisiting *The Conscience of a Conservative*, Goldwater mentions the Supreme Court case of *Wickard v. Filburn*. I've joked that I think I'm the only person who has run for the United States Senate in modern times to overturn *Wickard v. Filburn*. Perhaps my friends Mike Lee and Ted Cruz might take exception to that claim.

What is *Wickard*? It was a perfect example of government expanding its constitutional bounds. It was also really the beginning of big government in the United States.

In the 1940s, the courts told farmer Roscoe Filburn, who wanted to grow twenty acres of grain, that he could grow only fourteen acres of grain. Filburn resisted, insisting that it was his land and he could do as he pleased. In an attempt to avoid any lengthy battles, Filburn grew the fourteen acres the government dictate allowed, but also grew six acres more for his personal use. The crop grown on the additional six acres would be fed to his cows to avoid breaking any interstate commerce laws.

But a lengthy battle came anyway. Filburn's case went all the way to the Supreme Court. And the Supreme Court said, "By your inactivity, by your restraint, by not engaging in commerce, you could have indirectly affected the price of grain."

With this decision, the Supreme Court opened Pandora's box. We had gone from a limited constitutional republic to a purer democracy where the majority—or mob—rules and the Commerce Clause could literally mean anything. It was an absurd and unprecedented decision.

I've remarked that if my shoes were made in Tennessee, the federal government can still regulate my walking in Kentucky. Though it's meant to be a punch line, it's also generally true—that is the current expansive notion of the Commerce Clause. So much growth in government jurisdiction and power came about through this new and elastic concept of that clause. For the next half century and then some, not one congressional law was struck down as unconstitutional.

Think about it. In *sixty years*, not one law passed by Congress was struck down.

Why is this so important today? Because so much over-regulation and government growth that conservatives deplore today is a direct result of this interpretation of the Commerce Clause.

ObamaCare is a primary example. The legal battle over ObamaCare wasn't about health care, per se. It was about the Commerce Clause and the power to tax. It was a court decision based on the precedent set by *Wickard v. Filburn*—the idea of inactivity, of not participating in commerce by not purchasing health insurance.

Columnist George Will called ObamaCare "the last exit on the road to unlimited government." He's right. If the federal government can impose ObamaCare, what, exactly, are the limits of government power? Does the Constitution restrict and define the size and scope of government anymore—or not?

When Benjamin Franklin walked out of the Constitutional Convention in Philadelphia, he was asked what type of government he had helped to devise. Franklin responded, "A republic, if you can keep it."

We haven't kept it. Or at least we haven't kept enough of it.

I have often called myself a constitutional or libertarian conservative, because it is abandonment of constitutional principles based in individual liberty that has taken America down the wrong path. I believe it is also the reclamation of these principles that can restore the Founders' vision.

In our domestic policy, cases like *Wickard vs. Filburn* set the precedent for arrogant centralized authority to sap the traditional rights of localities and individuals. ObamaCare is a perfect example, where the federal government stretches definitions of the Commerce Clause to force people to purchase health care via individual mandate. There is such a wild imbalance today between what the Constitution allows and the federal government demands that we can only imagine what the Founding Fathers would think of modern American government.

GOVERNMENT EXPANSION IN FOREIGN AFFAIRS

This arrogance of centralized authority is by no means restricted to domestic policy. Conservatives of all stripes have long agreed that the primary function of the federal government is to maintain a strong national defense. But there is debate and division among neoconservatives, libertarians, and others about what this means. Our military should be used to protect our vital national security and interests. But should it also be used to police the world, nation-build, and export democracy? Is the power to declare war reserved for the legislature, as the Constitution states, or it is now within the powers of the executive branch?

The Founding Fathers gave the power to declare war to the legislature for the same reason they were so particular about delegated powers throughout the Constitution—to limit abuse and check power.

The debate within the Republican Party over whether to intervene in Syria was between those who believed we must follow the Constitution and allow Congress to declare war and those who believed the president could go to war without consulting Congress. To say that we don't have to follow the

Constitution because so many other presidents have taken military action without consulting Congress is essentially to say that ObamaCare is justified because of precedent going all the way back to *Wickard vs. Filburn*.

Is our justification for centralizing authority in our federal government simply that the Constitution can be ignored because it has been ignored for so long? If this premise is accepted, then there is little prospect for conservatives ever to stuff the federal government back into its constitutionally limited box.

There is now what many are calling a libertarian-leaning wing of the Republican Party. These Republicans have been some of the most vocal opponents of ObamaCare, and they have also been stringent in demanding that the president seek approval from Congress before going to war.

This is no coincidence. Domestic and foreign policies involve separate issues but not separate principles. In both our domestic and foreign policies, government must be restrained. It must be limited. The law must be followed. And the Constitution must reign supreme.

LIBERTY MUST BE DEFENDED

We need respect for the individual and the rule of law again. We need a more constitutional conservatism. We need a more libertarian conservatism.

When I held a filibuster in the Senate over whether or not the president should have the authority to kill an American citizen without due process, those thirteen hours on my feet were about more than the specific issue of drones. The filibuster was about what kind of power the president has. It was about how much power the federal government has taken on and how much of the Constitution it thinks it can ignore. And it was about whether we were going to let the president and the federal government get away with overreaching their constitutional bounds.

There are factions within the Republican Party that I believe give government too much benefit of the doubt.

When President Obama says he won't use drones against citizens, some Republicans give the benefit of the doubt to the executive branch. When the National Security Agency admits it is monitoring the phone calls of every single American, certain Republicans say we should simply trust it. When the Department of Justice seizes the phone records of the Associated Press and other newspapers, some Republicans turn a blind eye. When the Internal Revenue Service targets Tea Party groups, some Republicans deplore such behavior but insist it is just few rogue actors. In fact, some in our party don't even consider such behavior abuse anymore.

If we are a conservative party, there is something very wrong with the thinking of these Republicans.

If the GOP is the party of smaller government, we must also be the party that is suspicious of government at every juncture. Thomas Jefferson believed that the price of liberty was eternal vigilance. Republicans should be that vigilant party. Patrick Henry declared, "Give me liberty, or give me death." Today, too many Republicans say exactly the opposite—take my liberty or we're all going to die! Tap my phone! Spy on my e-mail! Drone my neighbor! Do it to protect me!

National security is the primary and most important function of government. But, as Benjamin Franklin noted, when you trade liberty for security, you get neither. A number of polls taken in the summer of 2013 in the wake of the NSA revelations showed that most Americans feared government overreach in trying to "protect us" more than they feared terrorism.

We must always have intelligence gathering and commonsense protections in place to reduce the risk or terrorism or any other threats to our security. But there must be limits. The Constitution must be obeyed. The Bill of Rights must be followed.

Conservatives must always err on the side of individual liberty and be suspicious of government, not the other way around.

ECONOMIC FREEDOM MEANS OPPORTUNITY

The good news/bad news scenario I tell people is this: the bad news is, we're in the midst of a crisis. The number one threat to our national security is our debt. But the good news is that we live in the greatest country ever created. We are exceptional because of the set of ideas that we embrace. We are exceptional *only* as long as we embrace those ideas. It is a generational, transgenerational fight and a war to see if we can keep a republic and stay true to our founding principles. It's been slipping away. The Democrats can have lots of the blame, but Republicans deserve blame also. This is a bipartisan problem;

we are letting our nation's exceptionalism slip away as we let the government do more and more things.

Our freedoms have also created incredible wealth in this country, which has bolstered our national security. We won the Cold War because our engine of capitalism defeated their engine of socialism. We had to have a strong national defense to win, but our emergence as the world's sole superpower really occurred because our nation's economic engine beat socialism.

If you come by your wealth honestly, if you work hard, if you come up with a great concept, if people buy your products, by all means, make as much money as you can and employ as many people as you can. Your success will increase our nation's prosperity. And let us not be embarrassed by that.

Not only should we refuse to be embarrassed by creating wealth; we shouldn't be embarrassed by insisting on economic freedom from government. We all need to understand that there is nothing that's really free given by our government. Somebody always has to pay for it.

The future of political conflict in America will be between two concepts. It will be between the people who believe that you can have success and that anyone can achieve in our society— the American dream—and those who want to just divide up the existing pie and try to redistribute it. I think there are enough people left in America who believe in the American dream. I think that the future of conservatism is about promoting a free market system that creates incredible wealth, and for that wealth to allow for incredible humanitarianism. If we make the national discussion about that, conservatism will win.

A COALITION FOR LIBERTY

Where the Republican Party has the most potential to grow is also where it needs to be more libertarian. We need to bring this message to the youth of America.

Young people do not believe the promise that Social Security and other programs will be there for them. They recognize that they are drowning in student debt and entering an unpromising job market. And they fear what a huge national debt means for their future. Young people have seen the promises of big government come up empty. They are ready for new ideas based on free market competition and more individual choice.

Younger generations want the government out of their lives in almost every respect. They don't want politicians involved in their personal lives or those of their neighbors.

Young Americans want more liberty and less government. And they want more opportunity.

There are countless independents and even disenchanted Democrats who would be attracted to a Republican Party that was more tolerant in its tone, more dedicated to attacking big government in all its forms (like abolishing mandatory minimum sentencing), and more serious about enhancing and protecting the liberty of all Americans.

Ronald Reagan's coalition featured this broad swath of Americans. To be nationally viable and to win elections, the Republican Party will need to broaden its base again. A more libertarian Republican Party can also feasibly make headway in blue states and places on the West Coast and in the Northeast, where Republicans have been uncompetitive.

"Extremism in the defense of liberty is no vice," Goldwater also said. In our own time, more liberty—and pursuing it in a more aggressive manner than we have—might also be the key to winning more elections.

By reviving Reagan's "heart and soul" along with Goldwater's pursuit of liberty, that movement can be revived to successfully limit government and return the nation to the constitutional principles of its origins.

More liberty is desperately needed. Our rights and protections that we have always enjoyed as Americans are under assault like never before.

Republicans can win again and so can conservatism, and it is libertarian conservatism that can best do it by defending our cherished liberties.

AFTERWORD

Governor Haley Barbour

◆ ◆ ◆

It surprised me when my old friend Mallory Factor asked me to write the afterword for his book on conservatism and the Republican Party. Even though he and I have been friends for years, he could have asked any number of outstanding, bright, young conservative leaders whose futures are still in front of them, unlike mine.

Yet I soon understood Mallory's thinking. He figured, correctly, that since I will never again run for office, I can freely offer the truth of today's political reality to the faithful in unvarnished terms.

Mallory's book is about the conservative movement, but my focus is its party, the Republican Party.

GHB'S UNVARNISHED TRUTH: *Purity Is the Enemy of Victory; the Goal Is to Win Elections*

Grassroots activists of either party must be reminded, constantly, that the ultimate goal is to win the ability to govern. In our system this means that victory lies in our party winning elections in order to control government and set its policies. The goal is not to be pure, for purity is the enemy of victory. The goal is to win elections. Period.

The Republican Party is not identical to conservatism, but it is the only vehicle available for conservatism. There is no viable third-party option. There are no breakaway mass movements that have the ability to shape law and governance. Like it or not, the Republican Party remains the only real repository of conservatism in American politics. That may be an ugly, unpleasant truth to some, but it's a truth nonetheless.

Let's discuss, therefore, the Republican Party.

In our two-party system, both parties, by reasons of necessity, are coalitions. Factions don't win elections, coalitions do.

It takes more than 60 million popular votes to win enough electoral votes to elect a president. (Obama received 66 million votes in winning a second term.) Both parties, therefore, must offer themselves as coalitions broad enough and diverse enough to attract the millions of supporters needed to win in November every four years. Not to mention electing fifty governors, 535 senators and congressmen, and enough legislators to control fifty state legislatures in the hundreds of other elections over the four-year political cycle.

Make no mistake: the Republicans are the conservative party in the United States, and the Democrats are the liberal party—or the Progressive Party, as they like to brand themselves these days. Though their numbers have shrunk to endangered-species status over the last ten years, there are still Democrat elected officials who are politically to the right of some Republican officials and some Republican elected officials to the left of some Democrat officials.

Of course, there was a much greater overlap thirty and especially fifty years ago when the South had a one-party system. G. V. "Sonny" Montgomery, who was my Democratic congressman in the third district of Mississippi, used to say, "When I came to Congress in 1967, there were 125 conservative Democrats in the House. When I left in 1997, there were only 'a Dixie dozen.'"

During the thirty years Sonny served in the House, Southerners, who had historically voted Republican for president, began to elect Republicans to Congress. In the House, more and more Republicans replaced conservative Democrats, and more and more liberal black Democrats replaced moderate and liberal white Democrats. So when older, more conservative Democrats retired, Republicans were elected to replace them. This shift was primarily a result of realignment between the two parties across the South and elsewhere.

Some of these retiring Democrats actually supported the conservative Republicans who replaced them. When the GOP picked up two of Mississippi's three open Democrat congressional seats in 1972, the retiring Democrat congressman in each of those two districts publicly supported his GOP successor in the election. (Of course, many Democrats in those days were not that loyal to their party in other ways. But that's another book and not what I'm here to discuss.)

GHB'S UNVARNISHED TRUTH: *In Congressional Elections Today, the Fight Is Usually in the Primary—Not the General—Election*

More recently, the general realignment in the South has had less to do with the election of fewer white Democrats to the House than it has to do with gerrymandered redistricting. This holds true outside the South as well, and it is another important unvarnished truth. Of the 435 seats in the U.S. House of Representatives, fewer than 100 are competitive in the general election today. The only serious chance of defeat for more than 75 percent of all House incumbents comes in the primary. This is true of nearly 200 House Republicans and more than 150 Democratic House members.

The Democrats, therefore, work hard to make sure no one gets to the left of them, while Republicans try to prevent anyone from getting to the right of them.

This brings out the worst in our candidates and congressmen, the worst for our party, and the worst for our country. It also gives people, including grassroots members of both parties, the impression that the party, in larger terms, is narrow and that almost everybody agrees on everything.

That is a mistaken belief, and it is ultimately a dangerous one.

Afterword

GHB'S UNVARNISHED TRUTH: *If Everyone in Our Party Had to Agree on Everything, We'd Have a Mighty Small Party*

Maybe the vast majority of Republicans whom you know personally do agree on most issues, but even among your closest friends there can be stark differences of opinion. And that is healthy, if for no other reason than it reminds us that fellow Republicans, including folks we know to be fine, upstanding citizens, can agreeably disagree with one another and remain loyal friends and party members.

Well, multiply your friends by the 60-plus million people who voted Republican for president last year, or even the nearly half million people who voted for me for governor in 2003 in our one little state. It is simply absurd to think everyone in such an enormous group could agree on every issue, let alone on every facet of every issue. Hell, my wife, Marsha, and I don't agree on everything, but Marsha says I have the right to be wrong sometimes.

As you read this book's thoughtful essays, filled with hard-fought lessons and hard-won wisdom, strong convictions and considered conclusions, forward-looking ideas and solid thinking, you learned a lot.

But it is highly unlikely you agreed with everything in it. And that's as it should be.

The conservatives who wrote these essays, all of whom are politically solid, don't agree with one another on every single issue. In fact, there may be significant differences on critical issues among them.

Yet all but one are Republicans in good standing—indeed, leaders of our party—and all are strong conservative leaders.

When I was chairman of the National Policy Forum (NPF), a Republican think tank, I edited *Agenda for America*, a book written under the leadership of a stellar group of NPF policy committee cochairs who explored, explained, and drew consensus on a range of topics regarding economic, trade, military, foreign, and social policies.

The authors of the chapters, written in 1995 by a task force of experts who served as NPF committee members, included many of the greatest thought leaders in our party: Jeane Kirkpatrick, Jack Kemp, Robert Bork, Tommy Thompson, William Bennett, Dick Cheney, and so on. Yet not all of them agreed on every single issue. Nor did I.

When I wrote the introduction to *Agenda for America*, I had to note in it that I didn't agree with everything in the book—and I was the NPF chairman and the book's editor!

The unvarnished truth is that ironclad agreement does not a good policy book or good party policy make. Moreover, my admitting it up front in the introduction made the larger point that disagreement is simply a function and healthy by-product of being part of a big party—the only kind that can triumph in a two-party system.

If everybody in our party had to agree on everything, we'd have a mighty small party. And left-wing Democrats would control government at every level, while we'd be split into a brawling, sprawling ragtag rabble of small factions.

The fact that our party must function well as a broad coalition led Lee Atwater, a great political operative but also a deep thinker, to declare that the Republican Party had to be a "Big Tent."

In the Deep South, when Lee and I were earning our spurs in the field as GOP operatives and, eventually, young leaders, our party wouldn't have dreamed of excluding converts for imperfection.

Better than anybody else, we Southern Republicans, trying to build a second party in a traditionally one-party region, knew our door had to be open and our tent large.

Conservatism, like the Republican Party that represents it, must be a Big Tent.

My old boss, Ronald Reagan, also understood this cold, which is why one of his favorite sayings was, "The fellow who agrees with you 80 percent of the time is your friend and ally, he's not some 20 percent traitor."

Reagan, considered the most conservative president of my lifetime and one of the most ideological, flew under bold colors and fought tirelessly for what he believed in. Yet as president he compromised on everything. With large Democrat majorities in the House during all eight years of his presidency, he had to master the art of compromise or get nothing done.

A former union president, Reagan knew how to negotiate. "When I began entering into the give and take of legislative bargaining in Sacramento," he wrote in his autobiography, *An American Life*,

> a lot of the most radical conservatives who had supported me during the election didn't like it. "Compromise" was a dirty word to them and they wouldn't face the fact

that we couldn't get all of what we wanted today. They wanted all or nothing and they wanted it all at once. If you don't get it all, some said, don't take anything. I'd learned while negotiating union contracts that you seldom got everything you asked for. . . . If you got seventy-five or eighty percent of what you were asking for, I say, you take it and fight for the rest later, and that's what I told these radical conservatives who never got used to it.

Through compromise, he got Congress to pass the Reagan economic plan that tamed high inflation and astronomical interest rates while launching a quarter century of economic growth not just in the United States but across the globe. It was not only "Morning Again in America" but around the world.

Through compromise, he rebuilt our military and won the Cold War, putting the Soviet Union out of existence.

Reagan achieved good policy, which led to good results. And, to do so, he repeatedly compromised with a Democrat majority in the House. I should know. I served as the political director of the Reagan White House part of that time.

Remarkably, he also united and strengthened the Republican Party in the process.

Beginning with William Howard Taft and Theodore Roosevelt in 1912, down through Dewey and Robert Taft in the 1940s and early 1950s, and on to Rockefeller and Goldwater, there had been two wings of the Republican Party for nearly seventy years.

Reagan's conservative policies, their impressive outcomes,

and his great leadership skills resulted in our party's coming together into one broad mainstream, which, in turn, resulted in GOP presidencies for five of seven consecutive terms, majorities in at least one house of Congress for twenty-two of thirty-two years, and powerful, creative Republican state governments leading all across the country.

GHB'S UNVARNISHED TRUTH: *Politics Is About Addition and Multiplication—Not Subtraction and Division*

Reagan knew what some seem to have forgotten or never grasped: you make your party stronger and more successful by making it bigger. Politics, after all, is about addition and multiplication.

Twice in my lifetime (and Reagan's) Republican candidates have received 60 percent or more of the popular vote for president, in 1972 and 1984.

I have always advocated that we manage our party—our coalition—in a way that 60 percent of voters would feel welcome in the party or at least be open to consider voting for the GOP nominee for president.

I still think 60 percent should be our number for the Big Tent, and we should run our party accordingly. There are virtually no voters in the other 40 percent who would ever vote for a Republican (unless he or she were unopposed). Be polite to the 40 but make sure that the 60 percent supermajority *is* welcome and *feels* welcome.

We are not all going to agree on everything, but everybody who wants to get his or her time at bat should get to have a say. And if a person's view is in the minority, it wouldn't be party policy but that view would be tolerated. Good, reasonable people can disagree agreeably.

More important, odds are we would still agree 80 percent or so of the time. Thus, we'd continue as allies, working together on all those things on which we do agree.

Senator Jim Jeffords of Vermont was up for reelection when I was chairman of the Republican National Committee in the 1990s. I was asked as chairman to go up to Vermont to campaign for him. When the word got out, a lot of conservatives criticized me for campaigning for the most liberal Republican in the Senate.

"It is absolutely true that Senator Jim Jeffords is the most liberal Republican in the U.S. Senate," I told my critics and the media. "But let me remind you, Jeffords is also the most conservative member of the Vermont congressional delegation. We will not elect anyone more conservative than Jeffords in that state."

Everybody knew I was right. The complaining disappeared, and Jeffords got reelected. He was later succeeded by Bernie Sanders, the first self-described socialist elected to Congress in six decades.

Regrettably, we have seen a new version of that scenario play out repeatedly in the last four years. And every time it's happened, it has allowed the Democrats to win a seat in the U.S. Senate that should have gone to a Republican. Hence, today, instead of fifty-five Democrats in the Senate, there should be only fifty or fifty-one. And maybe fewer.

It started in 2010 when some Delaware Republicans and the developing Tea Party decided Congressman Mike Castle was too liberal, a RINO (Republican in Name Only). Even though Castle, a multiterm former governor of Delaware and an eight-term incumbent congressman representing the entire state, was the overwhelming favorite to pick up a Democrat seat and succeed Joe Biden, who had been elected vice president, the fight was on to deny Castle the nomination.

Enter a young woman who had once worked at the RNC and had tried unsuccessfully to run before, in 2008. Add some political consultants more interested in making money than in the GOP winning elections. In a low-turnout Delaware GOP primary, Castle lost to a virtually unknown "non-witch" because of a narrow group who successfully portrayed him as not conservative enough.

While Castle was branded as ideologically impure, the Democrats elected a liberal senator who votes just like Biden, far left. The quest for purity among some Republicans gave the Left a seat we should have today. We lost in Castle a senator who would have voted right 80-plus percent of the time.

Regrettably, this is only one of at least four instances in the 2010–2012 cycles in which the GOP lost the general election because a skewed nomination contest chose an unelectable or far weaker candidate as our nominee. The same thing happened in Colorado in 2010 and in Indiana and Missouri in 2012.

In the Missouri Republican primary for the Senate, Democrat political action committees (PACs) effectively nominated the weakest Republican in the field. Astoundingly, GOP Congressman Todd Akin's biggest donors in the primary were independent expenditures by PACs controlled by Senate Democrat Leader Harry Reid of Nevada and incumbent Missouri Democrat Senator Claire McCaskill, Akin's opponent in November. This fact is documented by Federal Election Commission reports.

Having helped defeat Akin's stronger, more electable opponents in the primary, McCaskill handily defeated her cherry-picked opponent that fall.

The real kicker for our purposes is that Reid–McCaskill helped Akin win the primary by running TV ads that touted him as the most conservative Republican!

Indeed, many would add the 2010 Nevada Senate race to the list of seats blown by Republicans in the primary, when Sharron Angle upset Sue Lowden, again with Angle's effort being heavily boosted by Harry Reid's PAC.

Republican primary voters ignored the Buckley Rule: nominate the most conservative candidate who is electable. Had they heeded the advice of one of the country's greatest conservative icons, the late William F. Buckley Jr., we might have five more Republican senators fighting Obama's terrible left-wing policies.

As disgusting as Reid's shenanigans were in distorting GOP primaries, I am equally dismayed by the way some ostensibly Republican PACs used their money to defeat Republicans in GOP primaries.

In the last two cycles, a New York–based GOP PAC has spent piles of money, given by Republican donors, to defeat Republican candidates in primaries. And the damage done by full-throated attack ads run by Republican PACs against Republicans in primaries played a major role in the GOP's losing the seats.

Republican attack PACs even went after former Wisconsin governor Tommy Thompson, the father of welfare reform in the United States, as being too liberal.

Contributors to operations like these Republican attack PACs need either to exert more control on how their money is spent or to give it to other organizations. I can't believe any of these donors intend to help the Democrats, but in competitive races these PACs have helped elect more left-wing Democrats in the last two cycles than they have Republicans.

Reagan may not have written the Republican Party's Eleventh Commandment, but he inspired it, lived it, and was the political Moses who carved it in stone: Thou shalt not speak ill of another Republican.

Like some other commandments, it's a mighty good doctrine, though extremely hard to follow in practice. The reasons are threefold:

First, "Politics ain't beanbag," as the late Democrat House Speaker Tip O'Neill used to say. And he was right. Though viewed as sport by some, politics is not a game. The stakes are extremely high; the results of many a presidential election have set the country's course for generations.

Second, the media gives the most attention to the shrillest attacks, the loudest critics, the lowest blows. Wanting to win, candidates and consultants see what the media, including the social media, gobbles up; and they serve it to the media on a plate, hot and steaming.

Finally, in so many House races in partisan strongholds, it

is virtually automatic that whoever wins the primary will win the general election.

It isn't easy to always stay on the right side of the line dividing fair and legitimate criticism on policy from manufactured negatives and phony analysis, not to mention sleazy character assassination. In my opinion, party leaders should not take sides in primaries. The RNC never did while I was its chairman. They should respect the process by blowing the whistle on those who cross the line.

I'll repeat what bears repeating: conservative voters should follow Buckley's Rule on primary voting and support the most conservative candidate who can win in November.

GHB'S UNVARNISHED TRUTH: *The Closer One Gets to the Grass Roots, the More Conservative the Party Is*

After forty-five years of active participation in Republican politics, I know that the closer one gets to the grass roots, to the base, the more conservative the party is. This realization came to me when I was executive director of the Mississippi Republican Party in the early 1970s, and I've never seen it contradicted.

This explains why primary results are so often more conservative than might be expected and why the results of a caucus or another smaller turnout process are almost always even more conservative. Likewise, in the Democrat Party, the closer to the grass roots, the more to the left the base will vote.

So if I'm a primary voter or am attending my precinct meeting to choose a nominee, I am at the base, the foundation of the party.

In conservative states like mine, the primary voters are very conservative, with the candidates spanning the conservative gamut. We are the rural party, and in rural states mainstream conservative Republicanism is the midstream of political thinking for the state as a whole.

Therefore, in Mississippi and many other Southern, Great Plains, or Mountain West states in which the general electorate is fairly conservative, voters can pick primary candidates about as conservative as themselves and still follow Buckley's Rule by picking the conservative candidate with the best chance to win in November.

Not long ago we were also the suburban party. We don't dominate the suburban vote anymore, and the suburbs aren't as stable as the rural areas.

The fast-growing, fast-changing suburbs are not as conservative as they once were. They are far more diverse in a variety of ways: economically, ethnically, educationally, and so on. They are more diverse politically, too.

In some areas or whole states, moderately conservative or moderate Republicans have the best chance to win. That's just reality, and it will become a fact in some other areas as our country grows.

But the changes in America, particularly in suburban areas, are not just demographic. There are changing views on a wide spectrum of issues: national security, social, etc. As suburban and exurban areas attract more voters from the central cities and urban areas, political affiliations shift. Currently, these trends are making suburban America less conservative.

But America remains a center-right country. After all, more voters thought Romney would do better on the economy, foreign policy, and managing the government. Subsequent polling in 2013 confirms that most Americans prefer center-right policies.

In 2012, Romney received a wide majority of the votes cast by Caucasians, but lost by much larger margins among Latinos, Asian Americans, and African Americans.

Much of the reason for the poor showing among voters of color was not about policy. It was because large numbers of Asian Americans, Hispanics, and African Americans thought Romney and the Republican Party did not care about them or their problems.

Indeed, a stunning finding in exit polling done for the networks on Election Day 2012 was the response to this question: Regardless of for whom you voted, which candidate, Obama or Romney, do you think cares more about people like you?

The answer: Obama, 81 percent; Romney, 18 percent!

Even if all the Obama voters (51 percent of the total) said Obama cares more about them than Romney, the math tells us that 62 percent of Romney voters believed Obama cares more about them than the man they voted for.

In most elections, the GOP candidate, unlike Romney, will not get so personally and viciously smeared that 62 percent of his or her voters end up believing that the Democrat cares more about them than their own candidate.

Afterword

GHB'S UNVARNISHED TRUTH: *It's Easier for People to Vote for You If They Think You Like Them*

But we must recognize, the answer relates to the Republican Party, not just to Mitt Romney. The unvarnished truth is that minority voters see too few Republicans in their neighborhoods, and even fewer Republicans are at their events seeking those minority voters' political involvement or support.

The great former Republican governor of Georgia Sonny Perdue used to say, "It is easier for people to vote for you if they like you."

We now see a corollary to Sonny's Rule: It's easier for people to vote for you if they think you like *them*.

I doubt we'll see future GOP campaigns in which our candidate calls for "self-deportation" of millions of illegal immigrants. But in 2012 many Latinos heard Romney's statement as "Send Mama back to Mexico." It is a wonder Romney received even 27 percent of the Latino vote. All I have to say is those 27 percent are some strong, faithful Republicans.

GHB'S UNVARNISHED TRUTH: *To Succeed, the Republican Party Must Be a Big, Broad Coalition*

I believe the GOP future is very bright, with many outstanding Republican governors leading the way. But some of us have to come to grips with the realities of two-party politics. Although it has served our country well for more than two centuries, large coalitions are hard to manage.

When I was RNC chairman twenty years ago, I considered my main job to be managing our coalition. This was the only conclusion I could come to after what was then twenty-five years of organizational GOP politics. Every position I held prior to becoming chairman—field organizer in 1968 for Nixon for President in Mississippi; coordinated campaign director in 1972 for Nixon Reelect in Mississippi; executive director, Mississippi Republican Party, 1972–76; regional director for seven states, Ford for President, 1976; county chairman, Yazoo County Republican Party, 1976–80 and 1982–84; campaign chairman, Cochran for Senator, 1978, Mississippi; regional director, Connally for President, 1979–80; candidate for U.S. senator, Mississippi, 1982; chair, Southern Regional Advisory Group, Reagan Reelect, 1984; Republican national committeeman for Mississippi, 1984–97; deputy assistant to the president and political director, Reagan White House, 1985–86—taught me the same lesson: To succeed, the Republican Party must be a big, broad coalition, the Party of the Open Door, the Big Tent Party.

And managing a big, broad coalition is hard work!

Leaders in the two-party system must come to the same conclusion as I did. They have to understand and respect that not everybody is going to agree with them on everything or like their stand on every issue. Similarly, voters have to understand and accept that there will be no perfect candidates from their party.

As I have told conservative crowds for years, "Only one perfect person has ever walked on this earth, and He is not running next year."

You won't agree on every issue with any candidate. And every elected official will have to compromise sometimes to get legislation passed.

Especially in a divided government in which the GOP controls only the House while Democrats control both the Senate and the Obama White House, we can't impose our will on the Left.

Honest politicians admit this. We can block some legislation; we can reduce spending levels at the margins; we can expose wrongdoing; and we can fight against bad policy. But we can't impose our will on the Left when they have a president and a Senate majority of their own.

That said, sometimes we can achieve more by indirection or by giving the Democrats part of what they want in order to achieve more of what we want to do. This requires judgment, and, as Reagan reminded us, not everybody will agree with every strategy and tactic.

The bottom line is, we won't be able to put our agenda in place to get the country back on track until we win enough elections to control the government—White House, Senate, and House.

If we win enough elections to do that, you will not think every elected conservative is pure or perfect. Nor will they be. But some of the best, strongest, and most successful will, like Reagan, know how to get good policy enacted and achieve maximum results.

The majorities we put together to win center-right or conservative victories in other states will probably be a little different from the coalition in your own state. Like members of your own family, each state is a unique individual. And as we allow states to learn from one another, they can act as laboratories of democracy.

For instance, when we passed comprehensive tort reform in Mississippi during my first year as governor, many states learned from us and passed tort reforms that fitted their own situations.

Controlling spending and running Medicaid are problems every governor faces, and there, too, we learn from one another, though the solutions usually differ because our states differ.

It is critical for Republicans to stick together, grow our coalitions, and practice the politics of addition and multiplication. My number one unvarnished truth: purity is the enemy of victory and a dead-dog loser in politics and elections.

In closing, I'd like to illustrate this by telling the story behind one of the huge state victories Republicans won it 1994, the greatest midterm majority sweep of the twentieth century.

Minnesota is a tough state for Republicans. In 1984 it was the only state the Democrats carried in the presidential election. (Yes, Walter Mondale won Washington, D.C., but it's not a state.)

By 1994 we had elected a Republican governor, Arne Carlson. Carlson was pro-choice and rather outspoken about it. Indeed, he could be outspoken about a lot of things.

Abortion had been a very divisive issue at the 1992 GOP convention in Houston. Afterward, the liberal media elite continued to write about abortion as *the* issue dividing the GOP.

When I was elected RNC chairman in January 1993, I

made it plain, "If we let abortion become the threshold issue of Republicanism, we need our heads examined."

Since I had been publicly pro-life for more than a decade, most pro-choice GOP leaders recognized I was trying to unite the party around the issues we agreed on. My goal was for pro-life GOP voters to support pro-choice Republican candidates, especially if the Democrat was pro-choice, and for pro-choice GOP voters to support pro-life Republican candidates.

For lots of reasons, Minnesota turned out to be a crucial state in the watershed 1994 election.

This story explains why and how. The Minnesota GOP has a convention to choose its nominee for governor, but the results can be appealed to a party primary.

One Friday night in early 1994, Curt Anderson, one of the RNC's regional field operatives and the one responsible for Minnesota, called me from the state party convention. Curt cut to the chase in his plainspoken manner, "Carlson's going to lose the vote tomorrow. By a big margin."

"Have they had some sort of straw vote or pre-caucus?" I wondered out loud. "How are you so sure?"

"No, they haven't. But it's obvious. Carlson's got all the power structure, the rich guys, the ones who winter in Florida. They've got suntans. The regular fellas, the dairy farmers and working class, they're white as snow from being up here all winter. Haley," he said with a pause, "the pale ones outnumber the suntans about three to one."

I laughed out loud.

"I'm not kidding," Curt said before hanging up. "Wait until tomorrow."

Sure enough, Alan Quist, the pro-life challenger, beat the incumbent governor at his own state party convention by about two to one!

As you can imagine, the *New York Times* went wild, and I was on the defensive about Minnesota and abortion for a while. Later that year, Governor Carlson came back and beat Quist in the primary by about two to one the other way.

Minnesota, I realized, presented a special opportunity—for my goals as chairman, my party as an emerging Big Tent, and our future path toward majority control.

Republicans had nominated conservative, pro-life Congressman Rod Grams, a former television news anchor, to try to succeed retiring GOP Senator David Durenberger. Grams and Carlson would be running on the ballot as the GOP ticket. Carlson, not only pro-choice but the most liberal Republican governor in the country, teamed up with conservative, pro-life Congressman Rod Grams. And I loved it. The pairing of these two candidates was a case study to test my model for 1994 campaigns and voter behavior.

Senator Bob Dole and I jumped on a plane to Minnesota to raise money for both campaigns and the state party. The candidates and campaigns cooperated with one another, and both won in November. Carlson later told me that more than 90 percent of the Republicans who had opposed him in the convention had actively supported him in the November general election.

That year, a spirit of Republican unity and cooperation from coast to coast witnessed pro-life Republicans voting for pro-choice GOP candidates and pro-choice Republicans voting for pro-life GOP candidates. In 1994, purity was not allowed to prevent victory.

We party leaders emphasized the core issues that united us: smaller government, less spending, lower taxes, rational regulation, open markets and free trade, rule of law, private property, free market capitalism, peace through strength, internationalist foreign policy, toughness on crime, and strong families.

In return, the GOP electorate did not let the perfect become the enemy of the good. We did not let purity prevent victory.

Of course, unity is not enough by itself to ensure victory. That Big Tent party has to be well organized and effective, not only in including all the voters who share its ideas but also in motivating them to actively support our candidates and actually vote on Election Day.

We must raise enough money to be able to communicate our ideas to the American people, and we must use cutting-edge communication technology to deliver our message near and far, and by every medium.

Most important, we must regain our rightful position as the party of ideas—positive ideas and practical programs that will grow our economy and spur job creation; ideas that will extend prosperity to those who have had the least of it; and ideas that equip all our citizens and their children with the tools needed to share in the American dream.

The party of these ideas is the conservative party, which understands the roots, the lessons, and the future of American exceptionalism, the only proven path to upward mobility for all who truly believe that our country can once again arise proudly as that shining city on a hill.

And now, sit back, pour yourself your beverage of choice (mine happens to be Maker's Mark), reflect on what you learned in this great book of essays, and consider joining the political battle that will return America's government to the path that will lead our children and grandchildren to the better, more prosperous, and more secure future they can have and deserve.

ACKNOWLEDGMENTS

◆ ◆ ◆

I owe a deep debt of gratitude to all those who helped me develop the original Conservative Intellectual Tradition in America course at The Citadel, the lecture series, and this book, as well as to many friends within the conservative movement.

This book project would never have gotten off the ground without the support of Edwin J. Feulner, founder of the Heritage Foundation, who wrote the foreword for this book and also supported my early efforts to turn the course lectures into a book. Thank you for ever urging me "onward," Ed. I am grateful for the assistance of the Heritage Foundation in providing critical support of this book and for its fine work in conserving and renewing the principles of the American founding.

My remarkable agent, Mel Berger, found me the best publisher for this project, and I appreciate his sound advice on all matters involving publishing. The HarperCollins team was terrific. I am very pleased to have had the opportunity to work with Adam Bellow, Eric Meyers, Joanna Pinsker, and the entire staff at HarperCollins on this book.

Acknowledgments

The Franklin Center and its president, Jason Stverak, deserve my great thanks for their own great work bringing transparency and accountability to government and for bringing the themes of this book to a wide audience. I thank Christopher Long and Jeffrey Nelson of the Intercollegiate Studies Institute for encouraging and supporting the original Conservative Intellectual Tradition in America course and the recording of the lecture series. They played an instrumental role in getting this project started. I appreciate Bud Watts's support of this project and all the opportunities he creates for so many.

My guest lecturers for the Conservative Intellectual Tradition in America have earned my deep gratitude: Alfred S. Regnery, David A. Norcross, Speaker Newt Gingrich, Michael Barone, Burton W. Folsom Jr., Yaron Brook, David A. Keene, Phyllis Schlafly, T. Kenneth Cribb Jr., General Edwin Meese, Douglas J. Feith, Daniel J. Mitchell, Secretary Donald H. Rumsfeld, Ralph E. Reed, R. James Woolsey, and Senator Rand Paul. I am indebted to all of them for painstakingly revising their lectures into the essays that appear in this book. I thank Governor Haley Barbour for providing a lively and original perspective on the intersection of Republican politics and the conservative tradition in his afterword to this book.

I am grateful to Susan Burdock and Ellen Schweiger for filming these lectures and bringing them to a wider audience by broadcasting them on C-SPAN. All the lectures can also be viewed on The Citadel Web site at www.citadel.edu/conservative.

My wife, Elizabeth, and I both thank Ben Shapiro, who gave us valuable help on this project as he does on so many of our projects. Great thanks are also due to Stanley T. Greer and Don Loos, who have lent us a hand on many projects, including this one. We thank our valued contributing editor David T. Crater for joining the team and helping us craft the final manuscript.

Alan Crippen of the John Jay Institute and Douglas Minson deserve our thanks for their guidance on the course and original syllabus. We thank Lee Edwards of the Heritage Foundation for his keen observations on an early version of this manuscript.

Donna Wiesner Keene, David Keene, Richard Miniter, and Al Regnery deserve my thanks for their advice on the design of this course, the speaker series, and many other aspects of this project. I am also grateful to Jim Pinkerton for his guidance on the early structure of this course and on so many matters. I am ever thankful for Bill and Darla Shine, who have shared their tremendous media acumen with me so generously. I have also learned so much from the legendary Pat Caddell, who has graciously tried to teach me how the Left thinks, although I am still incredulous at times. I want to thank Dr. Rich Roberts for his political insights and for constantly striving to make a difference.

I am extremely grateful to The Citadel, South Carolina's Military College, for allowing me to serve as the John C. West Professor of International Politics and American Government. Although I did not have the privilege of attending this fine institution, I have become a very strong believer in the value of The Citadel education in building fine young leaders. A special note of praise and thanks is reserved for my terrific

Acknowledgments

students at The Citadel, who have taught me so much about honor and leadership. In our seminars, they have truly driven our exploration and learning. Thanks also to my wonderful student interns who have kept my courses on track and helped me deepen the learning experience for my students.

My sincere thanks go to General John W. Rosa, president of The Citadel, for his contribution to this work, his support of the seminar and lecture series, and his fine leadership at The Citadel. I am very grateful to Brigadier General Sam Hines, our provost, and Colonel Gardel Feurtado, my department chair, for their guidance and friendship. I thank Colonel Jeffrey Perez for his work in showcasing The Citadel through our video recording of the speaker series. I really appreciate the contributions of Brigadier General Thomas J. Elzey, Dean Bo Moore, Sarah Tenney, DeBose Kapeluck, Brad Collins, and many other trusted colleagues and friends at The Citadel. I thank The Citadel Foundation and Gary Hassen for their valuable support for the speaker series. I am also extremely thankful for the involvement and support of Tommy McQueeney, Marcelo Hochman, Reverend Samuel Rivers, Nancy Mace, and Rick Berman.

I am grateful to the alumni of The Citadel for their support of the speaker series on which this book was based. I am especially thankful to Bud Watts and Bill Krause for their support of leadership and ethics at The Citadel, as well as their embodiment of these virtues themselves. Their support has been especially instrumental in launching our new project to bring Citadel cadets to UK Parliament as interns under the auspices of the Young Britons' Foundation. Thanks to my trusted friend

Acknowledgments

Matthew Richardson for facilitating this invaluable opportunity for our cadets. In the UK, I am also grateful to Brendan Simms, Alan Mendoza, and Terence Kealey.

To my partners, sponsors, speakers, panelists, and participants of my political forums, the New York Meeting and the Charleston Meeting, thank you for your continued interest in conservative politics and for your belief that it is important to keep a lively dialogue going within our movement. Thanks to James Taranto, James Golden, Monica Crowley, Jedediah Bila, Jason Riley, KellyAnne Conway, and Robert George for keeping the meetings interesting. Thanks to Grover Norquist for inspiring me to start a center-right political forum in New York well over a decade ago. O'Brien Murray can hardly be thanked enough for his invaluable involvement all these years.

We are extremely grateful to so many people for their help in launching our previous book, *Shadowbosses*. We want to especially thank Sean Hannity, Michelle Malkin, Steve Forbes, David Keene, Frank Abagnale, Dick Armey, Herman Cain, Andrew Napolitano, David Horowitz, Colin Hanna, Sally Pipes, Mark Smith, Michael Finch, Mike Huckabee, John Stossel, Keith Urbahn, Richard Viguerie, Connie Hair, Kimberly Willingham, and Andrew Murray. We would also like to thank Lynn Bradshaw, Walter Carr, Ken Abramowitz, Nick Spanos, Ted Lachowicz, Stephen Whelan, Louis Topper, Jerry Lewin, Tony Fortuna, John Stavros, Anthony Lepre, and Darin Gardner for their valuable help on our projects.

To our growing and adventurous kids, and to all the other children in America who are our nation's future, this work is ultimately for you. May you read, think, learn, and embrace our conservative tradition for yourselves.

Finally, if we are going to succeed in putting America back on the right track, we are going to need to pull together. Let us all work together toward our common goals so that the pillars of our movement will continue to guide our nation toward truth.

◆ ◆ ◆

Chapter 1: The Pillars of Conservatism

1. A version of this essay was previously published in *Inter-collegiate Review* here: www.firstprinciplesjournal.com /journal/issue.aspx?id=bb15a739-3278-41f1-94d3 -bbcd1b7d4860&journal=IR.

2. Henry Hazlitt, *Economics in One Lesson* (New York: Three Rivers Press, 1988).

3. Friedrich Hayek, *The Constitution of Liberty* (Chicago: University of Chicago Press, 1960). See also Friedrich Hayek, *The Road to Serfdom* (Chicago: University of Chicago Press, 1944); Milton Friedman, *Capitalism and Freedom* (Chicago: University of Chicago Press, 1960).

4. Felix Morley, *Freedom and Federalism* (Chicago: Henry Regnery Company, 1959).

5. Russell Kirk, *The Roots of American Order* (Wilmington, DE: ISI Books, 2003).

6. George Nash, *The Conservative Intellectual Movement in America* (Wilmington, DE: ISI Books, 1996).

7. Raoul Berger, *Government by Judiciary* (Indianapolis: Liberty Fund, 1997).

8. Russell Kirk, *The Conservative Mind* (Chicago: Henry Regnery Company, 1953).

9. M. Stanton Evans, *The Theme Is Freedom* (Washington, D.C.: Regnery Publishing, 1994).

10. Will Herberg, "Conservatives, Liberals and the Natural Law," *National Review*, June 5, 1962.

11. Patrick Allen, *Catholic Intellectuals and Conservative Politics in America* (Ithaca, N.Y.: Cornell University Press, 1993).

12. Kirk, *Roots of American Order.*

13. Edith Hamilton, *The Greek Way to Western Civilization* (New York: Norton, 1942).

14. Gilbert Murray, *The Literature of Ancient Greece* (Chicago: University of Chicago Press, 1956).

15. R. H. Barrow, *The Romans* (London: Penguin Books, 1951). See also Raymond Bloch, *The Origins of Rome* (London: Thames and Hudson, 1960).

16. Kirk, *The Conservative Mind.*

17. Ibid.

18. Russell Kirk, *The American Cause* (Chicago: Henry Regnery Company, 1957).

19. Catherine Drinker Bowen, *Miracle in Philadelphia* (Boston: Back Bay Books, 1986).

20. Alfred S. Regnery, *Upstream: The Ascendance of American Conservatism* (New York: Simon and Schuster, 2007).

21. John Maynard Keynes, *The General Theory of Employment, Interest and Money* (London: Palgrave Macmillan, 1936), 383–84.

22. Angelo Codevilla, *The Ruling Class* (New York: Beaufort Books, 2011).

23. The Mount Vernon Statement can be found at www.themountvernonstatement.com/.

Chapter 10: The Cold War, Anti-Communism, and Neoconservatism

1. Edward I. Koch and Christy Heady, *Buzz: How to Create It and Win with It* (New York: AMACOM, 2007), pp. 2–3.

2. Irving Kristol, *Neoconservatism: Selected Essays 1949–1995* (New York: The Free Press, 1995), p. x.

3. Irving Kristol, *The Neoconservative Persuasion: Selected Essays, 1942–2009* (New York: Basic Books, 2011), p. 149.

4. Norman Podhoretz, "Kissinger Reconsidered," *Commentary*, June 1982, p. 23.

5. Ibid.

6. Ibid., p. 24.

7. Ibid.

8.   Ibid.

9.   "Transcript of President's Interview on Soviet Reply; Drastic Change in Opinion," *New York Times,* January 1, 1980.

10. Ronald Reagan, Address to the British Parliament, June 8, 1982. Available at millercenter.org/scripps /archive/speeches/detail/3408.

11. The Reagan administration conducted arms control negotiations with the Soviets, but it did so with limited expectations about the good they might yield and a sensitivity to the potential for harm. Reagan took pains, for example, to protect the U.S. missile defense program from being transformed into a "chip" that could be played away in a diplomatic game with the Soviets. In the United States and abroad, public opinion generally favored arms control negotiations, and President Reagan evidently did not consider it worthwhile to defy such opinion outright. But Reagan was committed to his strategic purpose of "winning" the Cold War, not the far more modest goal of arms control, which was trying to stabilize relations between the powers.

12. Kristol, *Neoconservatism,* p. 40.

13. David Brooks, "The Era of Distortion," *New York Times,* January 6, 2004.

Chapter 13: How Social Conservatism Can Win

1. Edward J. Larson, *Summer for the Gods: The Scopes Trial and America's Continuing Debate over Science and Religion* (New York: Basic Books, 1997), p. 233.

2. Ron Haskins and Isabel V. Sawhill, *Creating an Opportunity Society* (Washington, D.C.: Brookings Institution, 2009).

3. 2012 Post-Election Survey, Public Opinion Strategies, November 6, 2012.

INDEX

◆ ◆ ◆

Page numbers in *italics* refer to figures.

Index

Index

Index

Moral Majority, 187, 306, 315, 320
Morgenthau, Henry, 104
Mount Vernon Statement, 1–2, 25–26
Moynihan, Daniel Patrick, xvii, 235, 316
Mubarak, Hosni, 333
Musharraf, Pervez, 295

Napoleon, 37, 58
Nash, George, xvii, 149, 198–99, 201, 214
national debt. *See* deficits and debts, of government
National Review, xvii, 149, 151, 154–55, 160, 167, 187, 195, 204
mission statement of, 153
National Right to Life Committee, 316
national security, and domestic threats, 329–44
   electric grid and, 335–39, 341–42, 344
   oil and, 335–36, 339–41, 342–43
national security, and foreign threats, 208–9
   need for strong U.S. military, 332–35
   neoconservatism and, 219
   Reagan and, 210, 211
National Security Agency, 355–56
NATO, 298, 300
natural gas, 343
Nazism, flaws in pacifist ideology and, 225–26, 229, 230
neoconservatism, 215–42
   Carter and failed diplomacy, 233–35
   contributions of, 242
   "current of thought" and ideas of, 24–25, 219–21, 242
   and liberalism's nature in 1950s and 1960s before New Left, 222–23

military power's use and, 25
misrepresentation of during
   G. W. Bush administration, 216, 239–40
Nixon administration and détente, 226–27, 236–37, 293
Podhoretz on détente versus ideology of Soviet Union, 228–33
Reagan and "peace through strength," 235–39, 394n11
Reagan's "ideas cluster" and, 199
Vietnam War and antiwar movement's shift of pacifism, 223–27
New Deal Progressivism
   fiscal policy and, 261
   neoconservatism and failures of, 219–20
   resistance to, 96, 97
New Deal Progressivism, Folsom on, 101–120
   failure of policies, 103–5
   1920s policies and low unemployment and high entrepreneurship, 105–12
   1930s policies and effect of federal spending, 112–18
   post-World War II effect of changes in tax policy, 118–21
   and question of private versus government spending, 106–7
New Freedom, of Wilson, 96
New Hampshire, in American Revolution, 60–61
Newsweek, 296, 327
Nigeria, 39
1920s, reduced federal spending and taxation in
   increased entrepreneurship in, 107–12
   low unemployment and, 105–7

409

ABOUT THE AUTHORS

◆ ◆ ◆

MALLORY FACTOR is the John C. West Professor of International Politics and American Government at The Citadel, and is a Fox News contributor. Mr. Factor is the cofounder and host of the New York Meeting, a nationally recognized gathering of elected officials, journalists, business leaders, and conservative authors in New York City, and the Charleston Meeting in South Carolina. He is the author of the *New York Times* bestseller *Shadowbosses: Government Unions Control America and Rob Taxpayers Blind*.

ELIZABETH FACTOR is a lawyer and coauthor of *Shadowbosses*. She graduated from Columbia University and Yale Law School.